Praise for *Stuff Nobody Taught You*

"With equal parts humor, sass, and wit, Summer takes one through a journey to aliveness. There's no stone unturned regarding the hidden saboteurs that make us self-abandon, yet she makes it okay to be confused, conflicted, and simultaneously inspired with big dreams bursting at the seams. It's this permission that allows the reader to laugh at oneself, give up the B.S. that has been stopping them, and surrender in the most delicious way. And with practical prompts at the end of each chapter, the insights stick. I'd never have t' ⸻⸻⸻⸻⸻ onal transformation a 'page-turner,' but this

—**Barb Wade**, M.A., executive coach, speaker, and author of *Your One Year Permission Slip*

"Summer is a self-help stalwart: educating and inspiring people for decades. I'm so in awe of her graciousness, commitment, and loving spirit."

—**Leonie Dawson**, author of *My Brilliant Year*

"Summer's unique voice will speak to your soul! Unlike so many watered down, cookie-cutter personal growth practices and inflated promises, her techniques and ideas are truly effective, wonderfully original, and practically magical. She's a true pioneer in personal growth, and this book is her best to date."

—**Morgana Rae**, author of *Financial Alchemy: 12 Months of Magic & Manifestation*

"Summer warns you that she has a sailor's mouth. But if you can buckle up for a really fun ride and not get triggered by the f-bomb, she promises to take you on the ride of your life. Being in the world of personal growth for decades, Summer has valuable gems to share that you won't find on a Google search. You get to dig deep into your heart and soul while assisted by her prompts so you can map out your vision, get crystal clear about who you are, and know how to manifest what you want right now and in the future. The best part is that you will feel light and joyful while doing it. Summer cracks you open in the most enjoyable way, so you don't have to live an ordinary life."

—**Dondi Dahlin,** author of *The Five Elements*

"*Stuff Nobody Taught You* arrived at the perfect time in my life when I was questioning almost everything I was currently doing. It helped me navigate my life and reinvent myself in a new and confident way. This book is literally like having the best coach and accountability partner you can imagine walking along side you, while you are transforming and reinventing your life. A definite must read for all those looking for a new way of living in their world."

—**Keith Macpherson,** speaker, coach, author of *Making Sense of Mindfulness*

STUFF
nobody
TAUGHT
you

40 Lessons from M.E.School® to Help You
**STOP BEING MISERABLE AND
START FEELING AMAZING**

STUFF *nobody* TAUGHT *you*

SUMMER McSTRAVICK
Author of *FLOWDREAMING*

Health Communications, Inc.
Boca Raton, Florida
www.hcibooks.com

Library of Congress Cataloging-in-Publication Data
is available through the Library of Congress

ISBN-13: 978–07573–2468–0 (Paperback)
ISBN-10: 0–7573–2468–1 (Paperback)
ISBN-13: 978–07573–2469–7 (ePub)
ISBN-10: 0–7573–2469-X (ePub)

HCI, its logos, and marks are trademarks of Health Communications, Inc.

Publisher: Health Communications, Inc.
        301 Crawford Blvd., Suite 200
        Boca Raton, FL 33432-1653

Cover, interior design, and formatting by Larissa Hise Henoch

Contents

Part IV: The Weasels in the Road 107

Part V: Heal That Shit Up 143

Part VI: Weightlifting for Your Soul 225

Part VII: Dive! Dive! 267

A Few Thoughts

Welcome to a very different ride than the one you were perhaps expecting when you picked up this book with its perky purple cover and peppy, earnest subtitle.

Yay! Personal growth! you thought. And, Aww, I could use some direction. Gosh, I want to feel amazing.

Well, for starters, you will get heaps of both, but you're also going to get a ton of salty language. A fuck ton, to be precise. If that bothers you, put this book down.

I've always had a sailor's mouth; in fact, I learned all my bad words from my mom, who also believes in the magic of language. Thirty years ago, I went to school for writing, graduated with a bunch of writing awards, and have wondered ever since why I didn't actually go on to . . . *write*. Well, maybe it's because I stopped writing the word *fuck* all these years.

Words are here to make an impact. It's embarrassing that I even have to explain myself, but there it is. Every word I write is a trigger, or I hope it will be a trigger. Triggers make things pop. Salty language makes things pop. And you're here to pop.

In addition to filling you with bad language, I'm hoping to possibly excite your senses of indignity and judgment because that's often where the gold is for your next step.

(And if you don't feel indignant, then get ready for a plain ol' fun, happy, and saucy ride with me!)

Because feeling something is fun. It means you're alive. I'm alive.

We have so much work to do, and we've all been so afraid to do that work, dancing around the corners of our lives in mincing little steps, trying to stay safe and be liked (which we think will make us rich or loved, or both). I have done that for ages and am done with it. Maybe you are too.

So I want you to head straight in with me. Which is going to mean giving a lot of *fucks*.

Which brings us to some questions: *Why are you here? Why did you pick up this book? Why are you even thinking about giving me a whole gob of your time?*

I think, like me, you're here because you want to shake yourself awake again and maybe even figure out how you got here to this exact point in your life. Not only that, you want to know where to go next. And maybe even how to go about doing that.

You're at a pause point, the needle in the groove between the songs.

And in this moment, you hear your own tired exhale.

I know, because that's where I am, too, as I sit here in my baggy lavender pajamas on this Friday morning in the spring, typing and thinking as we start this journey together.

I'd rather be out walking the dog or chasing down fresh lettuce in my garden. But if I don't sit here and do this with you, then Monday morning I'll be doing the same things as always, feeling the exact same way as always. So I'm going to do the thing, to write the thing, with you at my side. And you, you've picked yourself as my accountability partner.

Very cool. Thank you. More on this later.

Now, a wee bit of practical: There are worksheets illustrating the end-of-chapter prompts that you can download here: www.flowdreaming.com/prompts. They're all prettied up and will make the work more fun. You might also want to follow up with my podcast, *Flowdreaming*.

Also, M.E. School is an actual, real thing. Everything you're going to read stems from my live, online M.E. School program that I teach to a cadre of very enthusiastic students as I guide them through these concepts and their own exciting inner changes. You're welcome to explore M.E. School too. I would love to see you take that next step at www.flowdreaming.com/meschool.

Now, let's boogie.

PART I:
Open Your Eyes

Chapter 1:
The Lavender Pajamas

When I think about the world of personal growth . . . wow, have I been thick in the trenches of it for a long time. I've probably read all the same self-help books as you. I've likely been to the same conventions, retreats, and summits. I've shaken hands with peyote, shaken my belly with tantra, and loosened my throat chakra with some *pranic* breathwork. I re-birthed my inner child, *reiked* my way to the fifth dimension, and used the purple light to reset my cellular clock. I've practiced the art of simplifying my life, created my morning rituals, and sat through more than one seminar on How to Achieve My Personal Best in Under 90 Days.

And that's only in the last few years.

My heart, like yours, is drawn to the unusual and the sublime. It's drawn to things that make us feel free, or happier, or both. It's drawn especially to practices and ways of thinking that help me discover my life and the universe through both energetic means as well as the practical, which ultimately helps me know myself a bit better.

To know yourself is to love yourself; at least it should be.

When I was in my twenties, I mailed a letter looking for work to a local personal growth publishing company housed in a boxy white warehouse by some scrubby canyons. I didn't know much about what they published, other than that a famous author had founded it. At the time, where I lived, there were only two publishing companies big enough for anyone to have heard of. After all, it wasn't New York City. It came down to this publisher or the other one who made children's picture books of stock-photo zoo animals for the Under-4 set. And I was a graphic designer, and twenty-something, and hungry to break into the publishing big leagues. Toddler books weren't going to do it. So, I asked the personal growth publisher: Did they want me to lay out their books? And . . . yes. They did. The answer was *Yes!*

You know those moments when a thread of fate seems to branch off onto that road of personal growth? It's nothing you'd notice in the beginning: just an opportunity, a new person you meet maybe, or that weird urge to try something new, like baking with butterscotch instead of chocolate.

You've heard of the butterfly effect? It's where one small change can lead to a vastly different outcome—the classic example of when the flapping of a butterfly's wings in Argentina can lead to rain in China. It's when a new, almost imperceptible wave of motion begins and the horizon in front of you shifts, and suddenly you're going somewhere completely different. Then, you realize you need to be a completely different person inside, too, if you actually want to reach that place.

That is exactly what happened to me when I started my career in publishing. My life went in a completely new direction, and it was startlingly and unexpectedly beautiful. And then the butterfly flapped its wings again about ten years later, and that particular pivot became one of the most hellish periods in my life when it felt like the world was cracking me open and dropping me like a runny egg with my gooey insides smashed all over.

Then I shifted again, six years later. And once more, I was stunned by unimaginable success followed by almost theatrical-like tragedy. Each time, however, there was one common theme: I had to *transform . . . to rebuild . . . to find myself anew,* to punch through into the new and discover who I was there.

My point is, like you, right now as you read this, I'm looking for the next iteration of myself. I'm ready to level up my game and go trekking over new lands. And the feelings that precede this? They're often the ones you feel right now: listlessness; indecision; frustration; not knowing what the "right" next thing to do is; feeling some sort of yearning for more but not knowing how to get there; feeling stuck in your job, marriage, or life; feeling desperately afraid to take some kind of risk or promising gamble; feeling anxious; feeling emotionally flat and empty; or being wildly unsure. You get the idea. These feelings are your mile markers, and it means there's a turn up ahead.

I know you've been here before. You've probably taken as many or more branching paths as I have. The difference is this time we are *provoking* your reinvention. This time, your inner transformation won't crush you like a tidal wave. No, this time, you have a surfboard. You're going to ride this wave, and it's going to be really, really exciting. You're going to learn a skill that will last the rest of your life.

You'll be taking the lead and discovering new bits and pieces of yourself, on purpose, with clear intention and desire. You'll get to rearrange that kaleidoscope of you into something more pleasing, more secure, more loved. You'll take stock of all you've done and been, maybe refurbish a few parts, and figure out if you want to go bigger . . . or just get your head above water.

It doesn't matter if you're twenty-five or fifty-five. On our road of growth, we all pause, stumble, and sit in the lonely dirt more than a few times.

This time, we get to walk it together. I'm enrolling you in M.E. School. So, you can wipe that dusty patch off your butt, get up, and start walking with me.

You don't have to be burned-out or soul weary to be ready for this work. Maybe you've simply maxed out your current success and have been on a frustrating horizontal plateau for too long.

Either way, we're going to look at your personal power, the way you think, your life itself . . . and we're going to figure out what's working and what's not. (Okay, you already know what's not working, I get that.) And we're going to find alternate ways of thinking and feeling that can and will make enormous changes and even tremendous pleasure inside you.

The goal is to get you out of your own saggy lavender pajamas and back into the thick of living joyfully, fully expressed, feeling safe and secure, and with so much dang self-love you practically stagger.

Let's do this.

Chapter 2:
You Are Not a Badass—
Yet! And You Know It!

This is where I feel like I need to start the chapter by telling you "you are a badass" or "you can heal your life!" or some rah-rah thing like that. But I know you've heard all that, and you still feel the same. Instead, I'm just going to tell you to be *open*.

Being open means being coachable, and *coachable* means being willing to try on some new thoughts and play with things that might work to heal you, release you, or just let you be your own damn self in the face of people or places that might not be comfortable with that. It means purposely deconstructing some head trips and things you've told yourself about yourself over the years.

If you were an athlete, being coachable means trying some different moves instead of stubbornly insisting on doing the same old things you think work, even when your coach is tearing her hair and screaming at you across the field to *shift your weight to the left this time! To the left!*

Being coached is fun. It's Red Hat Society–type fun. If you don't know what the Red Hat Society is, trust me, you will. For now, think about your saucy grandma with her drawn on eyebrows and stockings sticking out of the toes of her very practical sandals, telling you to stop giving a fuck, wear the goddamn shirt, and stop moaning about how thick your arms look in it. Those are the Red Hat ladies.

Amen.

Let's start with a deeper peek into M.E. School, I mean, that's part of the subtitle of the book, and that's what you're getting into, right?

M.E. School started with a simple premise: You learn to be more effective in your life, rid yourself of old fears and blocks, and set in motion a life of ease, joy, and security—with a dash or two of wonder—by working with both physical and nonphysical energy. And we did this; we actually accomplished this over and over as almost a thousand students passed through its doors.

Over time, a larger thread began to weave its way through: It became a school for reinvention. A school for transformation. It became a place and point where everything that's stuck in your life starts moving again, where everything unhealed gets healed, and new choices and opportunities take shape and begin to blossom. A place for you to gain mastery over your life. A place for you to take back your power. That is what you're going to do right here, with me, in this book.

In M.E. School, you're going to move through seven sections (Parts I—VII). In the first few chunks, we're going to peel away layers of old ideas, expose the feelings you have right now about yourself and your life, and pump you full of inner revelations. This is when we learn what we're working with, right now, inside you.

Then, we'll look at what I call all the Weasels in the Road—those things that make you stumble and that block, thwart, or disappoint you. And again, we'll dismantle them or their importance to you one by one. (You'll discover that untangling and revealing inner patterns and blocks is *my thang*.) Finally, you'll reach the last few sections: in these, I'll hand you tool after tool for gaining inner strength, developing (or redeveloping) purpose, and frankly, just lighting that fire of passion as you move through your own inner reinvention.

Each chapter ends with a call to action. These are prompts that mimic the worksheets I give my online classes. I urge you to get a journal and do all of them—they are the meat and bones of the work we do. It can also be fun to do this as part of a book club.

Finally, where will you end up? Well, like I said, you might fork onto a whole new path. Or you might become fully accepting of yourself as you are and finally see your own inner being in a fantastic and gorgeous new light. Or you might end up doubling down on your current path with renewed zest and fresh focus. I don't know where you'll end up. I'm really curious for you. Curious *with* you.

And that's why I'm doing M.E. School right alongside you. I'm peeling back the process so it's not something dictated from afar. No, I'll be right by your side, sharing how the shifts feel in me, how they've felt in my past students, and how I know what *you* might be feeling.

I've done this before. In fact, I've done this practically every year for the last ten years as I've taken multiple waves of students through this process. And this time my crossroads, my pivot point, my moment of reflection might even be similar to yours: I've gone through these last few crazy years with you. I'm stopping at the same checkpoint that calls for reassessing myself and my life as you. During the COVID pandemic, I unexpectedly home-schooled two teens and sent one off to college and became an empty nester. I put on at least twenty pounds and discovered I left my hair's flat iron in the drawer way more than I used it. Ditto makeup. I've been sitting my butt down in front of my computer to work full-time, even as I have days to wander my house and ponder the meaning of my life. I'm ready for my next reinvention, the next upleveling, *as are you.*

This is why it's our perfect timing, the perfect moment for us to both start M.E. School. We are exactly where we need to be. All this means growth is imminent—a fluttering, shimmering butterfly wing catching the light and asking us to *come hither.*

I'm so glad we're doing it together. ♥

We're starting with the first thing I teach my class: *Reinvention is possible! Do you want it?*

Chapter 3:
Yes, You Can
Reinvent Yourself

It's what, maybe a Thursday? It's late afternoon. Your week kind of sucked. Work was stressful, or insanely boring, as usual. Or if it wasn't work, it was school. Or spinning around at home all week, getting shitloads of nothing done, even though everything seemed important at the time. At any rate, you're at a stopping point. A *hold-your-horses* moment where the rider pulls back on the reins. You're facing your computer, or your phone, or your TV, wondering what's next for you in your life or if this is all there is.

You toy with the idea that you have depression. Maybe you do, maybe you don't. But you do know that what's in front of you for the next five years, ten years, is untenable. *I just can't do this anymore*, you realize.

So, how do you reinvent yourself? Can you, even? You google it. All the articles recommend that you take deep breaths, explore new hobbies. *What bullshit*. You feel incredibly underwhelmed.

This is another Thursday lost in time.

I know you know the feeling of doing the same things you've been doing for years and not being sure about their value. I know you also know the feeling of knocking your head against the same wall over and over, hoping eventually something will work out, go big, or get you to that next level of success via a bigger income, a happier home, a relationship—any of a hundred things that tell us we've finally broken through to the next level of success instead of spending yet another night in the foxhole *of nothing ever working out.*

You need to reinvent yourself. I need to reinvent myself. *How? How? How?*

You look back on all your past reinventions. They all happened without awareness. You were doing one thing, then slowly began doing another; then that other thing became your *main* thing. It was organic. You evolved. Why isn't that happening now? Why do you feel like you're clawing onto the present even as you're wishing it away?

Because this time, you're afraid. You have bills to pay. You have kids to support. You have less energy, your body is sagging and getting tired earlier, and the thought that you have the time or ability to pivot seems much harder to believe.

Your life doesn't feel rolled out in front of you like some long, deep-pile Persian carpet. It feels like a narrow, gray sidewalk choked with old gum.

You need to reinvent yourself. I need to reinvent myself. *How? How? How?*

First, I take that stupidly long, deep breath. And then I recognize that I'm different. I'm older. I have more seemingly rational reasons why I can't be successful piled up in the deep dark corners of my mind. I've built up barriers to change that hold me locked into a rigid walled garden of what I can be, and how much money I need to earn, and how long it'll take me to do anything else.

And those walls may very well be absolute bullshit. But for the moment, I'm believing them.

Until I stop.

Stopping means that I exhale. I give myself the time to evolve again, slowly like before. I still have the same pressures, the same responsibilities. I have the same fears that what I make or become next won't happen fast enough, be financially supportive enough, or be in any way as good as what I had before.

But then I see that what's really happened over time isn't about any of that. It's about *trust*.

Somewhere along the way, our trust broke. The trust that we could re-invent ourselves successfully.

There. Stop.

Feel it for a second. What if you have utter, total, deep, solid trust—*a knowing*—that reinventing yourself will be wildly and spectacularly successful?

Um hmm. You would do it in a hot second.

So now we see the key, what we're missing. We no longer have that *trust.* We used to, back when we just let ourselves shift and evolve without even really thinking it through. But now, every shift is calculated against our po-tential losses.

So how do we fix that?

We do it by getting right back to that old, original feeling:

> # reinventing *yourself will be wildly, spectacularly successful. Not might be. Not has to be. Just . . . will be.*

If you can't feel that, then you are totally 100 percent committed to staying where you are instead.

Nobody takes any leaps if they can't feel themselves successfully on the other side of the chasm. And just because you can't *see* that chasm doesn't mean it's not there.

Nobody put an expiration date on your life and said, "You can't have any success after this. No more pivots for you. Time's up."

Nobody said that but you, in your limited, small-minded, untrusting, fearful thinking.

Deep breath. You want to reinvent yourself? Here's how.

Make time for it. Create space for it. Carve time out in your day to let your mind wander and grow. Cancel the silly time-sucking things you have in your life that keep you distracted from yourself from dawn till midnight. You know what those things are. Tell everyone you know that you have a new hobby and it's nonnegotiable: You've committed to redeveloping trust that your reinvention is going to be wildly successful, and you're giving yourself the time and space to nourish this into reality.

Don't give yourself a hard deadline. Your deadline is whenever the pie is baked. It's unknowable right now. Just get the fucker in the oven.

Stop thinking that the reinvented you has to be more successful and bigger and better in every way. Maybe the newly reinvented you is shy and searching and lovely in your sweet naivete. Be okay with that. We don't know who's going to come out in the New You. All we know is that they've been waiting for you to open the oven and let them out.

And last, don't fear it. Don't fear him or her. She isn't losing anything. She's gaining. You give her time and space to emerge, and she gives you your new breath. Stop fearing that you'll lose your income, or your family, or that you don't have the time or space for this. Start reminding yourself that you've done this before, and it was easy last time, it just happened last time. You don't need the buildup of fear around it.

That fear is a new thing. And it's a lie.

You *can* pivot, right now. Commit, make the time, and do it. Remember, I'm doing it with you. Reinvention is a *thing*, a *real* thing, not just a hazy yearning. It needs its own space and a generous, warm welcome. Don't let it be some amorphous longing that you distractedly think about. Make it *real*. Make it like me, right now, today in my gray pajamas (Day 2) banging away on a keyboard to you.

I'm reinventing myself right this moment through this simple act of writing and reflecting.

Reinventing myself as what, exactly? I don't know yet. In the beginning, you usually don't know.

I haven't published a book in eleven years. Maybe I'm going to be an author again, maybe not. Maybe I'll pull my coaching company apart at the seams and rearrange it into something bigger, brighter, and more relevant than ever. Or maybe I'll pivot completely and become a virtual travel agent specializing in exotic truffle hunts. Maybe I'll go through this with you and discover that I'm just simply ready to retire. Maybe my reinvention is *not* to get to some bigger, greater, more wildly successful plateau—maybe it's to learn to just be, to savor the delicious ray of sun peeking through my office window as I listen to my dog slobbering in his sleep.

See? I'm open.

But no matter what it ends up being, I commit to it. I commit *hard*. For me, this feels like taking all the other options off the table. By this I mean, *I don't really have other options, now do I?* I can sit here in my pajamas for another week, another month, a year, just kind of longing and waiting and growing more frustrated and distracted. But that's not really an option, see? It's a default.

Whereas choosing that feeling of hope and commitment, right now, *is* powerful. I reclaim my power, starting right in my heart and gut, when I shake my tiny fist at the universe and say, "Oh yeah, buddy? This *is going to happen*, and it starts *now!*"

Commitment is something that blooms through you. Can you feel it? Can you feel that deep knowing that you are changing and growing, that it's a good thing, and that you are committed to doing it?

Prompts Are Your Friends

Yes, every chapter has a task, a prompt. Every student in M.E. School (that's you!) has homework to plow through in order to reveal something about them or their life, and/or to challenge, fix, heal, or grow that thing.

For you A-types: I know you want them. Get your notebook and pens, and let's start the process.

You B-types: You can just glaze through the prompts if you want, but don't be surprised if they come back to haunt you in the shower. That's a good thing. Let them.

Speaking of . . . reminder! You can find all these prompts in a sweet, downloadable format at: www.flowdreaming.com/prompts.

To use the prompts well, give yourself some time to ponder and answer each question truthfully. If you can't answer, or don't understand what you suspect I'm trying to get at, don't worry. I'm not looking for a right and perfect answer. I'm looking for *your* answer, even if it's "I have no friggin' idea" or "Too soon, Summer. Not going there yet." If you haven't journaled or done any self-reflection in a while, you might be rusty with letting the flow of ideas slip out. That's okay. Put on your uniform; first practice starts today.

In this chapter, your prompts are exploratory, meaning you're discovering where you are (what you're bringing to the table right now) as you get this ball rolling. Like I said at the beginning of the last chapter, the key question here is: *Are you open and coachable?* Or like I asked later: *Are you committed?* Dive into these ideas with the following prompts.

M.E. *School* Prompt

Your prompt is to commit to your reinvention and take inventory of where you are right now.

Journal on the following questions:

- Am I committed to my growth or reinvention, or am I scared or mistrustful? Or both?

- What does it feel like to know I want to change more than anything, and that I am 100 percent committed to doing it?

- What is my overall feeling about my life right now?

- How good am I at being coached or taught?

- How am I feeling/being when I shut down or reject new knowledge?

- How am I feeling/being when I open up and receive new knowledge?

Chapter 4:
Between the Reefs

Out past the reef is the blue, blue ocean. Wide, deep, beautiful. Also, scary, uncertain, directionless.

Little fishy, you've been on your reef a long time. You know its crevasses, the little hidey holes, even where the eels lay their scary heads. You've got the reef. The reef is good. All your fellow fishies agree.

Except: You're getting a little curious about the world. You keep looking with longing over there, past the reef. You little Nemo! What's out there?

One day, you venture off your reef. Your friends and family nag you and ask what's wrong with you. Your friends and family have seemed like scared little whiners lately. So annoying. Negative nellies. *Gripe, gripe.*

"Just do something about your problems!" you want to yell. And they don't. But you're doing something about yours. That's why you've found yourself at the end of the reef. And right now, you're floating in the vast blue ocean.

It feels vulnerable. You feel exposed and silly. You want your old reef buddies, but you know the second you go back you're going to feel even more out of place. You've already been too far out. You wonder if there'll ever be another reef.

You've entered the Grow Zone.

The Grow Zone is where you've never been before. It's full of new experiences. Many of these experiences make you feel insecure and uncertain. You have no prior experience with them. Back on the reef, you were in the Known Zone. The Known Zone is super safe. It's also super boring after a while.

The Grow Zone is always alluring because the more you experience it, the more pieces and parts of you get revealed. You didn't know you liked Italians until you dated one. You didn't know you could yodel until you went to Switzerland. You had no idea you'd fall for a gal who does cosplay on the weekends. You've discovered a lot about yourself. You've expanded. You've grown.

Still, there's this moment between leaving the Known Zone and encountering the new delights ahead where we . . . pause. Our little fins quiver. We want to reach backward, but we can't. Forward is still murky blue. A part of our mind is screaming that we should not have done this, it will be bad. That's the part that's built to keep us safe. And we feel anything but safe in this big, blue ocean.

But then, you spot it. A reef! A big colorful reef, with fish unlike any you've ever seen! And when you get there, your old reef friends are resentful. They feel abandoned. Truthfully, they could meet you on the new reef anytime if they wanted to. They don't want to. Yet. But someday they will, and then you can show them around your *new* Known Zone. Somebody always has to be the leader, even if they don't know they are.

So swim, little fishy. Your next Grow Zone awaits.

The Grow Zone

The Grow Zone, familiar? Or rather, it's never exactly *familiar* since being in it means you're in a new place, charting new waters. But the feeling of being in a Grow Zone is familiar. It's weird, funky, a little or a lot scary. It's where the stuff behind you is no longer working for you, but no new stuff has presented itself yet. It's the lost middle of the road trip between the two points of your destination.

Here's another example, my own.

After about a decade, I left the mega publisher who'd hired me. Or rather, they fired me.

It super sucked because I was no longer just a book designer there. Nope, I had risen. A super famous author who founded the company was my boss's boss. I had a weekly live radio show on the Internet and SiriusXM cohosting with another super-famous personal growth leader. I'd been given a multi-million-dollar division of the company to run, with a big staff, in charge of producing and delivering all their audio content, from audiobooks to live events to dozens and dozens of podcasts by people you've seen on TV, headlining major conferences, and generally game-changing the entire personal growth world.

Not only that, but I oversaw the building of multiple sound studios and had launched the company into the Internet with newfangled "online webinars" and an online radio station that was delightfully and hugely embraced by the wellness and metaphysical communities. I was making the company gobs of money by transitioning them into the digital world, and my yearly performance review was always five-star. I very much believed this was my destiny, and that I was doing a very good job.

I'll tell you the whole story later, but in a nutshell, I found myself suddenly unemployed, crying into my bathroom sink, feeling very, very much between the reefs.

Imagine the best thing you ever had—that you've stuffed a decade of your life into, that you just based taking a mortgage out on—being taken away in a heartbeat of an afternoon for no discernible reason.

Actually, maybe you've had that happen to you too.

It felt like life had said, "Fuck you, Summer. You've had enough of the good stuff. *Bye.* Oh and, good luck ever getting something like this again, babe." (Yes, my evil inner thoughts all sound like misogynistic men. Sorry, guys. I do love you.)

Sometimes, you end up between the reefs by force, not by choice. Like when you discover your partner is cheating, when your employer fires you, or when your doctor tells you they need more tests.

Unlike me, I don't want you spending the next three years with a horrible stress-induced health condition, not knowing what the hell to do next, not realizing that *life was indeed working just like it should.*

Because if that event hadn't happened, I'd never have built my own multi-million-dollar personal growth brand, Flowdreaming.

I'd never have invented M.E. School.

I'd never have awakened to my true calling—the very thing my prior career had quietly skilled me to do.

I probably wouldn't even be sharing this book with you right now, and you and I would never meet. And the changes in you, which I hope will flow from sharing this book, would never have come to be.

Instead, I'd still be humping my way into work at 6:30 a.m. and winding up at 6:00 p.m., missing my kids growing up, and throwing myself ever more into my job just to get ahead, which, by now, would have turned me into a bitter wad of despair.

But nah, life sent me between the reefs, where it was super lonely (life was not giving me any hint of direction) and super scary (the only way to pay the bills was by building my own company, because I could not think of any other thing to do, and well, my little idea called "Flowdreaming" was catching on).

And this is what brings me to the next stage in our journey: realizing that you're already enough, that you're where you need to be right now, this very second, and that you are worth every damn droplet of goodness in the universe.

But first, get your worksheets or your notebook.

M.E. *School* Prompt

Your prompt is to recognize your Grow Zone and your level of comfort about being in one.

Journal on the following questions:

- How do my Grow Zones feel? Am I in one now?

- What precipitated my latest Grow Zone? Was it a big life change or was it more like a slow creeping one?

- Am I trying to escape my Grow Zone as fast as I can because I absolutely hate it, or am I open to settling in for the ride?

- How uncomfortable am I comfortable feeling? Can I go past that and commit to feeling even a little more uncomfortable?

- Do I want something to change me? What am I waiting for?

Chapter 5:
Are You Worthy?

Let's play with an idea. Let's say you're born as a scrawny screaming baby with pretty much no worth. I mean, you may or may not even be loved by your parents. But if you are loved, are you worthy of that love?

In this scenario, no you are not. You see, your worth is going to be created as you grow. You're an empty character with no experience in the game. Do good things, become more worthy. Do bad things, become less. You're pretty much empty of worth, but ready to make yourself worthy by all your future life choices.

It's the old *good girls go to heaven, bad girls go to hell* model. We're basically racking up heaven points, or we're losing them.

Contrast this to intrinsic worth. With intrinsic worth, that fidgety little baby is born worthy. Just being blessed with your first gulp of air assures you that you are worthy enough to be here. You made it! Life or God or whatever felt you had enough merit to come here.

And maybe you got lucky and live in a plush, upscale home, or maybe you'll be walking barefoot down a sewage-filled street. Those are your external circumstances. They have no bearing on your inner intrinsic worth; all humans are created equal, of equal worth, with an equal right to pursue happiness. No one is inherently more worthy than another.

If this is the case, your only job is to fully express that worth in the world. To allow it, build from it, create from it. You have nothing to prove, no points to gain. You are already cleared for great things, and now it's just about expressing them and letting them out.

No one can doubt you or say you don't have what it takes. We all have what it takes.

If you live a scared, retractive, mean, small life, you've taken your intrinsic worth and misplaced it. You've ignored it, don't believe in it, and gone around thinking you have to accomplish things to get it. You're on a constant merry-go-round of trying to gain worth and then losing it through getting people to love you, validate you, give you money, or whatever. In this model, you never really win.

On the other hand, if you live a bountiful, fully realized, fully expressed life, then you've unlocked your intrinsic inner worth to impact the world in marvelous ways. *No one here gave it to you, so no one here can take it away.* This means if you want to be something great, you already have permission. If you fail at it, so what. You are still worthy to be loved, adored, cherished, admired, and supported. That never goes away.

Now, which model do you believe in?

You Already Love Yourself (Mostly)

If I were channeling Louise Hay, this is where I'd say, "You've got to learn to love yourself."

But I'm not saying "learn to love yourself."

The problem with that is that we all *do* love ourselves to some degree. We just don't love *all* of ourselves. We think we have to do more, be more, or climb more to become that beautiful, lovable person we want to be. We've taken our intrinsic worth, set it aside, and instead focused on a litany of all the crappy shit in us that needs fixing.

And then personal growth is happy to step in and tell you where you fail.

Well, guess what, in even the nicest homes, the toilet breaks. Having a broken toilet doesn't mean there's no worth there. It means you live in a body with a life where you sometimes do crummy things or crummy things get done to you. You are still worthy . . . of everything!

And you should love your broken, janky toilet self as much as you love your big bay windows self.

But I promise you, we won't be "shoulding" here. Instead, I want you to be thinking about how much you think you have to change yourself in some "better" way to finally get what you want or have your life look like you want.

A lot of us discover that personal growth is a moving horizon: We're always on our way to it but never reaching it. Happiness is always one mountain range away, because we have forgotten one very important thing: not only are you intrinsically worthy, but right now, in this moment, you are also at the literal apex of your life.

Right now, you have the greatest amount of wisdom you've ever had. You have the most life experience you've ever had. You've had the most successes and the most failures. You've had more experiences in relationships and how to navigate their tumbling waters than you've ever had before.

Your toolbelt for life is bulging with all the miscellaneous items you've picked up or discovered through the years. It has never been fuller or heavier than it is at this moment.

Kind of a profound thought.

Chances are, you have tools for almost everything and certainly more than you did five years ago or even twenty.

And the ways you dealt with things five years ago, or twenty, probably won't ever be repeated. How could they possibly be repeated? Back then you only had a hammer. Now you have a hammer, circular saw, and a whole freaking factory line. *You are not the old you, and you'll never be again.*

So why do you still think you're not going to be successful, or happy, or in love, or whatever else it is you want? You are the best person you've ever been, right this second. Yes, *the best.*

Even if you don't particularly *like* yourself at this second, you can't argue that you're not the most wise, most experienced, and most knowledgeable you've ever been. You've got more inner resources than ever, so why the self-doubt?

Don't you think it's silly that the more skilled we've become, the more we fear making changes and taking leaps? Leaps into new lives, new partnerships, new work, new anything?

We fear all the bad things that could happen again, instead of recognizing that we're better equipped than we've *ever been* to make those same things *never* happen again.

You've been working on this "culmination of you" for your entire lifetime. Every second you're bigger, better, and more capable than the second before. The slow drip of time itself has done that for you. You didn't even have to work for it. It just is.

I don't fear I'll ever be fired from my dream job again, since now *I made my own dream job*. I'm the only one who can fire me. I won't ever be that gal twelve years ago who didn't have all the insights, wisdom, and inner resources I have now.

I also don't fear that I'll never find a new career path, or "rebuild" my career from the ashes, because I've done that too. If I did it once, I can do it again.

See? You really are in the best place you've ever been. You literally *can't* be that old you. They're gone. You would never make the same decisions, be caught in the same circumstances . . . nope. Gone.

I think you may not realize that *you're already where you need to be, right now, right this moment.* There is no more waiting and no more fearing.

If you're still waiting to get ripe like a fat avocado dangling from a tree, consider this instead: *maybe you've already ripened, and now you hang there, still waiting.*

M.E. *School* Prompt

Your prompt is to ask yourself, "What am I waiting for?"

Use the prompts below to explore your intrinsic worth, your secret fears, and all those things you're waiting for so you can feel like the amazing, gorgeous person that you are.

☐ What do I think I need to do or become to finally feel security, greatness, life purpose, or whatever my goal is?

☐ If I believed that life would support me with anything because I am already worthy of it, what would I be doing or how would I be living?

☐ What are my secret fears, and what can't I do because of them? Where am I not good enough, smart enough, handsome enough, likable enough, popular enough, seen enough, etc.?

☐ Am I projecting my ideas onto other people and presuming they're judging me the same way I am?

PART II:
Grip the Tools

Chapter 6:
The King and the Queen

This morning, we settle in with black coffee. I admit I'm still in my nighttime sweats, but it's only 8:30 on a Saturday morning. I'll let it pass.

Finally, we're getting to the good stuff—the heart of M.E. School. The "where you go now that you know that, even though you're between the reefs, you're actually super ready to see what your already-worthy self is going to do next."

The heart of the work you're about to do requires your *emotion*. Not your thoughts, not your logic. It requires your heart, and the seemingly endless conflict between what you know, what you feel, and what you actually do.

There's a really rational reason for how you got into this life-stopping, soul-crushing standoff between your rational mind and your wistful heart.

Reinvention begins with igniting your inner queen. *The queen is your heart.* Yet trusting your heart to lead you is about the hardest thing you can do.

If you're an overachiever, I feel for you. I really do. After all, your intellect has led you to all the great stuff you have right now whilst your heart would have sent you down a thousand rabbit holes to nowhere. No wonder you trust your head over your heart. You've never given your heart a chance to prove itself. Why start now?

On the other hand, maybe you've trusted your head to make the so-called "right" decisions, but instead, it's made tons of decisions that were piss-poor bad. You won't listen to your heart, but you don't trust yourself to make good, rational choices either. Your heart is tied to a stake, bound, and gagged inside you as your rational self relentlessly keeps you on the so-called "right track," doing the things you "should" do that should lead you to growth and safety, but which instead lead you to daily mind-numbing misery. You're left lost in a fog of indecision, self-doubt, and failure, unable to make a choice you can stand behind.

How do we help these poor lost babies?

I call the head your king and the heart your queen. Together, they should rule the kingdom equally. And this isn't some gender thing. Think of it as an old-fashioned parable or myth where opposites take these roles. In fact, your queen may be a cis-man, your king gender fluid. It doesn't matter.

The role of your heart, the queen, is to tell you all those most important things like "I'm falling in love." Or "I love my kids more than anything on earth!" Or "I don't know why, but I have to say yes to this. It feels so right." She drives you into new territory. She makes you vulnerable and open. She's the fierce explorer who stands on the castle parapets and dreams of what's beyond those green hills out there.

Conversely, the king wants nothing more than to keep you safe and fed. He'll tell you, "Don't go out of these castle doors. You don't know what's out there. It will probably hurt you. We have food and warmth in here."

The two sit in despair on their thrones, hardly speaking.

The king has a strong argument for keeping you safe. After all, he takes all the things you've ever learned or experienced, adds them together, and says, "This works and this doesn't. Listen to me and I will read through everything that's already happened to you and extrapolate it into your future so I can tell you what you should do next." Smart man, this king.

The queen wails back: "Yes, but if I only guide my future by what's happened in my past, my world starts to shrink. You can only forecast based on what you've already experienced, and here we are going over the same hallways day in and day out, and my heart is dying inside. Life should be about *growth,* not safety."

The king stands his ground: "Life should be about *safety*, not growth."

All the birds in the castle are suddenly still. We're all holding our breath. Who should win?

The queen says to you, "Every day I whisper a breeze of intuition through you. I give you little tugs of good feeling that nudge you in a new, promising direction. I light you up with joy when you do or think things that feel fresh, fearless, or adventurous. In short, whenever you pursue growth, you feel me."

And you think to yourself, *Yeah, but I usually ignore that because, you know, the king is telling me to stick with what I'm already doing, he can manage that, we know that. Even if we hate what we're doing, at least the crappy known is better than the scary unknown.*

The queen sighs and slouches in her throne, her pretty dress moldering.

Your heart's voice is consequently pretty faint.

But your head's voice? Your intellect? The king? It's very strong. Because it's used to winning.

Your head's voice immediately goes into protection mode. It assesses risk.

After all, it feels that's its job: to protect you from all the heart whispers that will cause you to screw up, lose money, fail in your dream, or repeat whatever dumb moves you may have made before.

Your head's voice says, "Don't even try, honey. I don't want to see you fail."

Your heart's voice says, "Go for it. You've got this!"

Don't be mistaken: Your head's voice really wants to protect you. It loves you as much as your heart's voice does. It just wants to protect you from yourself, much like a parent who doesn't quite believe his or her child is up to the task.

Consequently, your head's voice keeps you small. But despite what the king says, it does not keep you safe.

It's actually your heart's voice that makes you strong and safe. Your heart's voice wants you to know that you create your safety by growing, not by standing still.

This is when you ask yourself, *Who's going to be the winner?*

Now that you know the role of your head's voice, you understand why it's in overdrive almost all the time, evaluating everything from A to Z, like: "How dumb is this? How stupid am I being? How expensive is that? Can I afford it? What will I get from this? What if I lose? What am I doing? Oh my God, I'm going to have to sneak this behind my partner's back! My parents are going to be so upset."

The jabber goes on and on.

You give your head's voice wonderful opportunities to continue to "save" you. And your head's voice is strong. It runs you because you almost *always, always, always* listen to it, and it's almost *always, always, always* right.

Or so you think.

Your head's voice has run you almost your whole life. And look where it's gotten you. Look at the situations you're in right now that feel totally unsolvable, where you feel trapped, where you've lost your love or your fire.

Look at the relationships that are broken, on hold, or nonexistent. Look at the life dream that you've stuttered on and off toward achieving for so long.

Look at how you feel about your money and income.

Look how people (partners, spouses, friends, bosses, family) continuously disappoint you and don't give you what you need.

And where is your life purpose? What are you really supposed to be doing with your life?

You will have felt some of these things. These areas are where your king has failed over and over. After all, if he could have gotten you out of these sticky messes, he would have already done so.

So, when this head voice of yours pops up with all its rationalizations and justifications for why you should back out, or "be safe" . . . please tell it to go find the queen.

You've trusted your head for long enough. Now your head needs to trust your heart. And she's so scary to your king. You'll do almost anything to not trust her. Because you don't "get" her. Your king is baffled by her. And because he can't figure her out (and rationalizing is what he does!), there is zero trust.

Your mind is a clever thing, and it will use all your oldest and most powerful rationalizations to raise fears about your heart. After all, fear has been its #1 tool.

Getting you *fearful* almost always works to get you to do what your king wants.

Whenever the king catches the queen mooning about on the balcony, looking longingly over the hills, he whispers, "I think I saw some real nasty bandits out there today. In fact, they burned a village or two."

And you freak out, and suddenly you're back in the "good enough to get by" zone.

Queen Takes King

So, let's talk about the queen. How did she get in this predicament? How did you stop trusting your heart? Is she not powerful at all?

Close your eyes and think about something really big that happened to you in your past. Not something you mentally know happened, but something you can feel—a moment that scared you, cut you, or maybe totally fulfilled you.

Notice that feeling. Notice that in that feeling your king steps back. This isn't his arena. Your queen is the one who says, "Every big thing that's ever happened to you is emotionally encoded in your memory. Faces fade, names get lost, dates are wrecked on the shore of time. But the feeling of what happened—how your heart was hurt or overjoyed or whatever it was . . . well, guess what's still running you."

Your queen is telling you, "You think you listen to the king all the time, but all the king is trying to do is protect you from me, from your heart. He can't handle it. He will avoid pain by any measure, even if it means stuffing your life with slow, smoldering unhappiness. He thinks that's better than the unknown. And you've believed him for a long time.

"Baby," she continues, "every big decision in your life has been me. When you fell in love? That was me. When you decided to break up? That was me.

When you realized you wanted a baby? Me. When you stormed out of your hateful job one day and then cried for hours and said, 'What have I done?!' That was me. Every big, life-changing decision was me. The king will always be trying to box you in, and I always come in and clean up the mess. And when I do, you know what you feel? Sweet relief. You get to exhale. The king carefully tends the festering wound. But I heal it.

"I run your life. I move you in the big ways. I'm the one who tells you what feels good, where your happiness lies, what chances you should take. And also, if you allow me, I'll heal you when the risks don't work out.

"You don't trust me because you've been brainwashed to think that your thoughtful, rational choices are always the way out of *every* situation. They are not. You know it. If they were, everything would be lollipops and roses right now. They aren't. Go tell the king to read a magazine for a while so we can get the work done."

All the biggest moments of your life have been your queen at work. Your emotions made the final choice. Every now and then the queen storms the throne room and puts the king away. And then the king spends the rest of the year telling you not to trust her.

Well guess what. Trust her. I know it's hard. I'm still struggling with that myself.

How do you ride on the faith of a feeling or your intuition? How do you trust your heart's voice when she says, "This isn't the right partner for you" while the king says, "Yeah but he pays half the rent."

Hear me: The queen always wins in the end. You can either cultivate a loving, listening relationship with her, or you can let her storm in and fix things over and over.

Me, I prefer the loving gentle caress of her leading me into things that feel good, that light me up, even though most of the time I don't understand where they'll take me, or why I spend money on it, and even feel guilty that it's not what I "should" be doing.

It's your king that's the "should-er."

Remember how I said seemingly successful people hardly trust their queen? It's because their mind got them to their current level of success. They followed it, and the more things worked out, the more often they shut off the queen in favor of the king. Except, they wonder why they feel hollow. Empty. Bored. Lifeless. In a rut. Sucking down the Wellbutrin. Overweight. Uninspired. Sick, burned-out. Lost. Without direction or purpose in life.

This is when you have that midlife crisis. When you self-sabotage your relationship. When you quit a good job for no reason. When your health crumbles and breaks. When you emotionally flatline and nothing seems exciting anymore.

Regain your queen. She is as strong or stronger than the king. She doesn't rule your decisions through fear. You've got to trust her. You can't move to the next level without inviting her into your life. You have maxed out the king level. Now, level up.

Meet your queen and ask her what she really, really wants. You'll discover it's exactly what *you* want too.

M.E. *School* Prompt

Your prompt is to discern who has been doing all the talking about running the castle versus who has actually been running it.

Once you do this, you'll understand what needs to happen to gain balance between your head's voice and your heart's voice. Again, we're looking for some "ah ha's" around which part of you you trust more—which part of you runs the show? (Or *thinks* they run the show?) And what part is shut down? Is it the queen? That's the one we want to wake up.

Journal on this.

- Why do I habitually let my heart or my head win and shut down the other? (Hint: It's about which one you trust more and what happened in your life to lead you to this trust.)

- Why don't I trust my heart? How often does my heart win?

- Do I let my head lead me into paralysis? What do I get from that?

- How often does my head use fear as a way to control me or my heart?

- What might happen if I go full-in to my heart and just start making decisions and trusting it for a while?

Chapter 7:
Fear of Feelings

I'm on my eighteenth day of writing with you. And I'm no longer in my pajamas all day: I've permanently switched to sweats. I feel a tiny bit better about myself, but there's more we can do.

Many, if not most, students in M.E. School come to learn about a concept called "manifesting," which is the idea that with proper energetic and emotional focus, you can influence the kinds of opportunities and events that come your way.

The thing is, most people I've taught the principles of manifesting to were still unable to properly use them. They'd think "manifesting" meant that marvelous things would just drop from the sky into their laps as a result of whispering their wishes to the universe fifteen times each morning in their journals, things like "I win the lottery. I pay off debt. I meet the handsomest smoochie dude who's not only my soul mate, but a bang up rich guy too," etc., etc. All well and good. Some of that stuff sounds pretty nice.

But . . .

Something got in the way, and those things never dropped in their laps, and the journal got discarded, and they said, "Lame. This manifesting shit doesn't work."

We do it differently in M.E. School. Here, you're going to learn about *why* we try to manifest things, and once that's clear, you'll learn a few methods for creating more of certain things and less of others in your life.

You're going to answer the question: *What are the things I want to manifest supposed to help me become or fulfill in my life?* Then we're going to strip away the woo-woo for a bit about the concept of manifesting and instead come to a new understanding about the power and impact of our emotions when it comes to either driving things to us or away from us in our lives.

In other words, start asking yourself this: *Is there something I can do— some way I can think or behave—that might start shifting the trajectory of my life to yield up sweet and beautiful things for me (instead of the crummy, crappy crud I'm used to)?*

The answer is . . . yes!

I start by asking my students to choose one thing inside them and one thing outside them that they want to manifest. The outside thing is usually easy to choose: "I want a house, I want retirement savings," and so on.

The inside thing is messier: "I want to feel happy and get out of this emotional dead zone. I want to feel confident. I want to forgive myself. I want to stop feeling like I'm a horrible daughter and being so mad at my mom. I want to heal this hurt around my marriage."

The inside is always sloppier because it's about feelings. And feelings are things most of us have learned not to trust. (Sorry, queen, we're still working on it.)

And the funniest bit is that a high percentage of the time the outside thing you want to manifest is actually all blocked up by the unresolved inside thing, even when they seem completely unrelated. Yep. You can throw all the energy, oracle cards, and affirmations you want toward the outside thing, but it's the inside thing that's holding it all in place.

And the inside thing is all about emotions.

Here's a story from a few years back that'll clarify this.

The Only Thing You're Afraid Of

It's July, and I'm sitting in a hotel conference room listening to a lecture about emotions taught by one of my peers.

I teach a lot about emotions, too, so watching sandy-haired Davey up on stage wowing his audience is positively fascinating. He's also unexpectedly hit on an idea about emotions that I'm embarrassed to say I hadn't figured out on my own. I mean, it's my job to know all this, but here I am in a stiff metal conference chair having a quiet, professional meltdown.

"The only thing you're ever really afraid of is emotion," he says.

I crane my head around to see if anyone else is reacting to this.

I mean, we're afraid of feeling particular emotions, but emotion itself? *Please go on, Davey.* Because now that he's said it, it seems obvious. We are afraid of feeling feelings. Period.

And why is that a big deal? Why am I having a holy revelation about this because, from the look of it, no one else is responding, or at least they aren't showing it on their faces. Or maybe they're all secretly and frantically doing what I am, tracing this idea backward in my mind, trying to figure out how deep it goes, and why I unexpectedly care so much about it.

I start by thinking about one constant feeling I've had lately: the money pressure. I don't like that particular feeling, that emotion: *pressure.* Is that what I'm afraid of feeling? I'm not exactly afraid of feeling it; I just don't *like* it.

I go a little deeper: I have a big staff to pay, a gazillion bills, and a whole family of four to pay for by myself. Money pressure makes me feel panicky, pressured, and incompetent.

It also makes me feel scared. I hate feeling scared.

There, that's four feelings I realize I hate feeling: panicky, pressured, incompetent, and scared.

Okay, I don't wanna feel those. Gotcha. But is that all?

Go Still Deeper

I'll start with the idea of feeling "scared" since that seems like the biggest of the four feelings. What happens if I look behind that emotion and ask, *Is that the ultimate emotion that,* as Davey says, *I'm afraid of feeling?*

Nope, not even close. I hate feeling scared because feeling scared means I'm scared of *not having enough.* That I'll lose things—like my house or business—and I'll feel *loss.* I'll feel the pain of disappointing myself, my family, and my staff. Other people will feel pain. And maybe that's the most painful—if my family feels pain, and I feel pain, and I caused it, then I'm going to feel hopeless, incompetent, and powerless.

Now we're getting close to the finale: If I feel hopeless, incompetent, and powerless, living will become vile and painful. *And that feels very, very unsafe.* That is my freak-out point: feeling unsafe.

There, now we've gone down to the final, deepest emotional point.

Feeling unsafe is the ultimate feeling I'm afraid of experiencing.

It turns out, I'm not afraid of the actual physical circumstance of not having enough money in the bank this month. I can handle an overdrawn account for a few days, or a little higher balance on my credit card. What I'm actually afraid of is what lack of money ultimately leads to, which is how it will make me feel.

Having money in the bank is the thing that I think will help me not feel that way.

Since I'm afraid of feeling unsafe, I make up all these rules, methods, and goals to make sure I don't feel it, which take the form of having stuff like lots of money and frantic, constant busyness, and all the other items on my to-do list that, if I only get them done, will supposedly prevent me from feeling what I don't want to feel.

This explains so much.

All the things we climb for and reach toward in life—objects like houses, cars, marriages, jobs, money, kids, etc.—all of them become our goals because we expect them to help us either feel something we want to feel or avoid feeling something we don't want to feel.

Almost all our actions and choices are helping us either go into feelings or get away from them.

This kind of means feelings rule the world, doesn't it? It means the queen must be the literal and figurative power behind the throne, right? Because everything we choose to do or not do is ultimately in anticipation of feelings —of having them or avoiding them.

What's more, we can take any "surface-level feeling" or desire and dig to its deepest point to find the core of what we're either trying to reach or avoid. And then, we can look at all the things in our life that we're striving for or wanting and see exactly why we're truly wanting them.

Let's say you're desperate for a romantic partner. That is the "thing" goal. But why do you want this partnership—what feelings will you get from it? Well, you want to feel deep, interconnected love and trust. You want to feel safe and accepted. The partner is the *means* to these feelings.

On the other hand, what if you're afraid you'll never find your soul mate?

Then you go deeper: If you never find them, you'll feel like life is withholding your one true love, which is nasty and unfair. It means you'll feel lonely. It means there's something wrong with you. It means you'll die alone. It means everyone else has something that you're too messed up to have. You're an outsider. You don't belong.

You see where we're getting to? You are deeply afraid of feeling these things. Having a partner assures you that you won't ever feel them. You aren't afraid of not having a partner *per se*, you're afraid of *feeling those yucky feelings*.

Light bulbs on, anyone?

Let's say you have a pretty basic list of things you want. Most of us have a variation of the following desires:

1. I want a great career (makes me feel fulfilled).
2. I want tons of money (makes me feel safe).
3. I want to be in love with a partner (makes me feel loveable).
4. I want good health (makes me feel safe).
5. I want close friends (makes me feel understood).
6. I want a loving family (makes me feel needed).

Notice how each "thing" has a feeling that you think the thing will create in you. ("A loving family makes me *feel* needed.") Each thing you're craving in life either leads you to emotions you want to feel or helps you avoid the opposite. In other words, if you don't get these things, the result will be emotions you don't want to feel.

What this really means is that it's never about the *things*. It's always about the pleasure or pain response. We line stuff up in our lives as goals so we feel more pleasure and less pain.

Never ever confuse *the thing* with *the feelings*.

Whenever you want a *thing*, ask yourself what feelings it'll give you. That's what you're really going for, always. Then remember that you've probably already tried the direct logical path to the *thing*, the path everyone told you would or should work. It didn't. You'd already have this perfect life if it had. Now, let's try this new way instead as we head toward feelings and let the actual right *things* slip into place around them.

I know this has been a lot to take in. Pay attention to the three biggest ideas in this chapter:

1. We're afraid to feel feelings because many emotions are so icky that we'll do everything we can to avoid them and move toward the happy ones instead.

2. You can always work backward from your surface level feelings to discover the bigger, deeper feelings that are actually pushing you around.

3. Feelings are always, always, always your ultimate goal, not things.

M.E. *School* Prompt

Your prompt is to identify the things you want, then right next to them, write the feelings you think these things will give you.

In this prompt, you're essentially taking a "Life Inventory" of things you desire in all areas of your life. You may want things like a good car, a loving partner, a fit body, tons of money in the bank, a promotion, or a raise. You're going to write those things down, then right next to them, our switcheroo is that we take these things to their true conclusion—the *feelings* you think the thing could give you.

Go as deep as you can with the ultimate feelings you think you'll get from the things you're wanting. Remember my example about money? Initially, I wanted money (thing) because I hate feeling pressured and stressed. But when I go deeper, I discover that I'm afraid to end up feeling unsafe, in pain, with my world and family shattered. Yikes.

Ultimately, *I want money so I can feel safe.* Safety is therefore what drives many of my financial and career decisions, and a certain amount of money or paid-off credit cards is what gives me that feeling of safety.

After you've written the list and the feelings, cross out all the "things" so you're only staring at the feelings. Feel the wobble in your heart as you do this. Feel the worry that without the "thing" goal, you won't have a visible path to these feelings.

This is a complex prompt. Take your time with it. In fact, here's a quick example of how it might look when you fill out each statement that follows:

Work or career things I want: I want $100k in savings and all my credit card debt paid off.

Feeling: I want to feel materially and financially safe forever with all my needs met.

Now, it's your turn. In your journal, fill out the statements below.

Health and wellness things I want (my appearance, health, fitness, self-image, mental health, and well-being):

_____

_____

And getting those will make me feel:

_____

_____

Financial things I want (money, income, savings, debt, security, and consistency):

_____

_____

And getting those will make me feel:

_____

_____

Work or career things I want (your job, school, career opportunities, achievements):

_____

_____

And getting those will make me feel:

_____

_____

Social things I want (your friendships, hobbies, community):

_____

_____

And getting those will make me feel:

_____

_____

Family things I want (with the exception of my partner or spouse):

_____

_____

And getting those will make me feel:

_____

_____

Spiritual and personal growth things I want (certificates, courses, breakthroughs, experiences):

_____

_____

_____

_____

And getting those will make me feel:

_____

_____

_____

Partnership things I want (to be in a relationship, to leave a relationship, to fix a relationship):

_____

_____

_____

_____

And getting those will make me feel:

_____

_____

_____

Chapter 8:
Just What Are These Feelings Called?

Saying "the feelings that you want these things to give you" is a real mouthful, so I've shortened it. I call them your emotional endpoints. Emotional endpoints are the *feeling goal* you have for just about every area of your life.

So that oozy sweet feeling of sunlight on your brow as you stare out over the sweet turquoise sea? That hot second of flaming, juicy joy watching your child win the championship? That peaceful moment after the big holiday is done and the candles are blown out when everything is *soooooo* good, you are *sooooo* content, and you wonder if maybe this is the happiest moment you've ever had in your life?

Emotional endpoints, all of them. And once you feel one, it has then been etched into your persona, now carried inside you for life. It's up there encoded in your neurons, stored for safekeeping. And some say it's also encoded in your soul, making up a part of you that you'll carry forever.

Your goal? More emotional endpoints like these, and less of the bad emotions that seem to slide their sneaky asses in when you aren't looking.

But mostly, you're going for more *day-to-day average happiness*. You know, just basic level happiness. That would be enough for most of us.

So how do we get there? Now that you've identified some emotional end-points that you want in different areas of your life, how do you start using them?

Let's go play with the idea of having a good romantic partnership (thing) so you feel adored, understood, and wanted (emotional endpoints). Now what if you said instead, "I want to feel adored, understood, and wanted?"

You could then say: "Damn, I can start getting that feeling anywhere. Maybe my family is already giving it to me. Maybe I can get that feeling at work. Maybe my community can step up and give it to me. Holy moly, I can get these feelings from multiple sources, not just a partner!"

Now, don't fret . . . I know you want to feel a *particular* kind of adored, not the kind of adored your kids or boss can give you. But this is where things get good: Now that you know to focus on your emotional endpoints, you can let life plug in multiple avenues to reach them, not just the narrowly defined ways of getting there that you used to land on. And trust me, life knows that a life partner will yield the *ultimate sense* of being adored, understood, and wanted, so that is going to be on the table for you. You may just get those feelings in all those other areas too. Not a bad deal.

Here's how this same idea plays out with a typical person, another M.E. School student, just like you:

Student: I need a guy who really loves me, he's going to live nearby, have money, have a good career, be super loyal, and I just love dark hair! He's also going to be taller than me and really in shape.

Me: How does this person make you feel?

Student: He makes me feel trusting, authentically me, safe, and adored. He makes me feel attracted to him. It feels easy and not stressful.

Me: What if we just say, "I feel loved by a partner who makes me feel trusting, authentic, safe, adored, sexy, content, and relaxed."

Student: But I like dark-haired guys.

Me: Don't you see that if you feel all those things I just said, then by default it won't matter what he looks like, where he lives, where he works, or anything else? You wouldn't feel those things if any of that didn't line up.

Follow? You can let go of every single detail that isn't emotion based—*every single one*—because all you're really going for is the emotions, truly, and the pieces that get you to those emotions will all just line up.

Need another example? Let's say you want a house in Hawaii to retire in. It's gotta be in Maui, on the shore, fit your budget, no fixer-uppers.

Why? Because when you retire you want to feel like every day is paradise. You earned it.

So, how about instead we say: *I feel myself fully safe, supported, and no longer working. I'm living in paradise. Everything about where I live makes me feel happy, relaxed, and proud. I love my affordable home. I feel so much love for it. It's so easy to take care of and be in.*

There—now you have just spelled out your emotional endpoints. This is how you want to feel. You've also opened up a thousand new potential places to retire in that could make you feel this way. Maybe life has a place in the Florida Keys for you that will make you feel this way. Maybe you'll end up in the Seychelles. Maybe you'll discover a little town on the Baja coast. All your feeling boxes get checked, so why should you care if it's not Maui? Instead of just one path to happiness, you blew the doors open to a multitude of paths that all have ease, affordability, and paradise factored in.

Sounds a lot easier to shoot for, doesn't it? It also sounds a lot easier for life to serve it up to you, being that there are so many options now instead of that one creaky little path you were previously on. Remember:

You are guided by either moving toward positive *emotional endpoints or by avoiding negative emotional endpoints.*

So might as well start focusing on them directly. Let life click things into place based on what your deeper self is longing for. Be flexible with the objects, places, and people that show up to fill the path there.

When you get your desired endpoint, you can be sure that the *details will always fit by default*—even if they're wildly different than you ever imagined.

The Crayon Box of Feelings

Right here is where you say, "Sounds good, Summer, but most of my day-to-day feelings are pretty *meh*, sometimes *bleh*, and now and then *grrrrr*. How do you expect me to make all these good feelings?"

You're talking about your personal, daily feelings—the way you feel from the minute you wake up to the minute you fall asleep. The way your day seems to slide and push you around, nudging you like a sail in a brisk wind into feeling all kinds of things, and you're at its mercy.

Let's differentiate *reactionary, response-based feelings* from *purposely created emotional endpoints.*

Response-based feelings are fiery little darts that keep getting shot out of a pistol over and over, and each one is drawn out by something happening outside you. It can feel like you're at the mercy of anything and everything that comes along to provoke one.

Let's say that mom calls; there's bad news about your dad. You feel upset, worried, and resigned. Or you're looking for a text from your boyfriend that hasn't come . . . for two days. You're pissed, hurt, and anxious. Then you look in the mirror and notice an extra chin forming. You feel self-loathing, disappointment, and more resignation.

Or maybe it's been a good day: You woke up early and exercised. You feel pleased. You ate a healthy breakfast and feel self-satisfied. You think about your grandma's birthday and feel warmth and love.

Every one of these feelings ricochets out in response to some external stimuli—the thing that happened that caused this feeling.

Not one feeling was self-generated, meaning you felt something without some external event triggering it. You're just one giant walking trigger. No wonder you don't trust your feelings anymore. You have essentially no control over them. You're used and abused, and you call this normal.

Except you do have control. Emotions aren't your enemies, they're your friends. You *could* choose each and every response carefully and thoughtfully. But you don't. You *could* feel things you wanted to feel without there being any kind of reason to feel them. Except that's weird.

What if every emotion you have is like a colored crayon in a box. There are hundreds of colors to choose from, and each one does a different thing for your life. Not only that, but there's no invisible hand drawing them out and scribbling your feelings all over all the time—that's just how you've been conditioned to think. You've never thought about your emotions as being useful, powerful, or proactive. They've always just been responsive reflexes.

Not anymore. See that bright, sunny yellow crayon? That's contentment. Contentment means that everything is good, everything is in its place. All is well. The feeling spreads on like butter and washes through you. You can feel contentment now if you want. Don't say, "Content about *what*?" Just say, *I feel content.*

Maybe try peace. Peace means feeling relaxed and at ease. Nothing to worry about, no stressors. Just an engulfing sense of pleasant, rosy pink peace. Feel it now.

I feel peaceful.

Don't feel peaceful *about* something because then you're making it into a trigger, a response. Just feel peace, generally, connected to nothing.

Weird huh? I bet you had to work for them. You maybe didn't nail them immediately because you had nothing to force them out, like normal.

Let's try another: *I feel fucking irritated.*

There, see how much easier that one was? It's easier since you're so used to feeling it. It's like the nubby worn-down little crayon. You use it all the time. It's easy to whip out, especially because you probably made it in response to something—a person or event that you inadvertently responded to as you thought about feeling irritated.

Negative feelings are usually a lot easier to call up on demand since we have these enormous storehouses in our minds of things we've already attached them to, like thinking of your body and feeling grossness about how you think you look, or thinking of your boss and sighing with frustration. *Boom!* Both of those come roaring in so easily since they have triggers for them you've already been carrying around in your mind. That means they're still *responses*. They aren't you truly choosing your feelings and taking back the control.

To do that, you have to pick a crayon that you don't normally use much—one that you don't have that many situations already stored up to respond to.

Let's choose a gorgeous peachy pink, the color of a tropical drink on a breezy day. This is the feeling of affection, which, if you bring it up and feel it right now, is a close cousin to love.

You might ask, "What should I feel affection for?" Well, let's make this game even more difficult: Don't assign any recipient to the feeling. Just feel *affection*. What's it like? A little like love, but not as intense? Is it a little gentler, a bit quieter? Do thoughts of people and pets and old homes still rush in to try to take advantage of the feeling? That's okay, you can let them. But really, just feel the emotion itself: affection.

The Power of Pre-Action

Why for God's sake would we want to practice this?

Well, look: You probably spend half your day feeling crappy feelings, since there's a lot in our lives that trigger those. You spend another quarter feeling not much at all, just closed off and neutral. And maybe you've got that last 25 percent for happy feelings: love, joy, security, pride, excitement, affirmation, stuff like that. Maybe it's even less for you each day. Some of us get a squirt of those maybe once a week or even less.

Did you feel any of those happy feelings recently? Or even today?

You are what you *feel*.

You've heard that before, right? You are what you feel.

What you feel is who you become, since literally your emotions are flooding through you twenty-four hours a day, influencing every action, thought, and decision you make. Look at your crayon box and see which emotions are the most used, the most constant. Are those the ones you want to be giving to yourself and your life so constantly? Or are they mostly all just knee-jerk response emotions to things outside you? Are you rattling around like a pinball, striking whichever pins you randomly fly into as stuff happens to you all day?

Let's change that. Let's open up all the other beautiful colors and start feeling them. And here's the catch: Don't wait for your life to give you a reason or permission to do so. If you do that, you're gonna be waiting a while. Instead, spend some time with that lush violet/magenta: *gratitude*. Or pick up healthy, energized emerald green. Allow these feelings to blossom in you multiple times a day.

And you bet, I've got a name for this too: It's called having a *pre-sponse,* or *pre-action,* which is the opposite of *response* and *reaction*. When you *pre-act* instead of *react,* it's like you're showing your life in advance how you expect it to make you feel later—you're sketching certain feelings in your mind and energy for the outside world to read and respond to. This is totally the opposite of your usual way of feeling things.

Flowdreaming

Over the years, I developed a potent, quick practice for creating pre-sponses and pre-actions on demand. It's called "Flowdreaming." It's a specific method that only takes about ten minutes a day. It combines guided day-dreaming with strong, pre-active emotion while you're in what's called "flow state." It's absurdly easy to learn, and most people pick it up after just a few tries.

Think of it as a little like guided meditation, except in Flowdreaming, your goal is to stay hyper-emotionally invested while you give your mind a ton of fun imagery to play with, even as you let go into a beautiful, timeless space inside you.

Okay, I just made it sound hard again, but it's not. In fact, most people say it's a strangely familiar state, as natural as sunlight on your skin. I'll distill it for you here.

How to Flowdream

To Flowdream, first find a quiet place and close your eyes. Relax your body. Take some slow, deep breaths. Let yourself drift. When you're ready, allow yourself to daydream that you're moving forward through time and space, maybe by imagining yourself floating in a meandering stream, or skating forward effortlessly through a soft, white landscape, or even walking forward on a perfect tropical beach right by the lip of ocean foam that rushes to the shore. The point is, imagine *anything* that makes you feel aligned, directional, moving, and in a right and good place. We want energy, focus, and imagination. You aren't hypnotizing yourself. And you're not meditating. Don't clear your mind, *fill it.*

You're actively engaged in a daydream that you're making up in real time and with a very specific goal of being able to create some pre-active emotional endpoints inside it.

Next, allow the emotions you want to feel to swell and fill you. *Become them.* Be them. Feel them pulse in your chest and expand through your body. You're *pre-acting* and *pre-sponding* to all the good things that haven't happened yet in your life. It can feel a little like practicing gratitude, except you're grateful for something that hasn't even happened yet. And you have a swirl of other positive emotions as well . . . maybe ones like security, healthiness, peace, or fulfillment. The list of potential positive emotions to feel is practically endless. You just have to match the right ones to the area of your life you're wanting to change, heal, or improve.

And last, if you do the first two parts correctly, you'll likely enter a state of flow. Flow state was originally identified by pioneering positive psychologist Dr. Mihaly Csikszentmihalyi, and the idea has been applied to all kinds of high-performance applications in the decades since. The state of being in flow generally means you're performing in a kind of peak efficiency that elevates you into a "zone" beyond the ordinary, whether while playing your perfect-scoring golf game or solving a previously unsolvable scientific puzzle.

However, you won't be golfing or making scientific breakthroughs today. Instead, we're going to use this state to create a kind of peak efficiency around your emotions—specifically, the positive emotional endpoints you've chosen to generate.

Let's review.

How to Flowdream

1. Close your eyes and relax in a quiet place.
2. Open up your imagination and let yourself daydream using whatever imagery makes you feel like you're moving in a positive, aligned direction.
3. Begin feeling your emotional endpoints either in a general way or get specific around a particular desire or situation in your life.
4. Release into flow state by sensing yourself fully letting go into the emotion, movement, and divine alignment around you.

At some point between steps three and four (feeling your emotional endpoints and releasing into that powerful, forward-moving feeling of alignment), something interesting happens. You know that feeling of waking up in the morning, and you hit your snooze button and think, "Just five more minutes?" Then you sink back into sleep, but as you do, there's a moment's awareness of passing back into sleep. It's the submerging, "sinking into sleep" feeling. Whatever it feels like to you, think of it as a sliver of overlap where your conscious is passing the baton to the subconscious, and you feel a sliver of that overlap as you shimmer through. Entering flow is similar . . . one minute you're aware of everything around you (the dog barking, the sirens wailing outside) and then the next moment you've let go, and now you're fully absorbed and enraptured with dazzling imagery and awash in all the big beautiful feelings you're producing. You sense a powerful, forward-feeling, divinely guided sense of perfect and positive alignment and direction. And you have completely lost awareness of the world around you, the outside noises, or even how much time is passing.

You'll know you reach flow state if, when you open your eyes a few minutes later, you've lost track of how much time has passed, forgot you have a body and the environment for a moment, and feel like you just returned from an extraordinary, emotion-packed daydream. *The whole process can take as little as five minutes.*

Emotional Reconditioning vs. Flowdreaming

Of course, there's a lot more to Flowdreaming than this. I've written two books about Flowdreaming already. That's why I'm just giving you the outline here. And maybe you just want to stop at Step 3, in which case you're doing what I call "emotional reconditioning." The process will still work even without adding in the flow part of it.

With emotional reconditioning, it doesn't matter whether or not you believe in manifesting, "alignment," or being able to shape the inner energies of your life. At the very least what you're doing is creating a little more emotional balance inside you. You're dropping your daily miserable feelings percentage from 70 percent to 30 percent. You're upping your positive feelings from 10 percent to 50 percent. And your mind responds to your continued daily practice of these feelings.

If you went to the gym and worked your biceps every day, your biceps would grow bigger and stronger. If you go to your emotional gym and work on your peaceful, anti-anxious feelings every day, then those peaceful feelings will likewise strengthen and grow in you. You've heard this before, but your brain is plastic, flexible, and responsive; when you start feeling happy, joyful feelings, your neurons shift and grow into those channels.

This is why your emotions are not your enemies. They're tools—important, powerful, daily tools. They should be treated as such. They don't run you. You run them, or at least you can run them when you try.

Now, to everyone in your life who ever told you, "Don't feel that way, you're stupid," or "Don't be a girl," or "Crying is for babies," or "Don't manipulate me," or any other bullshit like that, know this: Your emotions aren't silly, babyish, manipulative, or "too feminine." They're just emotions, and they're the biggest tools you have for shaping your life.

That's why people are always trying to make you stuff them, hide them, not have them, and give you crap for showing them. Emotions are raw power. They get shit done.

So go pick a crayon and begin working with it. Feel it over and over. Don't give it a reason to exist other than you just want to feel it now. Pick something glorious, like gratitude, love, or receiving. You're making something, *in you,* and you're also telling your life that this is what you want and expect more of. And the more you make it (pre-act it), the more it grows both inside and outside in your life.

It's time to let your emotional power finally bloom.

M.E. School Prompt

Your two-part prompt is to really let this concept of pre-action settle in and to figure out just how often you spend your time reacting instead of pre-acting. Then, set up a daily practice of feeling your new emotional endpoints, either through Flowdreaming or by simply honing in on those feelings by closing your eyes for five minutes a day and letting yourself feel them (emotional reconditioning).

This is perhaps the most important prompt in this whole book. We're starting it now, in chapter 8, and we'll return to this idea again and again as you grow more emotionally nimble through the chapters ahead. Just because I don't talk about this exercise constantly (because we have a lot more to cover) doesn't mean I'm not breathing down your neck to do it. Of all the exercises and prompts we do, *this is the one that has the biggest daily, cumulative effect in your life.*

Part One: Journal on the following questions. It's okay to feel clumsy with these answers right now. As you practice, you'll get a lot more clear on what, exactly, you want to feel.

    What situations typically cause me to be reactive instead of pre-active? What are the emotional endpoints I want to feel instead in these situations?

    When will I do this pre-active emotional reconditioning or Flowdreaming? Will I set up a daily time for it?

    What area(s) of my life do I want to start reshaping with this technique? Refer to the Life Inventory prompt from chapter 7.

Part Two: Select an emotional endpoint or pre-action you'd like to feel in the area of your life that you chose.

Now, close your eyes and feel your emotional endpoints using either Flowdreaming or emotional reconditioning for at least five minutes.

If you don't feel much or aren't sure if you're doing it right, don't worry. We have a lot more M.E. School ahead, and more will become clear as we move on.

Chapter 9:
The Dead Zone

The Dead Zone. No, it's not a zombie flick. It's how you feel when you're totally, completely wrung out and *over it*. You've got no fucks left to give, no emotional energy or feelings left to even play with.

If you're struggling to feel any emotional endpoints . . . wait; if you're struggling to even *want* to try to feel emotional endpoints . . . then this chapter is for you.

The Dead Zone

Up in the Pacific Ocean, somewhere out past Washington off the US West Coast, there's a big swath of empty ocean. It's a victim of hypoxia—a lack of oxygen. Fish that swim into it die. Corals and creatures that can't swim out die too. Snails that crawl too slowly . . . dead.

There are hundreds of Dead Zones around the earth right now.

And there may be one in your own heart.

Another word for Dead Zone is "no snap-back ability," which is a lot harder to say. You're like a rubber band that got stretched so much it can no longer hold your ponytail. It's limp, spent. You keep expecting it to hold, yet it won't.

Earlier, I was on the phone with a client, and she was telling me that she has no passion in her life. She doesn't even know what she wants, but she knows that where she's at is dry, boring, and repetitive. Her psychological immune system has totally crapped out.

My husband recently told me at dinner that new studies show that the most miserable median age in a person's life in the United States is 47.8 years. He tells me it's the lowest point, when life is most likely to be unfulfilling. It's when our bodies start to show their age, our kids have gotten very expensive, our elderly parents are requiring all our emotional resources, our marriages are aging and brittle, our finances are stretched thin and there are more bills than ever, the prospect of a poor-ass retirement is haunting us, and our work has settled into a seemingly permanent holding pattern with no advancement in sight.

Sweet Jesus, that sounds awful.

That's a Dead Zone. And your snap-back ability has been spent. Too much has been pulled from you, for too long. You've shouldered a thousand burdens, and you need a rest. You need a long holiday in France, walking the lavender valleys. You need a deep, emotional detox with no demands on you from anyone for a full year. You need golden coins to fill your bank accounts so there's no money stress anymore.

You're laughing at these ideas and sort of crying too. Or maybe, in the Dead Zone, you feel nothing much at all.

Resignation. Tiredness. No passion. No desire.

You're a flattened pancake. The idea of summoning emotion, *any* emotion, on demand is ridiculous. All that stuff about *pre-action*? Yeah, great, if you even had any emotion to work with. Now what?

Obviously, you don't want to stay here.

Clearly, you need to refill the well. You need to restock the shelves in your life. You've got to start gathering the components that will refill and rebuild your emotional self.

See, you've probably been waiting for a big cure-all to come to you, to reignite you and put some burn back in you—a *one-and-done*. But you don't have a wick anymore. What's a lighter going to light? You need a wick; you need fuel.

Restock Your Pantry

Here's what can happen instead: You're going to restock your pantry with the equivalent of cumin and cardamom, with spicy black beans and croissants. You have no idea how any of these ingredients will fit together. But no cook is inspired by empty shelves. They are inspired by a full pantry overflowing with possibilities.

The ocean needs oxygen. You need newness and possibilities.

You're going to begin by drawing up a list of the Dead Zones in your life: your relationship, your work, health, friendships, etc. Maybe it's every area—maybe the Dead Zone is your own heart, your own soul's burnout.

Now, under each area, you'll write down quirky ideas and ways to add color and interest to each of these areas. For example, if work is your Dead Zone, write down things like "Redecorate my cubicle. Spend a day searching for jobs way outside my expertise. Attend a webinar on entrepreneurship. Look up certification programs in a totally different field. Get a friend to go to a wholesale flower market with me."

Mind you, none of these things need to be in any way directly related to your current work. The things you dream up are all ways to add diversity and new components and connections into your life. If you only think up normal things that you'd normally do to make work more palatable, you're missing the point. Think up *ab*normal things. Think of things wildly unconnected to your daily life. If you'd normally decorate your cubicle at work with photos of your family, then turn it into a magical ski slope instead, with snow globes and photos of snowy pines.

I know, I know, this sounds ridiculous. Hear me out.

Be Wild, Silly, and Creative

Be wild, silly, and creative with this list. Definitely do not be *on point*. Instead, wander. If the Dead Zone is everywhere in your life, then go even further out with your ideas. Write down things like: "Book a trip to Panama. Join a church choir. Get fish tacos and eat them by the ocean on my way home from work. Buy a new painting to put over the couch, one with lots of color and life. Get some bright new pillows for the couch, too, while I'm at it. Take a different route home from work. Stop at a new, cute boutique on the way home. Go to a museum. Blow bubbles on the beach. Buy crafting supplies, and take a class in making mosaics. Get some oracle cards and begin playing with them. Go take a stroll, or jog by the lake or in the forest. Plan a day at my local spa. Join a bowling league. See a medium who can communicate with grandma. Drive to a new nearby town and explore it. Set up an appointment with a great doctor or naturopath and get those hormones checked."

Get the idea? Be silly. Be wild.

Write down things you haven't done in a long time, or have never, ever done. They can be things that used to make you feel good, or things that you have no idea how they'll make you feel—they just seem sorta interesting.

I know you don't want to do this yet. You're too low to even find them fun or interesting. It sounds like a lot of worthless work that you'll have to peel yourself off the couch to do. But stay with me.

Once the list is written, begin to *do* the things on your list. Drag yourself through the motions if you have to. But get some or all of them done. Plan to do two a week, or one a day. There's no absolute "schedule."

Yes, Summer, but how does doing a bunch of random new things reignite me?

Sometimes, external action is what changes the interior.

Don't pooh-pooh it as too obvious a solution, or you won't even try.

You aren't looking for that "magic bullet" thing that will instantly wake up your heart and fill you with passion again. You've been waiting for that for years, and it still hasn't arrived, so it's time to try a new route.

Instead of a magic bullet, you're now relying on **creating** an accumulation of new elements that will eventually reach a tipping point.

To return to the pantry idea, everything you do that's outside your box of normalness is like adding a spice to your cupboard. You're restocking the shelves, even if you aren't ready to cook with them yet. Every outing, every new thing you add in becomes one of the new building blocks you'll get to work with later.

My own pantry got filled a few weeks ago when I was in line at a drive-through coffee shop. Someone had "paid it forward," meaning they'd paid for my order before I even got to the window. Wow, how exciting! How fun. How weird. My experience getting coffee unexpectedly turned into an experience of generosity. Of course, I, too, then paid it forward. How long could we keep this chain going?

This unlooked-for bit of "spice" in my day went straight into the pantry of my heart. I discovered (remembered) that I love the feeling of creating surprises for other people. And that awareness became . . . a little bit of new feeling swimming in my heart. My Dead Zone shrank a teensy bit.

This is the process for rebuilding your wick. You're turning a gray empty closet into something filled with sparkling, exciting treasures and light, bottles of magical potions, and the drift of chimes ringing through the air. One day, after you've built this spicy little pantry in your life, you'll walk in and something bright will catch your eye. And that's when your Dead Zone shrinks again.

It will finally happen. You'll feel a rise in you. You'll realize that you're still tired, burned-out, and flat, but something feels good. And you'll do more of it. But since you don't know what "it" is yet, your sole job is to just start restocking your life with possibilities.

When you surround yourself with new ideas, new experiences, and new places . . . then new opportunities and desires have room to take root and grow. You have fed the soil of your life with the nutrients it's been starving for.

Or, another way of saying it is that the only way an ocean recovers is to refuel the Dead Zones with oxygen. One way to refuel your own life and get past the ennui is to add in more material to choose from and place yourself inside a fully stocked palace for the soul.

You can't light a candle without a wick. You can't find life swimming in the sea without oxygen. And you can't recover from your Dead Zones with an empty cupboard.

M.E. *School* Prompt

Your prompt is to write your list, then choose some things on it to actually do. And do them.

Write it.

Choose a few.

Do them.

Don't do two out of three. I'm looking for three out of three here. That's where the magic lies . . . *in the doing.* In fact, do *more* than one thing. Lots more. As many as you can handle.

Things that might, could, or just possibly may add some glitter and fun into my life are . . .

_____

_____

_____

_____

_____

_____

_____

_____

_____

_____

PART III:
Fuck the Fear

Chapter 10:
External Power Leaks

It began with a vague dissatisfaction about the idea of reincarnation, of all things. And this is when people in my world were constantly throwing around the words, "It must be from a past life." As if, "That means I can't do a damn thing about it because it's like *divine karma,* you know? I gotta suck it up and take it."

And I'd think, *Huh, what a crappy idea.* It means some "Other You" did something, and now you have to balance the old scales even though you have zero awareness of what happened.

It's like punching the brother for something the sister did.

More importantly, it means you don't have any power to change things. You shifted that power out of your life and back into some other time, some other place, some other person.

Now, this is a *way* simplified version of karma, I know that. But that's how people were using it—as a way to remove their power over their own life and destiny and place it into the hands of something they had no control over. If it was *karma,* you could shrug and stop trying. If it was *karma,* your only option is to navigate the oncoming shit because avoiding it is out of the question. It's got you by the balls.

I began to notice myself doing this weird transfer of power to other people and circumstances in my life, too, but in other ways than karma. I noticed how I'd feel angry, frustrated, disappointed—all those yucky feelings and reactions, and I'd just *wait* for the person or thing who caused me these feelings to fix things. The control was out of my hands and in someone else's. All I could do was wait for *them* to make the next move so I could feel better.

As in: "Darn it, Mom, if you would only stop being so negative, then I could feel less stressed!"

And "I need *you,* Hubby, to get a damn job so we can have some money, because I'm tired of always struggling!"

Or "No one is giving me an offer to speak at their conferences, and I'm so frustrated."

And even "I guess it's just not the right time yet for the world to see my true gifts. The universe just doesn't want me to have that experience."

Everywhere I looked, I was assigning my power to other people, other things. Everyone was "making" me feel a certain way, and if only they'd change or do the thing I needed them to do, then I could feel better. My feelings were hostage to their actions (or nonactions).

Mom holds the power over my stress level.

Hubby holds the power over me feeling financially safe and not struggling.

Conference organizers hold the power over whether I feel professionally validated or not.

The universe (or God) holds the power over whether I'm successful and able to share my teachings with a wide audience.

These are called *power leaks.* When I saw them in me, I began to really, deeply see them in everyone else too. I began saying to my clients things like "Why are you waiting for your kid to move out of the basement? Your happiness is hanging on the thread of what someone else will or won't do. Think about it—your kid has zero incentive to move out. And you're thinking he's going to magically wake up someday and realize your happiness is dependent on him, and then feel joyful motivation to change? Nope, not gonna happen.

You have a choice: either get happy about him living with you or tell him he has thirty days to move out."

That's the funny part: It's so easy to see where other people aren't claiming their power. It's just not obvious for *us* with our *own* power leaks.

Yeah, imagine that: Everyone can see our power leaks *but us.* How many times have you told someone to just fix their problem or stop complaining? It seems obvious to you that the issue is imminently curable (*take your ex back to child-support court, tell your boss they need to hire someone to help you, stop buying salt-and-vinegar potato chips and hit the gym*).

But they won't fix it; they feel they *can't* fix it.

So I devised a way to see our own personal power leaks. It goes like this:

1. Think about a situation where you've been unhappy for a long time.

2. Now think about why you think that is. What's causing it?

    Does the universe just not want to give you a soul mate?

    Does your boss just not want to promote you?

    Does your girlfriend make you feel insecure?

    Mostly, you're going to pin it on something that has to change, and it's something that won't change.

3. The exact amount of time you've had unhappiness about a situation is the exact amount of time you've had a power leak around it.

Now spin in a circle in your imagination and see all the areas or places where you're blocked from your true expression and happiness.

Maybe you say, "I don't have enough money to do what I want to do."

Okay, money is the power leak: It doesn't like you or want you.

"No," you say, "it's not money; it's that people or my work or life won't give me enough money."

Okay, so there are random people at work who won't give you money.

"No, it's that life doesn't give me a chance to get a better job to get that money."

Okay, so it's life's fault? Life doesn't want you to have money?

Eventually, you get to the root of whose fault it is. And when you hit "life's fault" you've pretty much hit the limit, since life is something you definitely can't change or control. It's all outside you, out there, unknowable, kind of like karma.

I saw, for instance, that I was waiting for life to give me a new publisher. Until I had that, no one was going to find out about my Flowdreaming work. I was stopped—waiting and frustrated.

It's why I haven't written for the last eleven years. I've had a power leak for eleven years.

And then one day, after eleven years, I saw the power leak: I had decided that my fate was in the hands of a publisher. And since my last publisher had let my prior books go out of print . . . well, the whole publishing mess was chock-full of icky, oozing, power-leaking feelings. Until a new publisher swept in to save me, I was stuck, waiting for that knight in shining armor named Penguin or Bantam to come give me the feelings of trust, hope, and validation I wanted.

But I realized: There must be a million other ways to get my work into the world. And that as long as "the thing" (getting a new book deal) was hung up on the power leak of me needing a publisher to give me the feelings I wanted from the thing, then I was at an impasse with life.

So I took my power back from that idea. I focused instead on feelings: *My work is widely known, respected, change making, and profitable.*

And however it gets to those feelings (via a traditional publisher, self-publishing, a cameo on daytime TV . . . whatever) is fine. Just get there.

Maybe this is sounding like radical autonomy. It kind of is: It's radical ownership. Ownership of all your feelings and understanding that you're waiting on all those things that are "making" you feel like crap to "unmake" you feeling like crap.

Most of those things *can't or won't*. And frankly, it's not their job to make you feel any certain way.

Let's go back to that one thing you've been waiting to have happen—the person or thing you're waiting on that holds the ball. Meaning, they hold the power, not you.

Remember that this is *your* life, not theirs. Why should they hold that power to make you feel a certain way? Because you gave it to them. You gave them that power. And there are only a very few people in the world whom you should love so much that you want them to have that kind of power over your feelings.

So now, every time you say, "This is what is making me feel like dog poo," instead say, "It's not their responsibility to make me feel the way I want to feel. Wow, I sure gave them a lot of power over me! Heck no, I'm going to choose how I want to feel, and then go find my own way of getting that feeling."

If you can't unpack this whole idea right away, that's okay. Or maybe you get it intellectually but can't see it in your own life.

Again, that's okay. Sometimes you have to sit in this concept for a while. My students often sit in it for a year or more before they start to see all their power leaks revealed and then discover how to take their power back. So, just let the concept *be* inside you. Remember, a big leak of mine took *eleven years* to become clear.

M.E. *School* Prompt

Your prompt is the next time you notice that something has made you feel bad, ask yourself, "Who's holding the power in this situation?"

Because if it's not you, it means you've given your power to someone else. And that is a power leak, and it is solvable.

Explore your power leaks with the following prompts. *Warning: this process can become delightfully addictive.*

What things in my life are not moving forward or progressing, or are continuously placing me in a position of having to wait or feel like my needs aren't getting met, and that it's in someone else's hands to fix? (Think, "I'm stuck here_____and here_____ _____."

Who/what am I blaming for this?

How have I given my power to them/it?

What can I do to take my power back from them/it?

What will I lose if I do?

What will I gain if I do?

Chapter 11:
Inner Batteries

Let's give this concept of power leaks a little more depth because honestly, you can't visit this idea enough. Everything you want to make, build, create, or grow next in life is probably getting snagged in a power leak. This is why I said before that while I can teach people how to manifest things using their feeling goals (aka, emotional endpoints), they won't manifest them as long as they're still unconsciously manifesting something else—something all tied up and stalled out in a power leak. And power leaks *steal energy*.

Pretend you have a battery inside you. Chinese medicine calls it *chi*—your life force. You're granted a certain amount when you're born, and when you use it up, *poof,* that's it, game over.

Of course, many traditions call it many other things. But in M.E. School, it's a battery.

You also have a daily battery. You wake up full, and you end the day empty. You sleep to recharge it.

Now what do you spend your battery on each day?

You do a lot of physical things, like working or eating. You do a lot of mental things, like talking and thinking.

And you do a lot of emotional things, like reacting and feeling.

And you do a lot of invisible things that leech your battery the same way that leaving all the plugs in your house plugged into the wall leech "phantom power" all day.

Power leaks are like those phantom electricity leaks—those plugged in but turned off appliances that are still pulling micro wattage.

Because you see, you *hold* them. They take space in you. They're a belief, an inner ceiling, a person or thing you've given power to . . . any or all those things.

We're expanding the concept of power leaks now, see? It's not just a person or thing you're waiting on that's a power leak. Even a messy room is a power leak.

Why? Because when you walk into a messy room your eyes and brain sweep through the placement of all the items. Your brain has to check them against language and visual memory to identify them. Your mind has to interpret the physical space around them so you don't run into them or step on them. It figures out how they're oriented. Upside down? Inside out? Or normal?

A lot goes on. Messy rooms are exhausting.

Think about a super clean room or a very modern room with not much in it. Notice how all the fancy rich-people magazines show modern homes with little decor—so clear, clean, and high class. It's like they're saying, "We can afford not to have all that emotional clutter in our lives."

Notice, too, that when you enter a room like that, you feel a little awkward, lighter, or empty. It's like—you guessed it—someone abruptly unplugged you from all those energy leaks, and you feel off-balance and weird. You don't like it. Or maybe you *love* it.

No wonder people love clearing clutter so much. It means you unplug a bunch of power leaks.

And when you start flushing out power leaks, guess what? You have more energy left in your battery for more important things.

Hunt for your power leaks:

- a messy room
- a messy desktop
- a messy kitchen drawer, or
- a messy garage or storage unit

But it's not just messiness. There are all kinds of other power leaks too:

- that person at work who constantly wants to corner you in the kitchen and complain about a coworker with you
- your parent who guilts you into being with them even though it's so draining
- the neighbor you feel silently resenting you for letting your tree block their view
- that friend who always asks you for favors but never does anything for you
- those people who expect you to look so good every day at work that you spend an hour doing your hair and making sure your clothes fit the unspoken style rules of the workplace
- your date, whom you want to see you in a certain way, so you do lots of things to try to control how they perceive you

Uhghghghgh. Exhausting.

And then, of course, the biggest leaks of all: all those people or things that have to happen for you to feel how you want to feel. Yep, we're right back to those ever-present, looming thunderclouds hovering in your awareness, a permanent wait zone, *sucking, sucking, sucking* your life through your unmet expectations.

Once I began seeing power leaks like this, I went wild trying to pluck them out. Trying to conserve my battery by getting all the phantom leaks to close up, I went on a bender of first identifying every time I felt bad, then noticing who I was waiting on to solve it. Was the power inside me or had I given the ball to someone else?

I realized that the only person who can give me the feelings I want to feel is *me*. It's no one else's fault or responsibility to do that, and asking that of others is asking too much of them.

Imagine if you had someone in your life who could not be happy unless you did all sorts of things to make them that way. How tiring. You'd get awfully resentful after a while.

Now, when my battery is starting to feel low, I look around. Where are my messes and space wasters? Where are people taking from me? Where am I giving my power away to others?

Whisk whisk, sweep sweep. Out they go.

It's a continuous process, since more power leaks always pile in. That's life. It's like a dirty house: The more your family plays in it, the more dirt you have to sweep off the kitchen floor. And that's a good thing.

Just, *you gotta keep cleaning.*

M.E. *School* Prompt

Your prompt is to notice the state of your inner battery and identify as many power leaks as you can.

- How low is my inner battery? How did it get that way?

- What tiny things am I constantly keeping track of in my home or life that could be easily solved to free up emotional space?

- What people in my life are constantly draining me?

Chapter 12:
Internal Power Leaks

A power leak can be a person, place, or thing you're waiting on to make you feel better. It can be anything from the lifelong pang of needing your dad to love you to the feelings of disappointment and resignation you feel every time you step into your crappy, always-breaking-down car.

But, a power leak isn't always outside you—it can also be coming from something *inside* you. These are your inner power leaks, and they're made of your beliefs and feelings about who you are, what's possible for you, and what you deserve or don't deserve.

Inner power leaks are things like:

"I've always been an outsider and a weirdo."

"I'm too short, and it sucks how hot women won't date me."

"My calves are thick and ugly. I hate them."

"I should have finished college. I'm such a dumbass for taking that crappy job and dropping out."

"There are way better people in my line of work than me. Of course that's why I struggle for clients."

"If I were only better at marketing myself, I'd have the career I want."

You get the idea.

People also call these *limiting beliefs*. I know you've heard that term over and over. Inner power leaks or limiting beliefs are ways of thinking and feeling about yourself that cast high walls about what you think is possible for you. It's where you pull up short and stop. You don't give your power away to anyone or anything else—you zap your power away right inside your own mind and heart and become your own jailor. Maybe this sounds like another way of saying "lack of self-confidence," but the effect of these limiting beliefs goes much deeper. That's why we don't talk in terms of confidence. We call this having *inner power leaks,* often in multiple areas.

Remember chapter 1, when I suggested that you can reinvent yourself? If your initial reaction was "Yah right, this is just another dumb book that I'll read and feel exactly the same after, because no matter what I do, nothing changes," well, that right there is an inner power leak: *Nothing you do works and nothing will ever change.*

What a bunch of crap. Everything changes. The good stuff changes and the bad stuff changes too. Inner power leaks will tell you all kinds of lies about yourself, but those lies seem very, very much like the truth, since you've had enough experiences with them to make them feel ironclad. They also usually make you feel contained, thwarted, small, unlovable, not-as-good-as, and a host of other crappy feelings. They explain away all the things in your life that aren't working, or that never change, or that always fall apart, and so on.

But inner power leaks, those limiting beliefs, are just beliefs. They are things you think are true, which may or may not be. And when you run up against one, it's a very, very good thing, because everything you want is going to be waiting for you on just the other side of it. I call finding one of these inner power leaks "hitting a ceiling."

The Other Kind of Glass Ceiling

Oh shit, is it a ceiling? I can't see up there. I don't see a thing, but I sure felt something wicked painful.

This is what churns through my mind whenever I'm in a particularly difficult situation. Your inner power leaks, or ceilings, are almost always invisible until you feel yourself hitting one. Then they're like smacking a glass windshield after a hard stop . . . or worse. But unlike a windshield, ceilings are meant to be broken.

Yep, shatter them right on down. Because each one is a prize. Ceilings are piñatas.

A ceiling is a graduation. It marks the point between familiar and unfamiliar, between where you've been and where you'll go next.

I think of a tall skyscraper. I'm tooling around on the bottom floor. I get to know this floor well. My life is on this floor. Over there is my boyfriend, there is my mom, there's my job and my boss, and that's my dog, Harvey.

I've spent years on this floor. My limiting beliefs (power leaks) have kept me cozy here and described the boundaries of what I can realistically have, be, or do.

Then one day, I feel something painful, something crooked. I realize I feel bound and squished and helpless. I realize I've been waiting for my boyfriend to propose (he hasn't), for my boss to promote me (she hasn't), for my mom to stop telling me how to live (she won't), and for my dog to finally learn to be a good boy on his leash.

It's like I'm in *Alice in Wonderland*, and I've just fallen down the rabbit hole. I drank the bottle of magic liquid and grew and grew until I'm hunched over with the side of my head painfully pressed against the ceiling. Like Alice, I've grown too big for the room. Ouch, it hurts. The room of course being the current shape of my own life, and the ceiling being the barrier between me and growth, change, and the next phase of myself. My room, my life, is too small now that I've grown bigger. And therefore, it's squishing me in painful ways. Now what?

Let's start with the pain: Why does transformation often come with pain? Why do we assume that after every painful thing we'll "learn the lesson?"

No pain, no gain, boy howdy.

But why pain, exactly?

If you were Alice, you'd notice how you no longer fit your space—how you've hit the ceiling. Meaning you've encountered a limiting belief or power leak that you suddenly see is keeping you small and stuck. Your inner power leak is shining clear and bright in front of you, and you can actually see it because it's the thing that hurts.

Hitting a ceiling and finding an inner power leak is just like that. Try shoving an elephant into a ring box and tell me if it feels good. And not feeling good is there to wake you up to the fact that you've hit the next level, and you've got a choice to make: stay and be in pain with that inner power leak, or move up.

Congratulations, you hit your head on the ceiling of the first floor!

Now what? You're supposed to walk up to the larger, more expanded second floor, because this will make the pain go away. You go from the Known Zone to the Grow Zone. You go from the reef to the open water. But right there at the cusp between the two is that little shimmery zone of "Ouch, goddammit, I hit my head on the ceiling."

Think about it: without that marker, how would you ever know when you're slipping from familiar to unfamiliar, from learning to mastery, from a power leak to freedom and self-assurance?

Because that's it: You've mastered something crappy in your life, and pain is now here to tell you to move on, move forward. How ironic that mastery is marked by a dangling star of pain.

But it often is.

Pain usually says, "Change it. Change this. You're done. You've done this, you've been here a long time, you're just repeating the same dance moves over and over to an endlessly repeating song."

You know that person who always has a crummy job? Always, always? And you tell him over and over to get a new job, and when he (finally) does, neither of you are surprised to find that the new job is as bad or worse than the old one?

Look at his pattern. Over and over. On some level, he's mastered it. So he says, "Let's do it again!" Because . . . it's familiar. It's expected. He knows what's coming and how he'll feel in it. It's comfortable. Even the misery of it is comfortable. What's not comfortable is smashing the ceiling and the inner power leaks that kept him under it.

So your friend looks up. Past that ceiling is the next floor. And he's cramped and rolling in circles, having mastered the crappy job pattern years ago. But that second floor? Wow, that's a doozer. Who the hell knows what's up there? Could be monsters. Could be a boss level. Could be anything. He doesn't even know how to function there—all his current moves won't work. He might have to be somebody else, grow into his 2.0 version. Maybe he'd have to lay his brains out for the world to see and invent something wonderful. Or he'd get that gig traveling and photographing wildlife. Or he'd press through that degree and go through the humiliation of fifteen job interviews at big corporations before landing a job. That second floor is terrifying.

And that's why ceilings hurt. They are the irritant that won't leave until you move into your Grow Zone again. Every power leak is hiding a ceiling inside it. Which hurts more: the pain of staying where you are or the fear of moving past your cramped space into your next level?

A lot of us pick the pain of staying where we are, cramped and all.

Your job now is to sigh and press the elevator button.

The Grow Zone

On the second floor, things are different. The pattern may still be in you, but you've shifted. You encountered that thing that felt painful, and went right in and through it. And now your new ceiling is way up there! High above your head. You have so much room to grow here! Everything you do will feel unfamiliar. You won't know if it works, if you're any good at it, if anyone will love you. But oh, the glorious space of the Grow Zone!

The funniest, weirdest, saddest part about ceilings is that we don't know they're there. It's the truth behind that old saying of "You don't know what you don't know." All we know is that we're not advancing in our lives or in ourselves.

We look up and see a flat ceiling in our life and we fail to see beyond it. We assume the ceiling is the sky. We can't even conceive of what might be past the sky in that bigger space in our lives. It feels unreal, a fantasy. It's as dumb as saying you'll be living in a Hollywood Hills mansion next year.

And so we don't conceive of it. We don't know what we're shooting for, because we aren't yet in a ripe, developed enough place to begin to see it. But one day, you will be. You'll bump your head on something painful, some inner power leak will suddenly become clear, and you'll realize that *you can actually solve it*. You'll poke your head through the ceiling, and it will be like the heavens have opened. You'll see and sense possibilities for yourself that seem almost possible. You'll imagine things for yourself that are doable. You'll find that the ceiling has dissolved—you've raised the bar.

The bar may or may not include your boyfriend, boss, mom, or dog. And if it does, they will not be assembled in the same old pattern as they were before. They will be in new places in your heart and possibly in new spaces in your life.

Having reached the second floor, you'll shake off the 1.0 pattern and dig into the 2.0 pattern. And now, when you look down below you, you can barely see that old ceiling; it looks like gossamer webs. You shrug because you finally got the hangy, glittery, shiny prize of the second floor, and there's much exploring to do.

M.E. *School* Prompt

Your prompt is to identify at least one inner power leak that has kept you circling in the same landing pattern for days, months, years.

What if that inner power leak were no longer true? Can you see the ceiling that the power leak is pointing to? If you shift this power leak, will you go beyond the ceiling? Use the prompts to help you see one area where you play small, rationalize your unhappiness, or otherwise keep yourself in a limited place.

- What are things I don't allow myself to do?

- What aspects of myself do I compare negatively to others? How does this affect what I allow myself to do, attempt, or dream of?

- Do I find myself trying to be what someone else wants? If so, who and why?

- What aspects of myself do I think are unattractive (physical, emotional, achievements, etc.)?

Chapter 13:
The True Meaning of Resistance

Right about now, you might be thinking, "But wait, Summer. Aren't some power leaks legit communication from the universe telling me to just stop, go back three squares, this isn't for you? I mean it's so freaking confusing! When is the universe telling me to go forward, and when is it telling me to stop? Ugh, I just can't tell the difference! Isn't having bad feelings telling me to stop? Or is it telling me that winners don't quit, and quitters don't win? Heeeeeelp!"

I know you've smacked up against some big-ass resistance in the past. Maybe you've even got some swirling on the stove of your life right now. Maybe that door slammed on your nose so hard that it's bloody, and you're somewhere between crying and punching a hole through it.

Maybe feeling yucky and frustrated isn't just a power leak, isn't a true ceiling to be smashed. Maybe it's life telling you to quit, stop, don't go there, back down, this ain't for you, hon. And this is when you start thinking in terms of resistance. Even if you solve all your power leaks, it's still there: this pushback from the universe saying "No. Not for you. You can't have that."

And it can be a tough call: Is this resistance really telling you to quit? Or should you double down and charge through it, discovering a ceiling somewhere in there? In fact, what even is resistance?

Delicate drops of resistance feel like pushback or tension.

In larger amounts, it's the feeling of being blocked, having nothing work out, feeling like nothing goes the way you want, being stalled by perpetual procrastination and even total flailing frustration. Everything you try fails. The road is hopelessly, inscrutably blocked by inner or outer power leaks . . . seemingly by life itself.

Sometimes we think resistance is good for us. When something rough happens, and we get through it, we console ourselves by saying, "That was a tough lesson!" And we feel proud for having conquered it.

And sometimes resistance feels really bad for us, like when we keep trying to build or create something in our lives, and it topples over like a house of cards again and again, pushed down, wrecked, or taken from us.

It boils down to two questions: Why don't I get what I want, and why is it so fucking challenging to get it? Is it all power leaks, or is it something more?

Ask yourself where you feel resistance right now. These are the things that are resisting your attempts to grow, change, get a better job, get a better partner, whatever. And you bet, each one comes with a power leak holding its clammy little hand.

Let's break it down.

Inner Resistance

There are two basic kinds of resistance, starting with inner resistance.

This is the resistance in our own hearts. Usually, this resistance is succored on fear. We have a big idea, but it's too risky! So we hold back. The resistance whispers, "Don't do it, that feels possibly unsafe." Inner resistance is often your king talking, telling you to stay in the castle. Inner resistance is often rooted in an inner power leak.

Sometimes, you can feel inner resistance about things that are exciting and growth filled, like leaping into a new career.

But you can also feel inner resistance when something isn't right for you—think about running out onto a busy road right now and dancing through the lanes. Your whole body should be shuddering, "No, don't do that!" You're resisting the idea, and rightly so. Your king is on the job!

And that's the conundrum: When is resistance saying to go forward, and when is it saying to fall back?

The key for you is to figure out if the resistance is justified or not. And this is where we get confused. Is the fear and resistance to moving to a new city for a job a fear of expansion and growth, or is some part of you warning that this is a bad idea, you're just running from your problem, and you should listen to your intuition and stay put?

Here's your litmus test: On balance, how does your inner resistance about something make you feel: good or bad? Feelings that fall into the good category include: exciting, risky, what-if-I-fail, uncertainty, insecurity, feeling like you don't know enough yet, feelings of not having a sure outcome, and so on. They are Grow Zone feelings. They are Between the Reef feelings, because the prize at the end (if you push past the resistance) should glitter and spin with good feelings before your eyes.

Now, contrast this to feeling fear for your physical safety or a gut reaction that something feels icky, backward, or wrong. It's a feeling that if you push past your resistance, you're going to land in an undesirable situation. There's no growth at the end of this resistance. The feelings of emergence and accomplishment are absent. You aren't striving toward something positive. There is no prize at the end.

Imagine you've just left an abusive relationship. You're sleeping on your friend's couch, and your ex texts: "C'mon back, hon. I'll change." So you lift your butt off your friend's gray velvet cushions and drive right over to your old partner. It feels cheap, too easy, a slide back. You feel resistance, but you go back to them anyway. You had *left* a power leak by leaving, *crushed* a ceiling of fear about possibly being alone forever, but now you're sliding backward.

Now contrast this: How do you feel right this second about asking for something that you've needed for a while that you've been afraid to request from someone? Right? That's also your resistance, your fear in the form of a power leak about someone not wanting you to ask, or about you not getting what you need. But the prize is that you get the thing you need. This discomfort says, "Do it. It's overdue. You need it." Doing this thing and overcoming this inner resistance is what *destroys* the power leak—it doesn't slide you back into one.

Contrast again: How do you feel right this second about jumping off a really high bridge with a poorly packed bungee cord? Right . . . that, too, is your inner resistance, your fear. There is no prize at the end. This resistance also says, "Don't do it."

Pretend you have a teeter-totter, and if it's 51 percent good, then the resistance is just your fear of moving into your Grow Zone. New spaces always seem scary because you simply haven't been there before. We usually experience self-doubt and fear whenever we change jobs, decide to get married, choose to move far away, push ourselves to grow our business or learn to make sales, risk having people laugh at or reject us, invest in ourselves, or risk speaking our mind to people we care about only to feel the sting of disapproval or rejection.

You can see how all these might carry inner resistance to do them, but we do them since the payoff of good feelings and inner authenticity is so great.

That question about "Is my intuition telling me 'No, stop, don't go there' . . . or am I just afraid?" boils down to understanding that you're going for another one of those feeling goals, ultimately.

"Do it" resistance leads you to feeling goals, those emotional endpoints that light up the sky with expansion, expression, growth, and potential joy.

"Don't do it" resistance is telling you there is no payoff ahead, steer clear.

The Two Paths (Flow vs. External Resistance)

Once we get past our inner resistance, we stand at the juncture of two roads. One road is smooth and inviting, swirling with rainbow colors. You see a straight, easy path flowing toward the horizon. Inviting, isn't it?

The other road has an old Do Not Enter sign at the entrance, and as you look down it, you see boulders have crashed onto the road, breaking up the grim and grisly blacktop. Tumbleweeds and old garbage pile up against the boulders, and a foul slime slinks over the sides.

You rub your eyes and open them again, spinning to look in a circle around you. Now, there are twenty, perhaps fifty other roads all extending out from the central circle in which you stand. And they are in various forms—some seem open and breezy but not quite as good as that first one, and some have a few big-ass potholes and rough gravel but aren't as bad as that terrible, slimy road. Each road takes you to one of your life goals—your emotional endpoints. But some roads have a lot more external resistance (pushback from the world) than others.

Think of each road as carrying a degree of resistance in it, from zero resistance to 100 percent difficulty, because every one of those roads, theoretically, does exist.

What road have you been on lately?

Let's say you've pushed past your good feeling, tingly inner resistance, and you have a goal, but you realize you've been on a really rough road. You don't know why or how you got on it, but there you are. This road has been filled with potholes, setbacks, and even U-turns. You're starting to think the universe doesn't even want you to reach your goal, that it's telling you, "Stop! You shouldn't go there; you shouldn't want that." And maybe you're thinking of stopping.

What would you be stopping? Is it a lifelong dream? Is it a goal of having a beautiful baby? Is it your idea for building a cool-ass jewelry business? In other words, does the goal bring you emotional endpoints, feelings of excitement and joy? If the answer is yes, then you need to get off the road you're on, and go over to that smooth, easy rainbow one that will lead you to the exact same destination, just a hell of a lot more easily.

It means that some things that you've been doing aren't a fit to get you to that dream. Some things you've been doing are the long route, or they're not the right match for you. Now, you may be tempted to double down and just do more of those things, screaming with balled fists at life that "I'm going to get through, goddamnit! Throw your worst at me and I'll conquer it!" If that's you, kudos for choosing the roughest road and committing to bruise and bloody yourself. Just kidding, don't do that. No kudos.

Instead, stop and listen. If you're doing things that consistently don't work out, see it instead as a kind of nudge. Life is nudging you off that road, away from that thing that isn't the best for you. *Nudge nudge.* Every difficulty you encounter is nudging you toward an easier road instead.

Life is saying: "*Shift.* Now shift again. Now pivot. Drop that thing; start this thing." Let go of your fierce expectation that something has to be reached a certain way, or a way that someone else told you or showed you. And . . . *now you're getting closer to your easy road.*

Listening to the feedback life is giving you doesn't mean you give up your dream. Not at all. It just means the current path to your dream is fraught with hardship, and you're going to keep stubbing your toes on that hardship until you change paths.

But! you wail, *I don't know of any other path! Everything I've shifted or pivoted to has also been shit, Summer. Now what?*

Stop and listen. Whatever you've been doing has been giving you massive resistance, and that resistance won't let up until you've tried enough roads. So, what *haven't* you done? What other ideas, means, or methods *haven't* you tried?

Chances are those other ideas are basking in the sun of the Easy Road, the road that flows and helps you. You just got stuck on your one path, with your one way of doing things to get there and your singular destination and your one set of limiting expectations about how the goal will be reached.

Your imagination has been stifled by all sorts of lack-thoughts and preconditioned ideas. You've been obsessing about all the things you've done that have failed, and you've forgotten to think ahead about all the things you *haven't yet done.*

Usually, we say to ourselves that all those roads not traveled are the things that won't work, don't seem like a direct path, are outside the norm for what your industry does, are wild cards that won't pay off, and so on.

"I'm just not ready for that," you say. Or "I just don't want to do that." Or "But no one else does it that way."

One of my clients is an actor. She used to land big parts in her twenties but not so much anymore. She's facing the endemic ageism of Hollywood, which, we agree, is a power leak. Sometimes power leaks are, in fact, real things like ageism, discrimination, or poverty. But for her lately, all the roads have ended in auditions with no callbacks.

She still wants to be an actor. She's waiting on God or lightning or something to turn her luck around and bless her with grace and fortune—that one job that reboots her career and gets her name wagging in the right casting circles.

As a result, she's getting more bitter and discouraged every day. It feels like nothing is supporting her dream, not even her own damn parents who are hoping she'll just meet a guy, finally have those grandkids, and get a normal job somewhere.

Should she give up her dream?

We talk about how acting makes her feel: seen, powerful, creatively fulfilled, juiced up on the actual work itself, which feels like play.

I asked her if anything else could make her feel like that.

Yes, probably something could, but no, she doesn't want any of those other things. She only wants the actor thing.

So we get stuck. All her roads are bumpy. They all contain loads of external resistance.

And her own inner resistance is preventing her from opening to change. *Stucky stuck stuck.*

Odds are though, there's going to be an easier road somewhere out there for her. She needs to try writing a screenplay. Maybe take a turn at directing. Audition for a stage play. I dunno, just something that can open new, fresh paths for her since the throw-myself-at-casting-directors thing isn't working. Shoot for the emotional endpoints, and life might just surprise her by circling her right back to a great movie role, even though she thought she was going into screenwriting instead.

Like her, you'll want to get imaginative. Release your white-knuckled grip on your current path. Just stop and do something you wouldn't dream would help you reach your goal. Maybe that's where the easy road has been hiding all along, because it sure hasn't been on the resistant road of "all the right moves."

Let me give you another example: I never intended to write my first book, *Flowdreaming*. I went to school to study English literature, and my family owned a tiny publishing company. I knew getting an agent and publisher to take on a book was a huge, horrible, soul-crushing, and luck-filled affair.

Yet, when I found myself working for one of the largest publishers of personal growth books in the world, I still didn't think about writing a book. I thought that (1) my workplace would never publish a book by one of their own employees, (2) I wasn't old enough and didn't have enough professional standing to be considered a viable publishing candidate, and (3) even if I got the book written, no one would be interested in my ideas anyway.

After all, I had already spent days of my early twenties sending manuscripts for short stories out to hundreds of publishers, only to receive the very rare, polite rejection letter. Most places never responded at all. I'd imagined that getting a book published was such a hard road that I never even took the steps.

Then one day, my boss told me that I should pitch a book idea to our CEO. I flatly refused. It couldn't possibly be that easy. I'd just be humiliated, and the humiliation would drag like an oily specter through the office in whispers and looks.

My boss badgered me. She even promised to sit beside me in his office while I made my pitch. *Poor baby, your boss is coming along for moral support.* How ridiculous I must have looked.

But guess what? The meeting took less than ten minutes. Suddenly, I had a book deal and a real, legit advance. I could not believe what I'd heard. That was not supposed to happen. I had just circumvented every tangled, weedy road out there.

I did the thing that wasn't supposed to work, that shouldn't have happened. I felt the glittery tingle of inner resistance in the Grow Zone that leads to glory. The queen's gamble had won over the king's threats of humiliation. I'd gone off my old path (of churning out proposals for agents, getting slammed by teetering walls of rejection letters) and tried a new one (a ballsy ten-minute, face-to-face meeting with my even bigger boss).

My story isn't unique. You've had this happen to you, too, somewhere in your life. Think about those fluke moments where everything just went right. Think about those blessed turning points that you didn't even know were so important until far later.

Something happened that pulled you out of your hard trudge, and that new place you found yourself in just worked. *It worked.* It flowed. And maybe a bunch of other good things happened along with it, everything flowing and rosy.

This is why I talk about *flow* so often. Flow is the easy road. It's a state of nonresistance, of fluidity. It's a state of things falling into place and working out. It's a real state of being. And when you're in it, you're like a bird on a windy day discovering that you can fly with the wind, going faster and farther, as opposed to flying against the wind, using the same amount of effort but getting only half as far.

Shifting to the Easy Road

So how do you go with the flow? How do you find the road of least resistance?

Simple: You put yourself on it. You shift and shift and shift again, like pulling cards from a deck until the ace comes up. Because the ace is there. It *will* come up. I don't know how many shifts you'll have to do to get it, but you'll pull it eventually. Our actor friend who hasn't gotten cast in a long time will get cast again. Thing is, can she wait it out? Can she wait in joy and contentment, or will she start doing the bad thing, which is to start front-loading her life with panicky frustration and despair, which the universe is just as happy to serve up for her because it thinks those are her actual emotional endpoints? Because, hey, those are the feelings she sends out most of the time, right?

Let go of your attachment to the *means* and stay focused on the emotional endpoints.

If something is giving you major resistance right now, you can either recognize it as a solvable problem and solve it, or you can recognize it as a boulder in the road and pivot to another road.

Some of us have gotten into a habit of expecting boulder after boulder and feeling like unless we clamber over every single one, we won't reach our goal. We expect and look for the next boulder. We expect and look for setbacks and difficulties. It's like we've begun telling life that if we don't encounter resistance, we know we won't get to where we're going. So we give life a free pass to keep heaping it on our plate.

And we never, ever think we could reach our goal without all these setbacks and traumas. Good things come to those who've suffered for them first.

Is that what you want to be telling the universe?

First, if you're feeling that scared-excited inner resistance, then you're good. You're on the right path, moving toward the right thing. If you're feeling unhappy, unmotivated, I-don't-like-where-this-is-going type of resistance, then heed the warning and stop doing whatever you're doing or living however you're living.

Good so far?

Next, remember your feeling goals—your emotional endpoints. Not just the things you want, but the emotional endpoints your end goal will give you . . . like happiness, fulfillment, feelings of monetary safety, time freedom.

Got that list? Good.

Now, notice the particular path you've chosen to get to those feelings. Has this path been fraught with trouble and setbacks? Is it stuck and not progressing? Are you front-loading it with frustration and lack thinking? Guess what—it's time to shift! Shift the method, shift the relationship, shift your mind. Just *shift*. Notice, too, if the goal itself shifts a little. Maybe you don't need to be captain of the team to get the cheerleader to date you. Maybe you can be a kick-ass chess team winner. Maybe the cheerleader is also secretly an intellectual like you.

Your end goal? The feelings of loving companionship that you think the hot cheerleader will give you. Your method? Captain of the team. No wait, shift, chess team champ. No wait, shift again, because why? Turns out the cheerleader really does like the football guys, but this incredibly cute girl on your chess team is absolutely dying to date you.

Bingo, goal achieved. Happy, happy you.

Break it down to the bones: hard road (captain), right goal (love). Shift! Easier road (chess), right goal (love). Shift again! Easier road (chess girl), right goal (love).

That is it. Taken apart like this, it's pretty simple. It's seeing the roads and recognizing the resistance that's the hard part.

Fortunately, your feelings will always guide you. Me? I'm shifting right now, writing this book with you, going through M.E. School with you, sharing my trinkets of wisdom with you. The pandemic brought me to a dead end in most of my other work goals. So I'm doing something I haven't done in forever: writing a book, with no real idea of where it'll lead.

The "thing" goal around the book? It's straight up success: I want some hungry agent to be peeing their pants over how hot and awesome a book this is. I want it on Target's store shelves, right under Brené Brown's books. Hell, *above* Brené. I want someone to be running around in Costco shouting, "Holy shirtballs, this is *The Artist's Way* but for your gosh darn *soul!*"

But my emotional endpoints? I want to feel the freedom to expand into new areas, feel unboxed in my career, feel like I'm allowed to shift into new horizons and daily work, and that it'll all be financially rewarding to boot.

Will the book help me reach those feelings? Would having it on Target's shelves help me reach those feelings? I have no frigging idea. But I do know what I'm telling my life, my flow, the universe, God, and Source each time I sit down with you to write. I'm saying, "This feels good. This is lighting me up. This tickles me into thinking that someone, somewhere, is gonna read a paragraph that will change their world forever." Dammit, that's hot.

And I want the easy road, the one without resistance or power leaks. I want that road that's smooth, flowing, and fast, and that'll get me to all these emotional endpoints *pronto.*

Now, let's pause a moment to savor all the juicy bits in this chapter. After all, we just ripped open your resistance and exposed its frilly panties to the world: inner resistance, external resistance, hard roads, and easy ones.

M.E. *School* Prompt

Your prompt is to identify the resistance in your life and suss out if it's internal or external, and if it's helping you or hurting you.

As usual, journal your responses to the prompts below:

- What hopes, desires, ideas, or goals do I have internal resistance to?

- Is the internal resistance telling me to plow through or run?

- What things do I experience external resistance with?

- Is the external resistance telling me to plow through or run?

- What shifts could I make that could still achieve my goal and put me on an easier road getting there? (This may not be clear yet.)

PART IV:
The Weasels in the Road

Chapter 14:
Lack Thinking

Part of my journey involved getting breast cancer when I was forty-three. One of the things it left me with is something called lymphedema. Basically, the doctors took out all my lymph nodes, and now my arm swells up like a crackling hotdog in the char pit if I don't get the backed-up fluid manually drained. Yeah, someone squeezes my arm to get all the backed-up lymph fluid out. I will do this every two weeks for probably my whole life.

The woman who pumps my arm is utterly wonderful. She's become a friend. And over the years, I've learned all about her enemy, the Weasel.

I nicknamed her this a while back. She's the other lymphatic massage therapist who does All the Bad Things you should not be doing in a hospital setting.

She dips her germy fingers directly into the massage cream jar instead of using the little popsicle stick thing to scoop it out.

She takes home the flowers you bring into the massage room to brighten it up, then denies taking them.

She both uses and scratches up your soothing massage music CDs and you don't discover it until you've got someone facedown on the table and your hands are all greasy and the CD is going *zzzpp-zzzpp-zzzpp.*

She's a weasel.

And we all have weasels like this in our lives. But a lot of times these weasels aren't people but ways of thinking that tear us from the easy road and tie us to the stake of hardship.

One of the biggest biggies of these is "lack thinking." But first, to properly appreciate lack thinking, we need to jump into the whole woo-woo world of *abundance thinking.*

Glass Half Full, Glass Half Empty

"Abundance thinking!" "Prosperity thoughts!"

Honest to God, these are the most misused, overhyped, and overplayed ideas in personal growth.

It's misused when it goes like this, "If you just had more abundance thinking, you'd join my $10,000 program!"

It's overhyped when it goes like this, "If you just had abundance thinking, your athlete's foot will be cured, your mother will love you again, and you'll lose fifty pounds in thirty days."

It's overplayed when everywhere you look, some guru is telling you how to have more of it, and yet everything you read fails to make any actual impact on how you live and think every day, and how your own damn scarcity thinking must be to blame, ya dummy.

This is the Holy Mama of the Temple of Personal Development: the abundance/scarcity dichotomy.

In psychology, there's something called *affective forecasting.* It means that all day, every day, we're projecting ideas about how we think we'll feel in the future. We make decisions based on how we forecast the outcomes to how different things will make us feel.

"Do I call my friend?" We only say yes if we think the call will make us feel good somehow.

Where scarcity (or *lack*) thinking comes in is that when we do this forecasting, instead of anticipating positive outcomes (Abundance thinking!

Prosperity thoughts!), we tend to expect negative outcomes, like all the time, unconsciously, about everything. This is called *negativity bias*. And when it gets out of control, it nose-dives into *catastrophic thinking*.

And then you have *loss aversion*. A pretty cool psychology study was done years back in which people got to choose if they wanted to gamble. It went something like this: Everybody got a dollar. If you rolled some dice, you could either win another dollar or lose the whole dollar you had. Guess what? More people chose not to gamble, even though the odds were 50/50. It was more painful to feel the loss of the dollar than it was to win the dollar. (How casinos get around this, I have no idea.)

But the result is that we all tend to go around hunkering down, preparing for bad stuff to happen, and trying to prevent good stuff from being taken from us. This also helps us understand why so many of us stay in crappy situations: I call that the ol' "Better to stay in the crummy thing you know than risk the scary something you don't know" mindset. Think about your bad relationship, your shitty job. Better to stay.

Couple all these ideas together (and more, these are just the biggies that will help you understand lack thinking best) and you have the epic Trinity of Lack: your negative affective forecasting is leading to chronic, constant negativity bias that is all wrapped up in your instinctual loss aversion.

Now, if you're a real psychologist sputtering and frothing over my over-simplification, I apologize. What I'm trying to get across is how so many of us are constantly pouring forth a stream of expectations that we will not get our needs met, that the good thing we want won't happen, and that what we had before (in our past) is always better than what we'll get in the future.

Call it lack thinking, call it scarcity mindset—it's all the same. There's just not enough to go around, and even if there was, you pretty much think you won't have what you need for your success anyway.

Some of us take this to an utterly epic level. We're bracing *all the time* for lack. We're Pavlov's dog, overly conditioned by past negative experiences to constantly anticipate and expect a lot of crappy stuff. We have anxiety. We have a perennial negative outlook. We have panic attacks and depression.

Where are you on this spectrum? To really see, you have to start catching yourself cruising in lack thinking throughout your day. Are you avoiding an e-mail? I bet you feel some guilt, worry, or stress around it. And why? There's something painful that you expect will come from it.

Grinding on the thought that you hate your job? Whenever that stroke of negativity crosses your breast, you're acknowledging that getting a new job is hard and unlikely.

Feeling frustrated by your computer? You're feeling like technology is too complicated and you'll never figure it out.

When you look at your child coloring at the kitchen table, you might feel delight at the drawing, but you might also worry about getting the crayon off the tabletop, or wonder if he's drawing people correctly yet, or perhaps he's delayed?

The examples that flit through your day are endless. Negativity bias crosses our minds all the time.

It boils down to this: The minute you feel a negative emotion, there's a 99 percent chance there's a lack thought attached to it. Spotting your negative emotions through the day is key to discovering how much lack or scarcity thinking you habitually spew out into your life.

I imagine us as little fire hydrants spraying lack out all through the day.

Lack thoughts are weasels.

What's the problem with this? Well, as if it isn't self-evident, most of us want to feel happy, content, secure, and nourished. We're reinventing ourselves, and by golly, we are reinventing ourselves to be filled with prosperity and abundance!

Lack thinking absolutely undoes all of that. What's supposed to be a small conservative "watch out" corrective tug in our psyches has morphed into a life-gobbling monster. Lack thinking is all up in your power leaks and busying itself in your ceilings.

This is where it gets interesting: What if you embarked on a personal goal of logging every lack thought you have during the day (meaning every negative emotion), then chose to turn each one into a positive, expectant, abundant feeling instead?

Your little notebook would be full in the first four hours.

But to really shift your life, this is exactly what you have to do.

You have to start gambling that dollar.

You have to recognize how often you're preparing for the worst, or at least for some sort of trouble or difficulty.

I know, I know, it's important to be prepared. What if we all went around in la-la land denial, oblivious to the dangers?! Wouldn't we be stupid? Wouldn't we be like that person who spends every dime they have on stupid stuff, then says, "Oh, the universe will provide," as they're declaring bankruptcy or getting evicted?

We have a deep resistance built in us to "not get too excited." We don't want to feel disappointed; we want to protect ourselves, and so, of course, we need to "bring our expectations down a bit to be consistent with reality."

Reality? What's real?

Reality is built on your expectations, actions, emotional energy, and results. If your expectations keep leading to lack-centered actions, then you will certainly get lack-infused results. It's a totally self-fulfilling prophecy. Around and around we go, and because all these negative results happen so darn much, so darn often, they get realer and realer.

Yep, pretty soon they are so real that there is no other real. Life just . . . sucks. Don't expect to get your needs met, have enough money, feel good or happy . . . and on and on. Because, shoot, your whole life has proven this to you. It'd be dumb to expect otherwise. Life is about prepping for disaster and hoping each one won't be too, too horrible.

There's only one way to change this: shift into abundance thinking—*true* abundance thinking. True prosperity thinking. Move into gratitude. Call it whatever you want—it's basically all the same. It's a feeling that everything is smooth and easy, the results will be anywhere from good to spectacular, and there is plenty, *plenty* for you. You will get your needs met. Things will make you happy.

Yes, it's called *positivity bias,* and it's a real thing too. We just tend to be a lot more stingy with it.

Here's the key: You choose to shift into feeling abundance and positive expectations even when there isn't one darn, single thing going right in your life. You need to do it *before* there's one darn, single thing going right in your life. Remember those colored crayons? You will stop reacting and start pre-acting.

You're a boat captain turning your big ship around at sea. You have to veer starboard for a long while to move the massive ship away from its current direction. It will look like you're still heading the same way for a while, but eventually that big sucker will fully turn.

This ship is your life. So, no matter what you see on the horizon, you feel abundance, fulfillment, and happiness instead. Feel it *despite* what you see. It's the only way to turn the tide of lack into abundance.

What you feel is what you create. Think about interlocking puzzle pieces: if your pieces are all shaped like lack, you'll get matching pieces in your external life clicking into place.

This does not mean you should be foolish. You're not going to spend your inheritance, take up eight simultaneous lovers, gorge on steaks and cocaine every day, and then say, "The Lord will provide" when it all goes to hell.

Most of us know in the midst of whatever we're doing if it's a good feeling or a bad feeling. You get a sense when you save money that it feels good and secure, which overrides the sense of deprivation at not spending it on the new iPhone. You know when you exercise that your body's thanking you even if your mind is telling you how incredibly boring it is to run on a treadmill.

In other words, good choices are good choices. Continue to make them.

Here's the takeaway: Lack thinking destroys many of us. We all know the chronic, negative people in our lives. And it's real for them—they really do get an absurdly large amount of negative crap. And they also expect it, prepare for it, and then delight that they were right about it.

But you, *you* can choose balance. You can choose to start preparing to feel good, having your requests fulfilled, and expecting happiness and security. The more you practice these feelings, the more you're steering in a new direction toward it all. And the more proof you receive that these good things really are there for you, the more you'll want to feel these good feelings. And now you are entering the Palace of Prosperity, the Abbey of Abundance.

Now you look at other people and see them stuck and wallowing and complaining about the same things over and over and over, and you wonder, "Why don't they change that?"

And they look at you and say, "Oh, you're just lucky. You'll get your own comeuppance one day," because they are going to do the lack thinking *for you*, if you won't do it yourself. And they will love to tell you all about it, and how you're a dumb, sissy fool.

You see, anyone who shows them that they can be anything other than broke or frustrated is . . . suspicious. Ever notice the lack thinking directed toward people who have happy, rich, fulfilling lives? It's not just jealousy. To the lack thinker, it's a direct strike against their way of living, one which says, "You don't have to live in Lack! Look at me? I'm not." And then the Lack People will want to hunt you down with pitchforks.

But let's not worry about that now. That thought can lead to more lack in you.

Lastly, you might also be wondering just how to heal and remove all these lack thoughts, how to get to that sweet balance I promised.

Fair question, but we aren't going to answer that until you *find* and catch those weasels on the road—your lack thoughts.

M.E. *School* Prompt

Right now, your prompt is to get your notebook and go on an epic Lack Hunt by noticing every feeling you have right now that's low, stressful, or worrisome, then finding the Lack Thought that generated it.

Notice how your unhappy feeling is connected to things you don't have, won't get, never got, won't happen, you don't have enough money for . . . and on and on. Jot as many down as immediately come to mind. These two questions can get you started:

I habitually go into lack thinking about:

_____

_____

_____

_____

_____

I have trouble trusting abundance thoughts about:

_____

_____

_____

_____

_____

Chapter 15:
Plan A, Plan B

I *know,* this might be feeling like the dense part of the book. The part where you want to put it down, come back later, and hope for something a bit lighter.

But that's not what we're here for. We're here to pull our wading boots out of the sucking mud and chart a new direction for ourselves. We're here to loosen the bags of garbage that time has left us with and find that sexy new part of our life (and ourselves) again. And finally, we're here because "good enough" is no longer good enough. You can be greater. And this is exactly why we're going to get into your Plan A and Plan B.

We all have (or had) a Plan A: That's the thing you really wanted to do or be in life. Maybe your Plan A was to be happily married; have a tight, close, happy family; and find yourself spending your days doing activities or work you utterly love. *Mmmm, yeah that feels good.*

But somewhere along the way you said, "Okay, I want that Plan A, but I'm not going to get it anytime soon, 'cuz it's really *too perfect.* Nobody gets that kind of perfect. It's gonna require luck and for everything to go right. Gonna have to meet that right partner, which will take a while. Have to work my way through some *meh*-ish jobs first. And I'll probably need to do a bunch of other crappy stuff to get there, like wait tables, save money, go to college for accounting, etc."

We have a Plan B. That's our fallback plan, you know? The one we go to in case Plan A doesn't turn out. The one we *live* while Plan A is "still in the making."

Funny, though, Plan B is a fallback plan because it feels so much more likely to happen. It's the safe bet, the one that can't miss. It's the "more possible, more doable" plan.

Huh. What happens with things that feel more possible, more doable, more likely? They become the main plan, the only plan, the plan we *trust.*

Which then means Plan A is the risky plan, the unlikely plan, the Hail Mary. It's the "if everything goes totally right" plan. The "if I'm the luckiest guy on earth" plan. It's the unrealistic plan. It's the less likely plan. It's the plan we took a stab at, had something not work out, so we hit the pause button on that plan and went to the oh-so-much-more reliable Plan B.

Guess which plan most of us will end up living? Yep. Plan B. We expect it. It expects us. It's where we've put our faith. It's where we put our hours.

Plan A does not get our faith. Plan A requires luck, money, and perhaps alien intervention.

This totally rattles some people. They've been hoping for Plan A all their lives, but in reality, they've been building Plan B every day. And if they do something toward Plan A and it doesn't work, they say, "Oh my gosh, see? It's sooo hard."

Whereas if you do something toward Plan B and it doesn't work, you say, "Oh, okay, I'll just apply at another restaurant/get another accounting job/ date someone else." In Plan B, things get fucked-up, but we expect that—it's Plan B. We nod our heads knowingly.

So, which plan have you truly been investing in? Which one is working out for you best? And if you hate your Plan B, why are you still doing it?

And if you love your Plan A, why aren't you doing *that* instead?

Life is a timed event. There is an end date stamped on us all. When does your Plan A get to start?

M.E. *School* Prompt

Your prompt is to really think about which plan you've actually been pursuing your whole life.

And if it's Plan B, then where is Plan A? Is it still around, hungering for attention? Or are you past it and about to decide on a new Plan A? Again, you're aiming to get revelation and clarity. *You must clearly see the thing you want to change.*

What I wanted to do with my life was:

_____

_____

_____

_____

_____

What I've actually done with my life is:

_____

_____

_____

_____

_____

_____

Chapter 16:
Backward-Looking Girl

And finally, I bring you one last weasel: Backward-Looking Girl. I know her really well; I've been her. And I still struggle not to be her because when you've lived a good life, there's a helluva lotta good things to look back on with love.

Years ago, one of my clients had been a writer for a very popular sitcom. Very popular. You'd know it if I said it. But then she met a guy, moved, and quit the job. A few years later, they split up.

She has been trying to get that job back ever since.

But you know what? The production company had moved on. They had new writers. She was older and not as cool now. In fact, no one was hiring her. And no one could tell her why she wasn't getting hired. It really, really sucked.

She's been rubbing this problem between her fingers for four years, over and over. Raw fingers, raw mind.

When we talk, it's all about how "Those were the best years of my life," and "God, I was so dumb to leave," and "Why won't anyone hire me?"

In my mind, she's a little ragdoll facing backward into her past, trying to reach for a part of herself that she already experienced. She wants to re-experience it since it gave her such pleasure. She wants to go back, do it again. Be there again. I know how that feels.

Life, as it turns out, really doesn't want you to experience the same things over and over. It wants you to taste new things, feel new feelings, and yes, love new people. Even if you feel like the good stuff is behind you.

Some things you'll love and experience forever, of course, such as the people you cherish or that old family home. But even then, you don't love them like you did when you were five, or fourteen, or thirty-two. You love them differently. Your family home feels different too. You're different *in* it.

Sometimes we get snagged like a little leaf on a branch in a stream. We don't know what's ahead, and behind was *soooo* nice. We can't let go when, honestly, that was the nicest, bestest thing we ever had back there.

But what happens is that the longer you're pining for "back then," the more the "now" becomes bitter and untasty. And what you end up doing is letting that thing that thrilled you become the thing that torments you.

That's hardly fair to do to the best part of your life.

I find these feelings come up in me when I start playing "comparison."

"My thirties were fucking amazing, and my forties sucked dogballs."

"My job at Big-Deal Company was the best job ever, and I've never had anything so great."

"My first husband was the best man ever, and no one will ever make me that happy."

"My body was so hot when I was twenty-two. Now my fat looks like wet Cheetos melting down my thighs, and I hate all my clothes."

"Everyone knew me when I worked at 'X', and it's been a slow slide, being eclipsed by younger people in my field ever since."

You get it.

Backward-Looking Girl is robbing herself of future great, new things to someday look back on. She's pinned the Moment of Perfection onto her past, and now nothing in her future is going to match that. Even if she has forty more years to go.

This is never intentional. It's always accidental.

Hey, let's try something different.

Look back on your childhood, twenties, thirties, your body, your ex, whatever, and say, "My God, I loved you. You were a blessing. That was a high point. And I know there will be *many more ahead.* They will be different things, with different people, in different places, but by golly they will be delicious and fruitful. I can't wait."

Can't believe it when you tell yourself that? The degree of disbelief is exactly the amount of Backward-Looking Girl (or Guy, or Person) there is inside you. It's your inner resistance to moving forward, revealing your fear about not being good enough or not being able to receive the same kind (or even greater amount) of joy in the years ahead. Now you know what to work on.

You will have various peak points all through your life. But that's the point: While there are still some ahead, you have to let go of the past ones to get into the new ones.

M.E. *School* Prompt

Your prompt is to identify one feeling of regret, loss, or disappointment that you've been nursing.

What if you finally put it to bed? How would you feel? Let's just see how much Backward-Looking Girl we can find. Jot down answers to the following questions:

- When was I at my peak, when everything was better, richer, fitter, brighter, and happier than it is now?

- What great thing happened to me once that will never happen again?

- When did I start thinking that I'd never again reach the level I had before? Why? What happened to crush me?

- How long have I been in this state?

Chapter 17:
Paper Tigers

I lied, which you'd know if you'd looked at the table of contents. There are a couple more of these nitty-gritty chapters, and I saved the best for almost last: it's about the *I'm Not Good Enough Show.*

You might not want to read this, since you're like "Aww, Summer, I've heard that a million times. Blah blah, *comparisonitis.* I know, I know, why make me read about it again?"

Because "I'm Not Good Enough" is a specialized, distilled, and highly common form of lack thinking that deserves its own special chapter.

Also, because "I'm Not Good Enough" is a boring, stupid joke, and no matter how real you make it feel, it's always just a paper tiger that you're letting ruin the shit out of your life.

Oops, did I go too far?

The *I'm Not Good Enough Show* morphs into various names and derivatives. Sometimes it's the *I'm an Imposter Show.* Sometimes it's the *Who Am I Kidding? Show.* (Okay, that's pretty much the *I'm An Imposter Show* rebooted on another network.)

It all comes down to one thing: What you want or who you are just isn't cutting it. You want to be, do, or feel one thing, and life is unkindly telling you that you're faking it, you suck, there are tons of other people more clever, crafty, rich, thin, loving, smart, go-getting, pretty, handsome, fit, healthy, young, in demand, talented . . . on and on *than you*.

Ouch. So, you're shuffling by, trying to pretend you've got this, your shit's together, you can do this . . . and at the end of the day you're tucked in bed with your knees to your chin, trembling and drinking your eighteenth cola today, thinking about how *it's all gonna fall apart*.

Remember when we talked about intrinsic worth? Get in there again with me for a moment.

I'm trying to feel my intrinsic worth right now. I know there are a bazillion self-help, pseudoscientific, trashy, pop-psychology books out there. And the *I'm Not Good Enough Show* is telling me right now that, honey, I better shut up and listen because I'm about to go down in a dumpster fire with all of them. Amazon will trash me. Readers will call me hackneyed and derivative. Reviewers will tear me up for my terrible overuse of cliches. To even think I could add something new or flavorful to the genre . . . well, my ego must be blowing soap bubbles with giants. Time to get popped.

I'm even afraid to tell you freely about people I know and work with, since I think you'll think I'm name-dropping, trying too hard. Real Deals don't name drop. I'm holding back half my stories so you won't think I'm an egotistical asshole since we all know that women aren't supposed to brag.

All this crazy self-protection and self-doubt is going on inside me, even when there's this much deeper part of me that whispers: *You've done some good stuff, Summer. You've worked with thousands of people, popped open their fears without them even realizing ('cuz you're such a damn good delicate surgeon), and sewed them right back up again. You've helped your clients earn millions and millions of dollars. You've seen them get married, helped them make that last and final frozen egg actually stick. Damn, girl, you're amazing.*

And then the other part comes up and continues the insecure self-talk: *Yeah maybe you're good, but not good enough to get an agent, Sum Sum, but if you do get one, and that's a goddamn big if, they're gonna make you take all this filthy, vulgar language out of this book, because they'll say you won't sell your books in Costco otherwise, and you're gonna duck your head down and quietly say, "Okay," because all this trashy big girl talk is just a power move to make you sound like a big shit.*

Well fuuuck me. It goes on and on. So much I'm-not-good-enough talk.

See what I'm getting at? This stuff is literally the kiss of death.

Sometimes we forget our intrinsic worth. I've let my fear of getting my ego bruised stop me from revealing who I am and what I know to the world. I've let the small, fearful me win over the loving, magnanimous, intelligent me who knows that if even one person's life is significantly changed by something they've read . . . well hot damn, it was worth it. (Okay, maybe ten people's lives. Writing a book takes a lot of hours.)

In other words, when I get small, I get selfish because I'm only thinking about *me*. My fear of getting exposed, ridiculed, or smacked down wins. Selfish, selfish girl. All the gifts I've been given stay inside me, and the gods shake their heads in disappointment. I can practically hear them intone in booming voices: "We gave her smarts! We gave her looks! We gave her socio-economic privilege! And even with all these generous advantages, she *still* she plays small, protecting her ass, worrying about what people think. What a waste."

That's the kind of smack talk that puts me in my place.

I can't play small. I can't give into feeling Not Good Enough. To get what I want, I'm going to have to *own* my vision and run with it, choking back my feelings of "Oh, shit. I'm gonna be exposed! It's gonna hurt, be embarrassing, prove that I'm a failure after all, etc. I can't do this!"

Back when I had a radio show with a famous cohost, and part of my job was to facilitate interviews with him at various live events, he really did push a lot of buttons in me.

I'd think to myself, "Man, how can you sit on the stage like some pompous ass with your calloused bare feet and board shorts, talking to rapturous thousands, when everyone knows you should be wearing polished wingtips and a suit. Where do you get off, dude, with your giant, big, balloony ego?"

And then I'd hear his answer in my head that sounded something like: "I get off sitting here in my goddamn board shorts and bare feet with my big scabby toes sticking out because I don't care. I literally don't fucking care. My clothes don't matter; I'm not using them to prop up my ego. What I offer the world speaks for itself. It's not about me. You either like what I share or you don't. And you, you're a judgy, jealous little lady, and you should just get over yourself and get up here in *your* swimsuit and toenails with their peeling polish and do the same. I'd like to see that. Maybe you'd finally get over yourself that way and get moving on your *actual fuckin' gifts.*"

Okay, that's pretty harsh. For one, he'd *never* use language like that with me. But the bigger point is that I realized my judgy feelings of "You're not supposed to do it like that!" exposed my truer feelings about myself of "I'm Not Good Enough" and "I'm Faking It and Somehow You Will All Know."

The worst part of the *I'm Not Good Enough Show*? It keeps you in check. It keeps you in Plan B. It keeps you always willing to hand the baton to someone else to take the lead in the relay race. It means you're unable to get over yourself, and your Little Self wins. And all that Big, Gorgeous, Awesome stuff you're trying to grow into gets stuffed into the bottom of the smelly backpack of life.

One of my peers once showed up to an online, recorded YouTube video interview with me with ratty uncombed hair in her pajamas. "Aw," she said, "I didn't know it was video." She recorded it with me anyway.

She also kills my company in terms of profits and smushes my blog size with her many more tens of thousands of ardent admirers. I don't think she's ever stopped to ask herself, "Am I good enough?" She just does her stuff, over and over, until she wears out her delight with it. She's blessedly immune to fretting over how others perceive her, so *she gets her true life's work done.*

Doesn't that sound kind of fun?

Hear me: You're good enough for whatever God set you up to do. Can you trust that? Can you trust that if you get an idea in your head, it's utterly perfect that you got that idea? And not only perfect, it's there to tell you to act on it, do it.

Self-Selecting

Hear this: Every major biggie wiggie you admire went through a moment of asking, "Oh, shit, can I really do this?" And the ones who never made it big are the ones who are still waiting for life or a boss or a casting director or someone, anyone, to tell them, "Yes, you are good enough. You are anointed."

The ones who've made it are the ones who self-selected—they selected themselves to lead and decided to believe in their work and their mission without holding back. When they were twisting their necks looking for the Keeper of the Keys, they realized that the keys were hanging right there. The only question they asked was: *Do I want to choose myself to take them?*

And they said yes. *I choose me. I will do this. My little fearful self will not tell me no. Someone has got to be the next [fill in the blank], and I choose it to be me. Let's hope others agree.*

Why are we always waiting on someone else's opinion of our worth? Someone else's validation?

Every big Hollywood star, every media mogul, every name-brand CEO, every star politician . . . they selected themselves to be there, to go for it. They didn't wait for life or God or other people to validate who they were. (Okay, if your dad is a rich movie star, you definitely have a leg up to be one too, but generally, we choose to be heroes, and there's no casting board qualifying or disqualifying us except ourselves.)

For the last time, can we put down the need to compare? Can we chill that angst of inferiority? Can you tuck that little freaked-out ego into the folds of your sock drawer and instead tell life: *I want this. I want to have this, be this, do that. You were right to place this (skill, art, ability, insight) in me, and I will take it to its limits! I won't crumple to the small me. I won't let protecting myself from pain or rejection win over my desire to let the goddamn queen out of her castle and see what I'm truly capable of!*

Ahh, that feels good.

I want you to self-select right now. Nobody is going to select you until you first select yourself—I mean, why would they? You'd be asking someone for something you won't even do for yourself.

Go take this thing that you want to do, be, say, have, or experience, and tell yourself you are 100 percent the right person for it. Go beyond telling yourself—feel it. Choose it. Validate yourself, and let go of the power leak of needing it from others first. It's an act of faith.

M.E. *School* Prompt

Your prompt is to get clear on all the ways you tell yourself you aren't good enough, someone else is better, it's not your turn yet, and so on.

Blow holes in them all. Then, engage in the feeling of choosing yourself. Play with how self-selecting feels. It may feel weird or false at first. Remember, this is a new idea. Give it time to take root in you. It will strengthen and grow.

Ask yourself:

- Where do I feel I'm faking it?

- What would I do if I knew I was guaranteed to succeed?

- Do I feel like I'm too old, too young, not thin or fit enough, not charismatic enough, not having the right skills, not talented enough, etc.?

- What particular part of me do I think is Not Good Enough and how is it Not Good Enough?

- How do I feel when I choose to feel like I'm as good as someone I admire and select myself to be in the "same league" as them?

Chapter 18:
What Will Happen When You Win?

I'm not even going to tell you we're almost done. Clearly, here's another chapter, and this one is somewhat related to paper tigers. Except it's about your fear of actually becoming a raging success.

What a weird idea, right? What will happen when you *win*? That means when you find your direction, when you have enough money, when you fall in love, get that awesome job, successfully and totally reinvent yourself, or finally solve that problem? What then?

I can't tell you how many times fear of success comes up in conversations with my clients. It's like the ugly stepsister to the *I'm Not Good Enough Show*. In fact, I think the *I'm Not Good Enough Show* is programmed to come on exactly before the *What Happens If I Win Show*, precisely to keep you from getting to that much scarier show.

At first glance, nobody ever really says, "I'm afraid I'll succeed."

We all think success is exactly what we're going for. However, when you squish up your eyes and peer deeper, you see all these things you do to ensure you won't ever win—or you'll win a little but not enough.

Sometimes people call this self-sabotage. But I hate that phrase, because "self-sabotage" implies that we're purposely inflicting pain on ourselves and scheming to prevent our own success. It's far more accurate to say that we do a series of weird things over and over that make us stay under some arbitrary threshold of success. These things are not always purposeful; in fact, they're usually invisible.

Let me give you an example.

Fear of Being Seen

One of my students is a kick-ass Aussie lady. (I love you, Australians. Out of everyone in the world, you're the most like us Californians in terms of temperament, outlook, personality. I know, I just generalized a whole country there.)

But my dear Aussie friend, Dana, has an idea for a new sunscreen. It's all natural and good for babies and old people alike. It's organic. It passed the development tests. It has branded bottling. It smells like sugar cookies. It's awesome.

And I've been helping her build her little company and get the word out.

Dana also works a day job for Australia's equivalent of Fish and Wildlife, but she isn't out counting salmon under the blue sky. Instead, she sits at a little gray desk every day, dreaming about suntan lotion.

She inches forward on growing her company each week, getting a piddly bit done here, a piddly bit done there. And she's spending a fortune on me to coach her. Finally, I lose patience and say, "Why are you going so slowly?"

There's no real answer. Or the answers are all about stuff that comes up that distracts her, that is momentarily more important: a work deadline, her mom needing a ride to the eye doctor, her sister coming into town to visit, her website people not getting the copy turned in on time. The list is weekly, and the list is endless.

It sort of sounds like procrastination, right? It's not. It's something that disguises itself as procrastination.

One day, I tackle her: "Why are you afraid of succeeding?"

"I don't know," she sniffles.

"Okay, I'll start with some ideas then. Ready?"

I see her brown bobbed hair and green eyes nodding at me in our video chat.

"You're worried that you might invest a bunch of money in this and find out no one really wants you or it. You'll be out of money and have had your lifelong dream crushed. And then what? You'll have lost your lifelong dream. So, better to always keep it in the 'almost succeeding' stage but never reaching the critical point?"

"Maybe."

Umm, I'll keep going. Fear of failure is not it.

"You're afraid that if you start selling stacks of this stuff you're going to end up quitting your safe job. And then what? What if your little company tanks after that, and then you won't have a job *or* a company?"

"A little."

Dana, you're a tough nut to crack. Fear of losing safety is not it.

"Okay, how about this: You think that if you get successful, you're going to have to hire people, become a boss, take on leadership. And you've generally hated your bosses and leaders. And you don't want to be the one at the top of the ladder with employees under you who only give you a hard time and secretly hate your guts and are going to stress you out day in, day out."

"That's starting to feel about right."

"And," I continue breathlessly, "not only that, but you think being successful is going to mean you'll have no time for life, you'll be constantly stressed, and you'll be miserable. What's more, your parents always told you that wealthy people are miserable, selfish, coddled, arrogant asses, and you'll be one!"

"Yes," she breathes.

I feel like Superwoman. Dana is afraid of *being seen*. If she's successful, she'll be seen; if she's seen, she'll be judged, which means feeling hurt, disparaged, hated, and unloved.

Being Seen

"Dana, let me tell you an old Chinese saying. It goes like this:

"'The *flower* that grows too high in the field is the first to be cut.'"

In other words, don't stick out.

Which is also saying, "Don't be seen."

Except that being seen is exactly what Dana is striving for. Maybe you are too. Anything you offer to the world, whether it's something you've made, written, done, quilted, shaped, led, baked, carved, studied for, coded, put together, auditioned, or interviewed for, etc., will gain an audience, perhaps an audience of one, or potentially an audience of thousands. Or millions. And if you want to go big with it, you'll need that big audience. You'll want people to buy into this offer—customers, admirers, readers, viewers, consumers, or even bosses. You'll want people to share it with. This idea isn't just for entrepreneurs either. It's for all of us who'll need to stick our necks out to get to the next level of success, whether by taking on more leadership or accountability at work or anything else.

You say you try to be seen all the time. "I write newsletters! I speak on stages! I get in front of the room to read my latest proposal to my boss and the team. I stick my hand up in company meetings, and I even have a gorgeous social media profile to showcase myself on."

But is that enough? Because at some point you back down. You give up. You slink away and say, "I tried and they rejected me. It always happens."

And that is that. You grow no taller than the flowers around you. To go any further would be too risky. Something would be put on the line. *If you grow too high, you'll be the first to get cut.*

Being seen is dangerous, really fucking dangerous. All kinds of bad things happen to people who stick out.

Right now, I can think of a dozen actions that Dana won't do because they seem too big for her, too impossible, too risky, too dangerous, too exposed, and too easy to feel rejection around.

She has something in her that says success is dangerous and miserable. It won't last, you'll be dumped, you'll be hated by your friends and family for being successful, you won't be able to handle that level of decision making . . . yeah, the cons of being successful outweigh the pros. So let's just sit here in this middle ground for a while.

Dana doesn't even realize she has such negative expectations of success. She wants it so bad, and yet she's *so, so* scared of all the terrible stuff it might bring to her. And for her, the worst are: "What if I get successful and then it doesn't last? What if I'm ripped down and ripped apart, I make stupid choices, my friends don't talk to me, and my parents say I got too big for my britches?"

Success will make her alone, lonely, hated, and vulnerable.

We can see why she's avoiding it.

Of course it isn't just Dana. I admit that there's a whole list of things I won't do for almost the same reasons as Dana. I'd be sticking my head out, and it would probably get cut off with mass rejections, or total silence, or I'd just look stupid, so why make myself feel that way?

Well, what if my next layer of success lives precisely up there, in the doing of all those things?

Nope, ain't doing them. Not ready to be seen, and potentially rejected, like that.

If you look closer, you'll notice that I'm prejudging people. I'm expecting, anticipating, that some people don't want to see me because I'm not important enough to be seen by them. (Lack thoughts, anyone?)

Then I realize that if I don't even consider myself a tall flower, why should they?

If I think trying to be seen, or success itself, will only bring me rejection, embarrassment, or stress, why should others work with me or help me achieve it?

I tell myself this is rational. And since I know I'm right, why put myself through the pain of rejection?

Except, in reality, I'm just scared. Just a plain scared rabbit, doubting herself.

The *I'm Not Good Enough Show* and the *What Happens If I Actually Win Show* have gotten together and had a baby. Me.

And what if I do go for it, and when these people still don't see me, refuse me, or in fact don't even acknowledge me at all, I've just gained proof that I was right? That is freaking scary. But on the other hand, what if I do actually succeed? Well, then all kinds of negative blowback will be on its way.

I can't risk potentially feeling any of those feelings. So I protect myself. *I'd rather live in the apprehension of not being valuable than have real proof that I'm not valuable. I'd rather not succeed than succeed and pay the price.*

Isn't the "being seen" conversation fascinating?

If we are seen, then we risk being judged, rejected, ridiculed, or disliked. We risk being the tall flower cut first in the field. We risk being disparaged, torn down, and seen for what we really are: sniveling pretenders.

But if we are not seen because we prevent and protect ourselves from being seen, then we are simply ignored. We might be sad, frustrated, or bewildered by our lack of success, but we at least aren't going to risk being judged, disliked, exposed, or thought of as too full of ourselves.

Being seen might mean losing friends and family who no longer "get" us or who are jealous or uncomfortable with our success.

Being seen might mean we can't hold on to the success, and we'll lose it, which might feel worse than not being successful in the first place

Being seen might mean we'll be exposed for the imposters that we are. They'll see we're just pretending to be so great at what we do.

Oh God, the risks of being seen!

No wonder we all chirp longingly for success like a flock of silly birds, but we never really go for it. And when we spot people who do, we spread judgment on them as thick as butter.

The only way you will ever be seen is when you can totally get over yourself and make what you create be more important than your own feelings. We're right back to that again.

In other words, when you start to feel that what you give or offer is more important than protecting yourself, then you will be seen.

But to have that faith in what you offer, you have to have faith in yourself, faith that you are simply amazing at what you do (or even that you're just getting better day by day) . . . that the world truly needs what you do . . . that people are better off because of who you are . . . that if you don't give what you do to as many people as you can, then you are failing in your calling.

That is some strong mojo. So, do you have that faith?

Maybe some days you do, some days you don't.

Like I already admitted to you earlier, as I write these words right now, part of me thinks that sharing myself with you like this is the Lord's truth spilling out my fingers, and another part thinks I sound like a pompous jerkwad and all this has been said before, so who am I kidding?

It feels much safer and easier to be humble and hide than it does to feel like God's gift to the world.

But safe and small is not where I like to play, so while I recognize the feeling, I've learned to shift the narrative almost as soon as it comes up. I've already bellied up to this inner conversation more than once, self-selected long ago, and still continuously self-select at every new level of success I reach. It's become the bedrock of my continual reinvention. Whenever this wiggling fear of being seen raises its slimy head, I see it, then choose to be the tall flower and do the scary thing, and once again I self-select.

You can simultaneously recognize your self-doubt and insecurity while at the same time recognizing your intrinsic worth, valued contribution, and worthiness of being seen at whatever level you choose.

I choose to feel a different sort of humble than the kind that involves hiding. My humbleness is not based on inferiority, but on simply getting over myself. My little self-protective ego-self won't win. I remind myself:

You're the messenger not the message.

What people think of the messenger is irrelevant.

The message is too important not to be carried.

And, gulp, you've selected yourself to carry it. Now what?

What would be released in you if you truly felt that way? Can you have that degree of faith in the message you carry or the abilities you're cultivating? Can you develop the feeling that even if your *raison d'etre* is evolving, you're still wed to the commitment of doing everything you can to get over yourself, to be seen, and to share who you truly are?

This isn't about just work or career—this is about *you*, all of you: The way you show yourself to your family and friends. The way you accept positions of power or avoid them. The way you drive forward into your next phase or inner transformation, even if that means going bigger or being seen in some way.

Do you believe you can continue to be the container that holds your bigger message, no matter what the cost?

Because if not, this is why your flower is small.

Fuuucckk that. Go let the sun pull you up into the sky, where all can see you. Shine your message. You've been selected.

M.E. *School* Prompt

Your prompt is to look deeply into your true feelings about being seen and successful.

Use the questions below to explore how you truly feel about success. You don't have to answer them all. Just answer the ones that hit home. As you unravel these deeper inner beliefs, you become able to make a different choice about them. In the last chapter, I asked you to self-select. Now, I'm asking you again.

Don't let what you discover in the questions validate your unworthiness. Look instead at your own answers and ask yourself where they came from, whether they are true, and if they're serving you. You're here to transform, grow past, and break down these old blocks and beliefs.

- Do I feel if I'm seen in a bigger way that I'll be rejected, hurt, or found out?

- Did I learn or was I taught at some point that "good people" don't stand out—only the egotistical seek such attention?

- What do my family and friends think about rich or successful people?

- Do I think successful people are truly happy?

- Do I think success always comes with a hidden, brutal cost?

- Do I believe I need to somehow "learn more" or "be better" before I'm worth showing myself? When or what will be the marker for that point?

☐ Do I ever see myself hanging back, waiting, "thinking it over," or slowing down just when I should be speeding up?

☐ Do I notice how, when I'm on the brink of success, I get distracted by other things, and by the time I've come back, the opportunity has passed?

PART V:
Heal That Shit Up

Chapter 19:
The Groove

Oh my God, we made it. You made it. You are now three-quarters through M.E. School. And yes, the center part was rough. You now have a neat little catalog of All the Stuff to Fix.

And here I am, sitting fully clothed in a bright red shirt and cutoff shorts, the July sun just setting behind my office chair. Spring has gone. I have an urge to throw my gray sky, despondent lavender pajamas from murky March into the trash, but I probably won't.

I'm realizing that I should've been writing these past eleven years, agents and publishers be damned. I'm realizing that it's also okay that I didn't. I wonder if you're starting to feel a bit better, too, about what you've been up to these last however many months or years.

The reality is that I've been doing something pretty wonderful this past decade. I was busy learning about people and skilling myself up in exposing all the things we do to keep ourselves small, stuck, and lost.

And, more importantly, how to get past and through them.

I now want to shove this book I'm writing with you in my own eighteen-year-old daughter's hands and tell her to *read and underline as needed.* As if. Eighteen, sheesh.

I'm 100 percent sure that whatever you've been doing, whatever led you to this moment of saying, "I'm ready to shift into my next form," is exactly what you needed. Doesn't matter how long it took. Doesn't matter how many times you fell off your path. The point is, you're here. Be gentle on yourself.

Some of you right now are probably forty- or fifty-year-old gals like me. We did the getting married thing. We did the raising kids thing. We did the career thing. And now we're asking ourselves, *Uhh, is that all there is?*

And some of you are just twenty-two or thirty-two, and you're looking ahead and wondering, *What the F do I do next? How do I make it all come together? Isn't there a guidebook somewhere?*

Hey, what were we talking about way back in the preface? Oh yeah:

I think, like me, you're here because you want to shake yourself awake again, and maybe even figure out how you got to this exact point in your life. Not only that, you want to know where to go next. And maybe even how to go about doing that. You're at a pause point, the needle in the groove between the songs.

This groove, pause, or pivot point between yesterday and tomorrow can be a lot of things:

Maybe it's post-divorce.

Maybe it's graduating college.

Maybe it's being laid off.

Maybe it's being home in bed with a spankin' new autoimmune disease or long-haul COVID.

Maybe it's being stuck in your job or career and failing to go bigger no matter what you try.

Maybe it's even "having it all" and yet still feeling dissatisfied. Something is missing.

Or maybe it's you taking flight to a new town in a new state.

Maybe it's you on the verge of walking into work tomorrow morning and saying, "Screw you, I'm done," and finally going out to get the kind of job you've actually always wanted. *(Plan A, here I come, baby!)*

Or maybe it's you expanding your business or practice with a new $100K loan even though you're choked up with fear.

Maybe it's just this vague inner whisper saying, "There's more to life. You know it. Why aren't you doing it? Why are you sad? Indecisive? Going through the motions of this relationship? Going through the motions of this job? Just making rent each month? What the hell? You aren't getting any younger. See those new fat rolls on your back? They weren't there last month. What do you want, *what do you really fucking want from this whole life thing?*"

Well, what do you want?

Oh yeah, emotional endpoints. Those things. They're a good start.

But maybe you're not quite ready. Maybe this book is a darn good read and all but, *boy oh boy, all that crap we just uncovered? How is it ever gonna be possible to beat that?*

Hate to sound cliché again, but trust me. It is. Most people never even get to the point of seeing their crap, let alone moving past it. You're now already ahead of almost everyone you know. Swim, little fishy, swim.

M.E. *School* Prompt

Your prompt is just to breathe.

Take a breath. Notice that you've arrived at the pause point, the moment between who you used to be and who you're becoming. Just acknowledge it. Settle yourself and feel what it's like to be really, really ready for the next reef. Because we're going there, now.

Chapter 20:
You Will Fix It When You're Ready to Fix It

My therapist looked at me across the table and said, "You'll fix it when you're ready to fix it."

We were sitting in a pair of creased brown-leather chairs with a few sad plants, tissue boxes, and some new-agey trinkets decorating the room. I was broken into pieces, newly fired, emotionally far, far away from my husband, mother to a toddler and a first grader, and recently diagnosed with interstitial cystitis that made me pee blood all the time. Yeah, scroll back in time with me a little.

I was fired three days after I got out of the hospital, where I'd been since I'd been urinating tons of blood. Like, lots—the toilet bowl looked like it was swimming with maraschino cherry juice. And did I mention it hurt? The kind of hurt that's like one bladder infection got hitched to another bladder infection who then adopted three more bladder infection children. Except this wasn't a bladder infection. The walls of my bladder had just given out. They'd been shredded with bloody ulcers from years of unrelenting, mind-boggling stress. Finally, I'd been released from the ER, staggered into work with thick pads bulging in my underwear, got sat down by HR, and had to clear my desk the same day. Fuck lot of thanks for ten years. It was total shit, in other words. I was just thirty-eight.

My therapist, Liam, listened to me cry and rage about how it was all so goddamn unfair. So unfair. Husband was a selfish ass who came home at 2:00 a.m. half the time. And all my previous beliefs, about how if you give your job your all then you'll get rewarded, were irrevocably smashed. I'd made millions of dollars in revenue for my company, restructured and built whole departments from the ground up, but the one area I'd failed in rather spectacularly was stupid: *office politics.*

Even some of my own employees had decided they could outsmart and out-angle me to their advantage, and they were right, because I simply didn't understand the political game. It had never even entered my awareness that the game was even important. *Shit, shit, shit.* I had severely and seriously misjudged and mishandled a lot of things in my life recently, and the truth of them had caught up.

And yes, I was rocking just four hours a night of sleep with a toddler who would only go back to sleep if I let him up to play for an hour at 3:00 o'clock in the morning.

Home alone, bleeding, fired, husband out God-knows-where, two crying kids, no path forward.

I woke up to no awesome job to go to anymore, with no true explanation, and my reputation smeared across my professional community as people whispered about my unexpected firing. No way to defend myself without pointing fingers or getting a lawyer, which felt like piling shit on top of shit, which I was unwilling to do.

I was walking around hunched in pain all day, and holding in my heartbreak since the one person I was supposed to be able to talk to was instead completely sick of me saying anything to the point where he wouldn't even come home.

What I kept asking Liam is "How do I fix it?" And he'd say, "How do you think you should fix it?" *What an asshole.* And then one day when I'm feeling so much self-defeat and total shaking disappointment in what I'm letting happen in my life, Liam says to me, "You'll fix it when you're ready to fix it.

We don't know when that is yet. Until then, we'll keep talking about it. You keep pushing yourself to fix it, but you're not there yet."

You will fix it when you're ready to fix it.

It's more of a gut understanding of what that means than the words themselves. It sort of translates to "You'll fix it when some part of you finally says, 'I'm ready to do X-Y-Z now.' Stop feeling like such a wussy turd and getting so down on yourself. I know you're a badass, but you aren't a badass right now. When you're there, it'll get done. Ride it out. At some point, you'll stop all this and set the ship straight. We just don't know when that is yet."

Fast forward exactly thirteen years. My toddler is grown and in high school. My husband is loving and fixes us dinner every night and does all the laundry. My old job, and my old firing that so fucked with my sense of self, was exactly what I needed to make me finally grasp the future that was mine, all mine. I could kiss that old boss now.

And now my client, Laura, is here on the phone with me, in an eerily similar situation as my own: Her husband has hit her, the cops came to swanky Malibu for God's sake, and she completely financially supports him. She also has a multimillion-dollar home overlooking the Pacific Ocean, and two other vacation homes, and works for a multinational corporation as some bigwig, and she is a *no-bullshit gal.* And she just wants to fix this.

And I remember when I felt exactly like this. Like I'm such a powerful person, and yet my life is bleeding. Why can't I fix this? When will I fix this?

Listen to Liam: *"You'll fix it when you're ready to fix it, and it'll just be right."*

Laura is so embarrassed. I'm proud of her for even telling me the one little area where she's fucked up. Usually, we hide that. Things like booze, cigs, bulimia, picking, OCD, partners who abuse us, being violated or controlled, eating after 11:00 p.m., faking your workouts, pretending your guy is loyal when you know he isn't—it's all so embarrassing. All so *not strong.*

Laura and I have worked together every month for a whole year. She's baby-stepping it, and that's okay. She can't tell her husband she's ready to leave. She feels guilty for getting him to marry her. She's assuming 100 percent responsibility when it should be shared. But she knows he can't or won't share it.

We ask the universe to give her the perfect next step, the one she can do, that will alter things just enough to get her to the next point. *We ask for it to be easy.*

And you know what? That's allowed. You can ask for the next step to be simple, obvious, and easy. Just a little step, one that works. You don't have to bite off the whole cookie.

Laura gets a job offer out of town, and she snaps it up. Now, she and hubby must live apart at least five days a week because, ultimately, he wants to stay near his country club. What an absurdly easy way to alter her situation by shifting the blame to her *job,* since she is still too fearful to fix it.

And that's allowed. Baby steps.

We get back to our session. She shares that she'll feel like a failure if she tells him he's not a good partner. She feels responsible for him since he and his mom are financially broke without her. She's giving him no chance to grow from his actions since she believes he can't. And she's still willing to sacrifice her happiness and the occasional bruises, every day, for this. Because this is what makes her a good person, in her mind.

"You'll fix it when you're ready to fix it, and it'll just be right."

I think about how my own drama played out.

I nursed my wounds for *three years* before I began to come out of it. Three years is a long time to be in a hateful pity party with yourself. I buried myself in kid-rearing, writing, my podcast, helping others, and having screaming fights with my husband.

And then one day it happened. I was ready to fix it. I called my husband out on the carpet and gave an ultimatum: The kids and I would move in with my mom if he continued to stay away from home. In exchange, I would try to be easier to live with. It would all work out.

Then I stepped into my calling and recognized that the success of my work was not just a fluke of having some really bright and starlit people around me. I was my own bright thing, my own light, with my own message. Those superstars had been surrounding me for a reason. But they were not making me who I am.

My bladder healed. My stress dropped. My toddler was a tantrum-throwing kindergartner with his own set of new dramas, but at least we were both sleeping without a Disney film running.

It was like I was suddenly just there, ready. It wasn't even sudden, really, it was more like a slow drip of moments over days and months, a zillion baby steps that finally led somewhere. And one day I blinked where I was standing and saw that it was different than where I'd been before.

I hear people tell me this all the time when they say, "And then one day I just knew I was going to divorce."

Or "That was when I realized my dad would never be who I wanted or needed him to be."

Or "I decided I could just put it behind me."

And "I just went to the doctor and got the damn test."

And "The next time he hit me, I left and I did not come back because I realized that I deserved a different kind of love than what I was experiencing."

All of these people had finally awakened to that moment.

"You'll fix it when you're ready to fix it, and it'll just be right."

It's coming. Stop pushing. Stop being so mad at yourself.

When you need to fix something, you might bury it, delay it, hide it, deny it. But it's always still there. You know it is.

So you might take the easy way and baby-step it.

And finally, when you do reach that point of gorgeous inner strength, readiness, and trust in your life, you'll fix it.

You always do.

M.E. School Prompt

Your prompt is to get really clear on what you're ready to heal, solve, or fix.

We may have looked already at the things you want to make, create, and feel, but here we're looking at what needs healing so that you can build your gorgeous new self (and life) on top of a solid, strong foundation. The questions below are tough, but you're ready for them. Everything you want is on the other side of them. Remember that.

- What issue around my healing or broken parts do I know I need to address?
- What scares me about it, and what do I fear might happen?
- Am I feeling mad or guilty at myself for letting it go on or for not handling it well?
- What would it take for me to feel ready to heal this?

Chapter 21:
Learning to Be Wrong

Congrats are in order. That was some hard shit to look at. Even if you didn't write anything down, I know it still flitted across your mind and you saw it, even briefly.

Now you're saying, "Okay, Summer, you got me into this, how are you going to get me out? How do I lay these problems to rest, exactly? Is there really a one-size-fits-all answer?"

Well happy day, you've actually been doing many of the things already to help you shift upward all through these chapters. All that "seeing yourself" stuff? That's been hidden information about yourself and life until now. Or, if not hidden, then not as deeply understood as it is now. See, you're shifting your understanding of it. You've added a whole bunch of new contexts and ways of seeing things that probably weren't there before—using ideas like pre-action, emotional endpoints, the king and queen, Backward-Looking Girl, lack thinking, fear of feelings, and on and on.

Something my M.E. School students hear me say constantly is "Everything you want is just on the other side of *that*," and then I point my finger at something in their lives that's ugly, unhappy, scary, and way overstayed.

It's true. Most problems fester in *front* of whatever you're seeking. They also don't magically go away, though sometimes we think we can just wait them out, and eventually they'll change—which sometimes does happen and is a valid strategy, unless you feel like your life is biting at the bit to move forward, and you ain't getting any younger.

Then you feel compelled to go through the icky thing simply to get to the other side where your rainbows are. And we've looked at various ways these icky things get piled up, in the form of lack thinking, avoidance, procrastination, power leaks, and more.

Like I've hinted, my little toolbox has gotten stuffed over the years with ways to break patterns, reveal ceilings, regain passion and direction, and push through all the gunk that's accumulated in our hearts. My hope is that one or more of these tools will work for you. I honestly never intended to go looking for these techniques. It's more like I just kept casually picking them up and sticking them in my pocket as I walked the road of life. And working with thousands of people intimately, in their minds and hearts, has really helped.

So let's start the healing.

Learn to Be Wrong

Getting through that gunk in your life almost always starts with healing. And the very first thing we need to heal is *your need to be right.*

Being right is what has landed you on the shore of this moment of your life.

Being right has had mixed results.

Being right is something the king loooooves to do.

Instead, we are going to practice being wrong—being wildly, spectacularly wrong—about most everything!

That's right, you don't know shit! Your assumptions are wrong! Your understanding of "how things work!" and "that's reality!" Wrong again!

You have never been more misinformed in your entire life.

All the stuff we've been talking about until this point has been about where or how you've derailed, or gotten stuck, or just reached the *blahs.* And to make sense of it, you've created some really watertight explanations of *why.*

It's one thing to feel stuck, frustrated, or unhappy, but if you can tell your-self what made these happen, it makes them much more bearable. And you don't want anyone taking that explanation away because you've worked hard to establish it.

Unfortunately, the more right you feel about your explanation, the harder it becomes to think anything else. You've explained your misfortune so thor-oughly to yourself that now, when you want to dismantle that explanation so you can move forward, you find that everything you try to tell yourself just keeps slapping that impenetrable wall of "no, that's the way it is."

Now, we're going to go to the other extreme. You're going to take every-thing you say to yourself about "why things are the way they are" and instead turn it around and be incredibly, patently wrong about why things are the way they are.

Go back to some of those power leaks. Remember how you had pinpointed an internal or external reason for each thing that wasn't working for you?

Well, as of this moment, those reasons are total shit.

You couldn't be more wrong about either or both of them.

As an example, let's say you're wrong about something icky you've always believed about yourself—one of your internal power leaks.

I want you to be wrong about that idea you have that you always start things and never finish them. Be wrong about feeling disappointment in yourself that you just aren't good enough, or perseverant enough, or what-ever to stick with something and develop it.

Now, why did you pick that about me, Summer?

Because a lot of people have this little cavity of "being right" about the idea that they never follow through with things.

Well you're right, I don't have a lot of faith that I'll start and finish some-thing big. I mean, look at my life. I've got certificates in Reiki, hypnosis, EFT, and purple-wanding, and I've spent a boatload of money but never did any-thing with them. I've had, like, thirteen jobs. I never got into environmental engineering like I wanted to because I never finished those last two years of college. I was working, and it was just easier to work.

Right. How can you be wrong about the feelings you have about yourself for being a loser?

I never said loser. I said I haven't lived up to my potential.

Okay, Ms. High School Principal. Can you be wrong about this?

Uh, I have lived up to my potential? I have successfully finished things?

Keep going.

Maybe my expectations have always been too high, so every time I don't finish something I get mad at myself? Maybe the things I didn't finish were not a big deal anyway, and I can stop feeling like they were, even that degree, because I've carved out a pretty nice life anyway?

Getting warmer.

Maybe I've persevered with a lot of things. Like having my best friends, Nan and Jessie, since high school. That's long-term. I've invested in those friendships for twenty years. Or my working out. I've done my 5ks for ten years now.

Exactly! That's it. Glass half full! See all the things you've persevered at, grown, and continued? They're everywhere, littering your life! You've only popped that magnifying glass on a few specific things you didn't finish, then allowed those self-recriminatory feelings to balloon way out of proportion.

You are incredibly wrong about yourself not being a finisher or being able to stick with things or make something substantial. In fact, you've actively been choosing to drop things along the way since they didn't quite suit you. Powerfully choosing, over and over. And sure, sometimes you chose to drop things out of fear that you wouldn't succeed and all that, but that's only because you hit a wall of fear that you then continued to work on surpassing.

We are breathless at the revelation.

You are not a loser, you are not a giver-upper, you have been actively deciding or avoiding making things in your life based on a whole set of conditions. You are gorgeously wrong about that old shitty belief about yourself. Now, why don't you just hold that awhile and see what it brings you.

Because that's what we're after—the results of changing your mind.

Here's the takeaway: Being right has kept you stuck. It's kept you spinning the same narrative around and around. You've hit a wall with this narrative. You're right and you're stuck. The only way out of it is to be freakishly, stupidly wrong. And doing it ridiculously, full throttle, by stating the exact opposite about yourself via "you're wrong" seems to be exactly what it takes to make it stick. No more years of therapy slowly unraveling the bits. Just say "I'm totally wrong."

Zap Those Rationalizations and Justifications

Before we wrap up, let's look a little bit deeper at your rationalizations and justifications. They are, after all, the things you're going to be wrong about.

But sometimes they aren't so obvious. Sometimes they're devious, tricky little devils because they want to stay right at all costs. And they'll head trip you hard to stay right.

Here's one last example, because yes, I'm going to beat this concept into the ground. I don't want you to ever forget it.

I'm in an argument with a client. This is the sucky part of my job.

My client, Jenny, is trying to convince me why she can't change careers. She has a long list of why she can't do it. But changing careers is exactly what she wants to do. And she is challenging me to break her extremely well-developed rationale for why she can't do it.

Yay me.

It goes like this, "You don't understand, I can't do this because . . ." and then, here comes the list:

> I'm too old.
> I'd have to go back to school.
> I can't afford not having a paycheck.
> I'm late to the game and everyone else doing
> this work is way ahead of me in their careers.

> *I'd have to start all over with a new audience or*
> *clientele.*
> *I can't do it while I'm paying for college.*
> *I have Lyme disease. I have cancer. I have*
> *a heart problem. I can't walk.*
> *I have to pay off other bills first.*

On and on.

The more I refute her, the more adamant she gets. She is dead set on telling me why she *can't do it.*

I am so glad the call is recorded. When she hears herself, she is just going to die with embarrassment.

But when you're in this kind of moment, it's like shoving all your deepest fears and rock-tight reasons out into the world and saying, "Look, it took me years to figure out why I can't get this or do this. Now that I know, I'm sure as hell not going to give up these really good, super, solid reasons. They've been helping me live without this thing I want, and the more solid my rationale is, the more relaxed and settled I feel about not getting what I want. And now you want me to not feel that way? Hell no."

The people with the strongest rationales are the most desperate to break them. Their reasoning has boxed them in and they can't get through it. They've made it too damn real and unbreakable.

So I say, "Jenny, what if you're just wrong? Like, all this stuff you believe is complete horseshit. You're totally wrong."

"No, I'm right!" she howls. "I've seen it again and again, it's been proven to me how right I am."

"Bullshit. *Stop defending your limitations.* Be wrong. Feel how freeing and light things are when you're just so, so wrong. Pretend with me. No, *feel* it with me. All your rationalizations and justifications are just bullshit. I don't believe them, and neither should you."

I tell her a story of my own.

Once, long ago, my soon-to-be husband would tease me that since I grew up as an only child, I was much more selfish than he was. He is the youngest of three. "I lived on hand-me-downs," he said. "I had to share everything."

"Wait," I said, "I have a half-brother! And I lived with three other step-siblings for most of my childhood! That's *four* brothers and sisters, more than you ever had!"

"Yeah," he replied gleefully, "but to your mom, you were an *only child*."

Somehow I accepted this bizarre logic. Okay, I was selfish, I couldn't share. And I thought that about myself for years.

And then one day, I was thinking about my work and my life, and I realized that my entire career has been built around helping other people. Putting myself in the line of fire with people like Jenny because I am a *giver*. What I do can be rough work. But I do it. I like to help people change. I share day in, day out. It's practically all I do.

And then I looked at where I spent my money—and it was on my kids and family, on anyone but me. My son needs some spankin' new tennies? He gets them. Meanwhile, I'm deciding to "wait until later" on those new flats.

Over and over.

My God, I thought, *I'm so wrong. I've been wrong all this time. I was never selfish. I'm very generous. I even over-give. I give people the benefit of the doubt even when it fucks me in the end. I plan vacations where my family wants to go, not where I want to go. Holy crap.*

And then I thought, *What else can I be* wrong *about?*

I wrote down every crappy thing I believed about myself or my life, and I said, "I'm totally wrong about that. I'm flat-out wrong! What I thought is so untrue! Wow! How wrong!"

It was like an iceberg melted off me.

Why had I been so invested in being right? What had that gotten me? I decided I'd *hate* being right for a while. I was going to be wrong about as much as possible and see what happened.

My dad doesn't love me? I'm wrong about that.

People think I look fat? I'm wrong about that.

I'll never have as much fun as I did in my twenties when life was spicy and fresh? I don't want to be right about that any longer.

No one will ever read the book I'm giving my heart and soul to writing? Wrong, lady.

And on and on.

All these glittering pieces of hope began to open up again all around me like little shimmery stars of things I could feel good about and look forward to. What's more, I changed things I did, said, felt, everything. I couldn't keep acting like I was right, now could I? As wrong, I had new ways to relate, hope, and interact with my life.

I called my dad on the phone and told him I loved him.

I put on that sleeveless tank and let the world see my svelte, sexy arms.

I had friends over for a game of Cards Against Humanity while we drank champagne cocktails around the firepit.

I wrote the damn book.

"Jenny, you're so wrong about all that stuff," I told her. "You don't want to be right about it anymore, because being right has stuffed you up with all sorts of limitations. You're so right you can't move anymore!"

"Yeah," she whispers, "I'll try to be wrong, but I still secretly think I'm right."

"Then you won't change anything. You've got to be fully, totally wrong. It's the only way you can let fresh air into your life. Let the breeze blow and let life start proving to you how wrong you've been. Wouldn't that be nice?"

"Yes and yes," she breathes.

Be wrong. Lose the justifications and rationalizations. It frees you. It freed me. I hope it frees Jenny.

You've got nothing to lose by trying it and everything to gain. Because being right has gotten you nowhere.

M.E. *School* Prompt

Your prompt is to discover what you can be totally, completely wrong about, and then swap your thinking into actually feeling like you're wrong.

What follows is a list of quite a few rationalizations and justifications that make you feel *right.* Choose something that you want to feel wrong about, then see if you've applied any of these rationalizations or justifications to it. If so, rephrase the rationalization to its exact opposite. In other words, think of one thing you want but can't get, feel, do, or become. There's a "why" attached to that . . . as in, "Here's *why* I can't have, be, do, become . . . ," etc. Find it, then flip it and be totally wrong about it.

Here's a good starting point for how to frame this sentence: "The thing I want but can't get/have/be/do/become is _____ because _____."

Use the checklist below, or write in your own specific rationalization.

- [ ] I've been waiting for the right or perfect conditions, and they aren't here yet.

- [ ] I'll upset someone and they'll be angry at me or even leave me or fire me.

- [ ] I'm indecisive: I don't know if I really want it or not.

- [ ] I fear losing out: If I choose this, then I can't choose the other thing I might want.

- [ ] The thing or person I'm looking for (my ideal job, my ideal partner) just isn't out there.

☐ I'm afraid I'll make the wrong choice and everything will fall apart, or I'll go broke, or (insert your specific fear of failure).

☐ I can't change because I'm stuck or held back by external constraints or commitments. ("My career only pays 'X' amount, I have two kids and can't support them on my own, etc.")

☐ Some things just *are* and can't be changed (born with a disease, overweight, not pretty, not socially at ease, or anything else "wrong" about you that's seemingly unchangeable).

☐ My personal failings (procrastination, lack of organization, lack of confidence or belief in myself, etc.) will always hold me back.

☐ I wasn't born into the right family, socioeconomic level, skin color, sex, religion, or place to get the things I need for this.

☐ Someone else is always going to be better at this than me.

☐ It takes too long, or takes too much work, or takes too much sacrifice (like dieting), or I hate doing it (like going to the gym or making phone calls).

☐ The universe just won't offer it to me or give me a chance, even though I keep waiting.

☐ It would be selfish of me to do this thing I want to do.

☐ My own reason: _____

_____

_____

Chapter 22:
Healing Is Like Showering: Do It Daily for Best Effects

Being wrong is like stepping up to the diving board. Healing is making the dive. And the fun, weird, interesting thing about healing is . . . it never stops. And if it does ever stop, it means you're dead. Or you're living a ghost of a life, which is almost like being dead.

Whatever brought you to pick up this book and join me in M.E. School in the first place is probably going to be solved by some form of inner healing. Your growth and reinvention hinges on it. Whether it's healing your broken confidence, healing your trust, healing your anger, healing your fear of having missed opportunities . . . whatever you want is probably on the other side of some form of healing. The icky, crusty, gunky stuff that you've been picking apart this whole book is finally meeting its match: healing.

Here's a little story about what healing truly is, and it has to do with the Happiest Place on Earth.

Healing Is Like Disneyland

Hey, baby, I know today is hard. And it should be. What an awful mess. I mean, it happened again, that thing you feared. You got dumped. You dumped someone. Someone you love is hurt or, worse, has passed. You were fired. You had an argument. Someone you were really into is ghosting you. You're grieving. The scale doesn't matter. You're hurting to a greater or lesser degree, but it still *hurts*.

You're also enraged. It's not fair. Any one of a thousand thorns has struck you, and now you wonder if you'll ever heal.

Maybe you just woke up to the idea that you've played small with so much of your life. You had a bad hand of cards and got hurt. Now, no matter what good cards come up, you won't play them. Why risk being hurt again?

Sweetums, I'll tell you.

Imagine a big adventure park like Disneyland. See the crowds passing through it, kids running and shouting, parents pushing strollers, people stopping with smiles gaping for a million photos? Tired people, happy people, hungry people. Food wrappers on the ground and gum stuck to handrails.

Now it's dark. The crowds have gone home. The night janitors come out and dump the trash, sweep the countless pieces of litter off the grounds, and replant the broken flowers.

In the morning, it's the Happiest Place on Earth again. I know, because my husband designed a coffee table book for Disneyland once and got to peek in after hours. And this is really what happens. Their gardeners replant the broken stuff before dawn. Their janitors street sweep the roads in the dark.

This place is *you*.

You thought that once healing happened, it was complete, as in all done. Like you "moved past it," or are "no longer affected by it," or will no longer fall into "that pattern again."

No, my love, you are like Disneyland. Every day you live, the millions of experiences you have leave all kinds of breakage and residue behind. Living creates breakage, like those candy wrappers blowing across the cement and the goo from sticky hands on the rides' handles.

Having to clean up is a sign of living well and fully. It means you took risks, had adventures, fell in love, stood your ground, did something fearless, or tried something that didn't work out.

> Every day you grow a little, break a little, and **heal** a little. In other words, having to heal continuously is a sign that you're living.

Sometimes, whole roller coasters break down at Disneyland. They take a long time to repair. The engineers can't fix them overnight. That's you, healing the bigger wound, the deeper cut. You'll make some slow strides, then maybe some big breakthroughs. You'll do some test runs once you feel stronger. And eventually the ride—your life—will reopen. Yet the ride will probably break down again. You may think you've healed that big deep breach fully and completely, but usually all it means is that you've reached a deeper level of healing.

What if you allow yourself to imagine that you will never finish healing —and that's a good thing? What if you just drop the big goal in your mind of "finally healing from XYZ" and instead acknowledge that you're going to keep healing and healing and healing, since you keep growing and growing and growing. And those big ugly things from your past are going to work their way out slowly, over years, or even decades, and you may never know when you finally reach the bottom of them and whether they have healed wholly and completely.

But one day you realize you're happy in a way you haven't been before, and you think to yourself, *Hmm, maybe those wounds have finally fully scarred over.*

Maybe they have, maybe they haven't. There may still be an even deeper level of healing you'll reach with them. Complete healing isn't the goal anymore. Daily healing is the goal.

And don't make the mistake of thinking healing only comes from heartache. When you come down from a high peak, you also grieve. Even the most gorgeous, highest, happiest points in your life have likely caused you to grieve when they ended. That counts as healing too.

Take the wound you're carrying right now. Call it inner disappointment, a horrible mistake, loss, a broken heart, or longing for the past—they're all variations on something broken. And know that each day you breathe, you'll heal a little deeper layer of it. And each day when you feel the frustration of it, cheer yourself on instead. Because healing will never go away. It's built into you.

The crowds at Disneyland will never stop smashing the grass or dropping their lunch bags. So drop the expectation of total, final, pristine never-get-dirty-again healing. You don't want that to happen because, the moment it does, it means you've stopped living.

And to stop living means you're busy dying inside.

Look forward to healing. It's a sweet breath of cool air brushing over your skin. It's a weight that lifts from your spine. It's that feeling of blessed relief that lets you relax and take your eyes off the wheel for a minute. And it happens *every single day*.

Unlike in chapter 20, where we warily circled and approached our biggest broken bits and admitted whether we may or may not be ready to "go there," in this chapter, we look at the smaller day-to-day breakage and get comfortable with the idea that healing isn't a huge, scary deal. It's a soft, easy, gentle, daily thing that's a sign of a well-lived life.

Ask, "What's broken in me, in my heart?" Find those little cups of sadness and lay them out on paper for me.

And what's more, when it does come to the big stuff, instead of searching for a "final one-and-done healing," can you instead delight in the idea that, layer by layer, you're continuously healing and shifting the meaning and impact of that sadness, regret, or loss?

See if you can release the self-battering feeling of "not having healed enough" and instead feel delight at the amount you *have* already healed. Can you acknowledge that you're likely going to keep breaking things and cleaning up the candy wrappers off the grass, and that your goal from here forward is simply to get exceedingly good at the continual, daily breaking and healing you're doing?

Yes? Do I hear a yes? Because that is the key: get exceedingly good at your continual, daily breaking and healing. Let yourself become as nimble and efficient as the groundskeepers at Disneyland.

Once you adopt this idea, you stop fearing all the things that could hurt you in the future. You stop bashing yourself for still feeling pain or loss about the things in the past. It all begins to make perfect sense. It's a process, ongoing and perpetual. Your heart is made to heal, so go about your life, and let it do its job afterward.

Healing is *good*. Healing means you're living full-out and *wonderfully*.

M.E. *School* Prompt

Your two-part prompt is to identify a few things you need to heal, and then shift your understanding of healing to embrace them with acceptance.

Part One: Journal on the questions below:

Sadness about _____

_____ lingers in my heart.

I'm still disappointed by_____

_____.

I feel cheated by_____

_____.

I wish I'd only had this _____

_____ in my life.

I'm still so angry/hurt that _____

_____ happened.

If only _____

_____ had never happened.

I wish I'd never _____

_____.

☐ I miss_____

_____ so much.

☐ I feel so guilty for hurting or losing _____

_____.

Part Two: Spend five to ten minutes feeling how okay you are about all that you just wrote. What emotional endpoints or pre-action would you rather be feeling around those things? Go there. Feel that instead for a little bit. Flowdream around it. Don't expect to solve and release decades of trauma here. The goal is to practice allowing a little bit of healing at a time.

Keep these thoughts and feelings in the forefront of your mind:

How wonderful it is that I'm still healing this!

How wonderful it is that I'll be healing new things in my future.

How wonderful it is that I've been alive enough to feel the breakage.

Chapter 23:
Your Heart Is Meant to Break

Speaking of healing, let's talk about your heart again for a moment.

Your heart is meant to break.

Yes, I know that's a weird thing to say. But we have this crazy notion that our hearts are like blown glass, and we have to carefully shield them and never, ever place them in someone else's hands.

What if . . . what if you're wrong about that?

Your heart is a delightful beating part of you that not only pumps fresh oxygen into your bloodstream to feed your cells but also removes the cellular debris and contaminants that your busy cells make every moment. In other words, your heart both feeds you and takes out the trash. Pretty incredible, huh?

Now, imagine another aspect of your heart—the emotional part. Imagine that your heart opens to love, intimacy, and connection by both giving it and creating it with others. But when that joy turns to loss, or the intimacy turns to betrayal, or the connection turns to coldness, your heart is also there to process it and carry the emotional debris away.

You need to let your heart do its job, both creating love *and* cleansing the heartbreak that love sometimes entails. It does a damn good job of it. Having trust that your heart will heal, no matter what, is the only thing that gives you the courage and trust to go out and fall in love again, or to trust someone with a secret again, or pursue your dream career again, because all these may not work out. But don't worry, your heart's got this—it's meant to break, and it's equally meant to heal itself from the break. In other words, you don't need to protect it nearly as much as you do.

When I was diagnosed with metastatic breast cancer, which means it had spread elsewhere in me, I was just forty-three. My daughter was starting middle school in a few weeks and my son was entering fourth grade. My babies needed me. I was also the only breadwinner since my husband was with a very iffy start-up company that ultimately failed.

I was paying the mortgage. I was paying for daycare and groceries. I was spinning a dozen plates on my hands and feet keeping it all going. And then, "You've got cancer. It has spread."

Talk about feeling your heart break. There is this feeling that happens when all the life and the decades ahead that you'd always expected to have suddenly wobble and crash. I stood in my bathroom in front of the mirror and realized that I had a million unspoken, assumed beliefs about how my life was going to go. I was going to live into my nineties like my grandparents all did. I was going to see my grandkids be born, and maybe would have traded up my old house for a nice beach house in my old age.

And now, all that was suspended, hanging in the air like a bunch of smoke disappearing before my eyes.

My heart broke into thousands of pieces. I could feel it crumbling in my chest, and I wailed. I cried and fell on the bathroom rug and hugged the tub, my tear-soaked hair sticking to my cheeks and chin. I cried and cried and cried. My heart broke and then broke again, big waves of feeling pulsing through me, heaving and sobbing.

I'd felt heartbreak before, but this was bigger. This was me understanding that my assumption that life was a *given* was totally, cruelly incorrect. This was me enraged that this was actually, crazily, undeservingly happening to me—so unfair. This was me wondering who would raise my kids when I died, and would they be okay or would they be hurt and lost forever? Me wondering what empty-headed twat my husband would marry after me, inheriting all my hard-won assets and retirement savings as she wooed him with casseroles and blow jobs?

Oh yeah, you can tell I was pissed. A-N-G-R-Y in all caps. Pissed off at God, the universe, my own body, and even my poor husband who did not yet have an evil new wife gunning for my place in our family.

I felt scared. And deeply wronged. My own body had betrayed me.

And do you think I was done after I picked myself up and staggered out of the bathroom?

No, not done. I did the same thing again three days later. I felt a whale leap from my chest and split me open, unexpectedly, out of nowhere. *Why now*? I wondered. But there it was. Grief had resurged.

If you've felt this, you know it's grief. Grief doesn't ask for permission. When it wiggles out, it brings you down, totally and fully, and leaves you in a hollow shell of sniffling and blank, insensible numbness afterward. So why, oh why, would I ever encourage you to feel it? It is rotten and horrible, and, at its finale, it makes you stare into your deepest fears of loss, agony, and even your eventual death.

But after my grief had passed, I felt something unexpected. There was a lightness in my heart that I had never felt before. It was as if I had popped a cork and grieved for every bad, stinky, fucked-up thing that had ever happened in my life. And there were a lot: emotional abuse, sexual abuse, betrayal, rejection, disillusionment, guilt . . . all those things in my life that my heart had steadily packed away for me had risen to the surface. I could not believe they were still there, buried in the folds of my cells. Only by feeling their absence as I grieved them out did I realize they had even been there.

And the absence was light. So sweet.

Not long after, I found a book called *The Untethered Soul* by Michael Sing-
er. He explains:

Long term, the energy patterns [emotions] that cannot make it through you
are pushed out of the forefront of the mind and held until you are prepared to
release them. . . . The energy first tries to release by manifesting through the
mind. . . . When the energy can't make it through the mind . . . it then tries
to release through the heart. . . . When you resist even that release, the energy
gets packed up and forced into deep storage within the heart . . . an unfinished
energy pattern that ends up running your life. . . . [I]t is your resistance to ex-
periencing these patterns that causes the energy to keep cycling around itself.

In plain language, this is roughly translated as: *All the shit that hurt you*
passes through your mind first as you hash and rehash it for practically forever.
But, because your mind's the king, it's unable to process it (because while he
tries, that's not his job), so it drifts down to your heart—the queen. But you
don't give her any cred, so she won't (or can't) fully process or grieve, so the
heartbreak settles into a holding pattern, circling around, taking up energetic
and emotional space, getting packed down into sedimentary layers, which you
eventually forget are even there.

My heart is made to not just create emotion but to process it out as well.
Just as the blood that your heart circulates not only flushes your body with
fresh oxygen and nutrients, it also picks up broken, discarded cellular debris
in your body and carries it back to be processed. And like carrying that debris away from your cells, your heart should also be carrying away the debris
of your emotionally broken bits and healing them every single day, if only
you honored it and let it.

Yet that healing often gets stuck. It swirls in circles in our hearts, unable
to be fully released, because we are ignoring it. We push down the grief; we
reject the hurt. We pretend it's gone already. We're strong and even proud at
how well we can carry it when in reality we should be feeling it and purging
it. If we were young when the hurt happened, we might not even have known

what to do with it; we were too immature and the events were too mature to process, so the heart stored it for us for later when we could circle back around to it.

The heart holds all our grief, loss, anger, betrayal, and guilt for us patiently. And like planes circling to land, as our emotional debris builds up, like more and more planes circling the same small airspace, we are weighed down with unseen, unresolved, uncompleted emotion.

Then, pop. Out comes the cork. The planes land. And you are on your knees, grieving for not only what has just happened, but for every goddamn, stinky, crappy piece of shit thing that has ever happened to you. All that old, layered-up Samskara shit comes draining out in a big, heaping, emotional meltdown.

Rise now and blink those tears from your eyes. Because right on the other side of that is a nectar of joy that's almost incomprehensible. It is heaven in a bottle. You don't think so? I know it because in the years since then, the oddest, most unexpected thing has continued to happen to me: I have been able to go into ecstasy, on demand, ever since—pure ecstasy, the kind where tears stream down your face.

This kind of ecstasy is dependent on nothing. It's about nothing. It's just a feeling that exists, one that I found once all the black tar had swirled away. And now that I've felt it, I'm able to identify it and know it so that when I go looking, I find it again and again. I admit it's extraordinary.

Will this happen to you? Who knows. But I do know that you don't need to fear your heart breaking anymore. I know it will heal; it was built to heal. You see, without that ability to heal, it would never otherwise let you take risks. You couldn't risk falling for someone and seeing them not love you back. You couldn't risk sharing your feelings in a deep way and perhaps be painfully rejected. You couldn't risk living in that deep, delicious, filled-up way we all crave, because what if you lost it again. But your heart is there whispering to you, "Go for it, you've got this. I'm built to break and built to heal. You just gotta let me do both."

Grieve for the Gold

In the prompt, you're going to do a little exercise called Tell Me All the Ways Your Heart Has Been Broken. Yes, I mean *your* heart, the queen, that bright beautiful object in your chest that pumps your blood and circulates your emotion, the part of you that has hoped and desired, and been betrayed and hurt, the part of you that needs a cleanse even more than your cells . . . and there's only one way to do that: grieve.

Grieve for everything past and present. Grieve for the dreams you never reached. Grieve for the people who passed you by for another. Grieve for the person you loved who left you before you were done with the relationship, or maybe even before they seemed done with their own life. Grieve for the parent who never loved you as they should have, and for all the "should haves" for anyone and everyone in your life. Grieve for all their failures. Then grieve for your own—you have so many—and know each one is proof of you having really lived.

Grieve for it all. Grief loosens the tight grip on your heart and clears it. You're squeezing the sponge dry and releasing the rain from the fat, dark clouds of memory.

Some of you know your grief is raw and just below the surface, and you're afraid to touch it. And some of you have buried it so far down that you can't even find it with a flashlight.

Grief is energy and emotion that gets stuck. It needs to be set free to move through you and out of you. Your heart owns its own time and will pace itself, but you still have to give it the opportunity.

Your grief may be loud and palpable, or it may sit like a frozen emotionless lump in your chest. Remember, grief writes its own terms. Don't expect it to look one way or another: tears for some, emotional hollowness for others. Just landing on your grief like a fly on a plate is enough.

M.E. *School* Prompt

Your prompt is to complete the exercise called Tell Me All the Ways Your Heart Has Been Broken.

This is important: Please do this exercise with professional oversight if you know it could unleash more than you can bear. Or do it in layers, starting with smaller hurts.

Remembering your list from the last chapter, write a catalog of all the ways your heart has been broken: broken by others, broken through promises, broken by death, broken by incomplete communication or lies, broken by people (or even you) not meeting your expectations, broken by feeling that a person who should love you, doesn't. Write it all. And let yourself grieve. Grieving is healing.

Dear Self,

My heart has been broken by . . .

_____

_____

_____

_____

_____

_____

_____

Chapter 24:
Selfishly Forgiving

There was once a real fucking bastard in my life. The kind who's vile, who tells lies, and whose selfishness runs so deep they're the fucking Grand Canyon of selfishness and narcissism. And what they did to me was so shifty, shitty, hurtful, and painful that it broke my heart and my life into tiny pieces like the remnants of millions of seashells scattered on the shore.

So I forgave them.

I know, WTF?

The actual "what happened" is irrelevant, because this person is actually more than one person. They're an amalgam of multiple people who've betrayed me, shit on my home, and ripped away my trust in others.

You also have this person, these people, in your own life. Different places, different acts, same horrible mess.

And like me, I bet you held on, or are still holding on, to these heartbreaking piece-of-shit tragedies. After all, it's the reason why you're fucked-up, untrusting, overweight, maimed, broken, grieving, violated, lost, incomplete, or whatever it may be.

These people, this person, is a real villain. And forgiving them would be like rewarding them. And the fact that you can't forgive them makes you feel even worse, because golden-haired angels say forgiveness makes you a good person, and we only open the gates of heaven to you if you're a good person. Which you clearly are not.

And besides, why should such an awful person get something so sweet and fragrant as forgiveness? No, they should get hated for a long, long time— they've earned it. *It's your just rewards, buddy.*

Except . . .

Your villain is probably long gone. How many months, years, decades has it been now? And even if they're not gone from your life, they're probably *over it.* After all, no one likes to dwell on how shitty they are, especially villains. Instead, they're hopping around town eating birthday cake and getting swooned over by their bosses and friends, which just pisses you off even more.

Go fuck yourself, you think. *Here's some more hate, dude. If no one else will keep giving you what you deserve, I will.*

At least I will secretly. In my heart. In my thoughts. In how I tell myself how you robbed me and screwed me over. I will keep blaming you. You deserve to be blamed.

Holy crap, this villain is really profiting. I mean, not only did they screw you over once, but their gift keeps on giving! They keep filling you with hurt, anger, rage, and all those other feelings day after day, year after year. They don't even have to lift a finger anymore to do it to you. You've taken it on to do it for yourself.

This is where you hit the pause button. Look at the math:

Villain makes your life fall apart once = villain's fault.

Villain makes your life fall apart every time you think of them = that's you.

Stop making your villain so powerful. Stop letting them hurt you. The only way you can do that is to forgive them. Forgive them for *you,* not for them.

Forgive them so you can allow them to stop torturing you. Because every time you feel powerless, angry, or sad, you're giving them more of your power.

They're your power leak, and you're letting them control you and move you into bad feelings. You're giving them control over you long past the point of the initial crime. You're letting them hurt you every day, even now.

Stop it. Just stop.

You don't forgive them to absolve them. You forgive them to make them stop hurting *you*.

Think about that sweet, luscious orange blossom-scented feeling of forgiveness. It feels like softness, release, wisdom. It feels like "I'm a bigger kid now, and that old betrayal doesn't need to keep hurting me. I don't need to keep pinning my current unhappiness on it."

It won't go away until you let it go.

Your villain has probably already let it go. Your sense of righteousness or pain that keeps it going is all *you*.

You're making yourself feel bad. You're making pain for yourself. You're fighting someone whom you may never see again. It only poisons you.

Once more,

you forgive your villain

for **yourself**, *not them.*

You do it for you.

You say, "I'm done blaming you. I'm done letting you hurt me. I'm over feeling cheated, betrayed, torn up, victimized by you. You don't get to have those feelings from me anymore. We're done."

It's selfish, crass, and oh-so-empowering. When you can get to that neutral space in your heart, you have finally robbed your villain of all power over you. You are done with them.

As the mafia says, "You're dead to me." Except with the sweet scent of orange blossoms and heavenly wings.

How to Forgive

In the last chapter you grieved for all your hardships and losses. Now you'll do the final street sweeping with thorough forgiveness. Grief and forgiveness are different, but they're brothers from the same mother.

And if you find you *still* can't forgive, even after trying, then make it a point every day to practice forgiving. Yes, just like you have a morning ritual of green tea, gratitude, and journaling, add it to your list. "I practice feeling forgiveness toward . . ." and then spend five minutes feeling the emotion of forgiveness. Empty out the villain from your life and heart.

Remember how we practiced feeling our emotional endpoints in earlier chapters? Well this is just one more emotion to practice: forgiveness, or acceptance.

You're doing this for you, not for them. You're depriving them of any more ability to continuously hurt you. It's powerful stuff.

You may find yourself wrestling back and forth with feeling forgiveness, then ten seconds later feeling how the thing or person doesn't deserve it as you unleash the hate and anger again. This is totally normal. After all, you've been punishing them for a long time. It's what you're used to. But, this is a process. It's similar to healing. You'll do a little of it every day, and eventually, a morning will come when you reach a beautifully neutral spot.

And once you reach that point of neutrality, your forgiveness will be practically complete. The only sweeter spot you can reach is when you are able to say, "I feel all the blessings in that experience. And while I may not ever have wanted or chosen it, I can and do feel *all the wisdom that came from it.*"

If you think that next-level kind of forgiveness is impossible, it's not. Even if you've lost someone you love, or been betrayed, or abused, or otherwise wrecked, something has come from it, something *you made* from it, that contains a bright bit of strength, goodness, or beauty

Maybe it's the compassion and deep empathy you can now feel for others who've suffered like you. Maybe it galvanized you to be a better person and propelled you into a lifetime of beautiful self-growth and commitment to truth. Maybe you became a champion for a cause. Maybe it provoked and inspired you to become that loving parent that you never had.

Dig out the nuggets of beauty from your pain and claim them. They're the diamonds in the dung heap.

As for me? Not only did I have to forgive a bunch of villains who'd wronged me over my life, but I had to forgive my own body for handing me cancer. I plucked the beauty from the diagnosis and thanked my cancer experience for opening me to so many new wonderful ways of seeing life. My illness radically adjusted my priorities in life to focus on my home, family, and inner pleasures. It allowed me to live like tomorrow isn't guaranteed. I don't sit around in "wait mode" much anymore—life is too precious for that. Instead I gobble life up and every holiday, every family trip is so much sweeter. It also opened me to deeply knowing how other people feel when they are robbed of health, trust, or anything else.

There's a lot more, but you get the point.

Now, let's go see who and what you will forgive.

M.E. School Prompt

Your two-part prompt is to identify who you need to forgive and begin creating the feelings of forgiveness.

Part One: Ask yourself, who or what still conjures up anger, hate, and negative feelings inside me?

Part Two: Write a letter of forgiveness to this person or experience. As you write, feel the emotion of forgiveness wash through you. Keep in mind that it may feel unnatural. You may swing back and forth between anger, blame, and release. It's okay.

Dear _____,

_____

_____

_____

_____

_____

_____

_____

_____

_____

Chapter 25:
Understanding and Owning Your Life Major

Now that you've practiced being wrong, quashed your rationalizations, grieved, healed, and practiced forgiveness, you're really starting to roll with this. Even if you've just scraped the surface of all these, at least you know how to do them, and you can begin doing them all over and over until you're starting to till the soft, rich earth of your life.

Now, you're ready for the next phase, when you can practically feel the tingle of divine inspiration slipping through, the sense that your life is moving again like a glass elevator suddenly coming to life and shooting for the sky. You are going *up* since all the heavy stuff was put *down*.

But, but, there's one more biggie. You've probably heard of the idea before. Okay, you've probably heard of the idea a hundred times before. Just, no one tells you what to do with it.

It's called seeing, recognizing, and coming to peace with your *patterns*.

Isn't it funny how we tend to do the same dumb things over and over again, even if the things are kind of sucky? Why do we do that? Why don't we move on? Why do we repeat the same dumb moves, the same dumb relationships, over and over?

Oh, patterns! You little devil dogs. A pattern is when the same stupid things happen over and over in your life: The "everyone I love betrays me, cheats on me, or lets me down" pattern. Or the "everything gets taken away from me" pattern. Or the "every partner I pick ends up being an abusive, scary, narcissist" pattern. Or even the "I make money and then lose it over and over" pattern.

How *ridonculous*. How disappointing. How stupid. Life must hate you. *Stupid, fucking pattern*. Each time you think you've broken it, evolved past it, healed it, whatever. But it's obviously still here, because here it comes again.

There are so many patterns to pick from. Probably thousands. But you know yours—it's the one that keeps happening (albeit with constantly new casts of characters) in your life.

But why? Why, oh why does it happen? And why can't we get rid of them or grow past them, especially if we do tons of inner work and healing? That's what all the personal growth people say is supposed to happen.

Meanwhile, your psychologist will say: "These things formed in childhood so you're just gonna be stuck with them for the rest of your long, unhappy life. Now tell me about your mother."

Who's right?

Let's reframe the entire idea. What if you decide that you aren't expected to finally and forever grow past your patterns? What if patterns are more like things you're supposed to create mastery around, over the long haul, and the more you bulldoze through, the greater your mastery becomes? Sort of like . . . a college major.

Yeah, a college major: You expect and intend to take classes around the same subject, over and over. Each class gets harder. And every class grows your knowledge deeper about the subject. And yes, you get really sick of it by the end and regret ever choosing it in the first place.

Eventually, though, you're pretty darn smart about this major. And you sure aren't crying and railing on yourself after class about what a dumdum you are for taking classes in your major *again*. Because that's what you do. You take the classes until you master the material.

The only sucky thing is that our "life majors" usually tend to have pain in them. Sometimes, they are *soaked* with pain—drenched, sopping, and mud-splattered with pain. We chose a life major in loss, or illness, or insecurity, or lack of love, or abuse. It's almost as if the mastery of pain is the *real* major, and whatever patterns we have are just the means to master pain.

Think on *that* for a minute. Yes, go full Buddhist on me. It's all about *mastering suffering*. That's the major of all majors, and this major is always at least a little bit *built into* all the other majors.

Say you have the "I always make good money, then lose it all" pattern. Built into this is (1) you're supposed to learn how to live without re-creating scarcity over and over, as well as (2) you're supposed to learn that the pain built into this pattern will goad you to finally, eventually, master it someday.

That's right: Pain propels you through your pattern. It drives you to master it, fix it, and pass the fucking class finally.

As you grow in understanding, getting more and more expert knowledge around this one area, you eventually start getting less and less "emotional charge" from your pattern—in other words, the pain decreases. The class becomes boring. You know the material so well that it's boring.

Congratulations, you passed. Pattern 202 starts next quarter.

Put another way, let's say you have the "narcissist partner" pattern. What if the next time your narcissist acts abusively, you see it right away, draw firm boundaries, and/or completely just leave them without looking back. And you'd do this because it feels *obvious* to do so. And now you've mastered the abused-person pattern, the loss-of-personal-power-to-someone-else pattern, and the "I'm not good enough" patterns. Yup, nailed them all.

You firmed up or left because finally, after fifty rounds of these kinds of relationships, there's nothing left to work out. There's no electricity, pain, or charge around the relationship. The minute you see shitty behavior, you're out. Done. No second chances. You saw the pattern and don't feel any compulsion to stick around and be nice and loving and do another round with it because, by golly, you've already mastered it. It would be like taking a second-grade class in basic addition again. Too easy. Boring. Did it already. No growth, no mastery to be had.

And what if eventually, the next time a person pops up who normally would've barreled you right into this pattern, this time, you barely glance at them. They're not even attractive to you. In fact, the way they act is just weird and puzzling. You don't see what anyone would see in them. Which is exactly how all your friends and family thought about your narcissist partner in the first place.

Let's take a look at Dakota, another past M.E. School student, who has a rotten boyfriend. We've all had a friend like Dakota, whose partner, Grayson, is a total ass. But Dakota loves him and goes bonkers that he doesn't text or reassure her when he should, and he keeps her on high alert and high anxiety as to his feelings, and he often hangs out with his ex-girlfriend overnight, which Dakota is supposed to be totally cool with because she's "not insecure."

You'd tell Dakota to dump Grayson. But she can't. She's used to having to do more, be more, prove herself, and have to win over someone who's too immature to be won over. So she and Grayson dance this silly dance together. From your standpoint, it's a dumb game, and he's super unattractive, and Dakota is a twit for being so sucked in.

This is how you feel since *you don't have the pattern*. Whereas she's hell-bent on mastering it and mastering it through the pain it brings her; it's sort of like her second-year college course in the subject. Someday, she'll get to a point where old Grayson looks as boring to her as he does to you. And not only that, but guys like Grayson won't even come rolling into her life anymore . . . because they're only looking for other matches to the pattern, and she's no longer one.

Dakota would have graduated her life major.

Except most of us don't ever graduate. That's why it's a *life* major. It's meant to be big and juicy and scarring enough to last a long time—like a lifetime long. And the bigger and longer it is, the bigger the graduation ceremony at the end. (Since you took the hardest classes, right?)

From this perspective, your major is there to provide you with tons of learning opportunities in areas where you're obviously weak or broken. And it's probably going to stick around at some (hopefully, decreasing) level your whole life.

And yeah, nature and nurture both come into play: you happen to be born into a culture that fostered your patterns, to parents who reinforced your pattern, and in a body that craves this pattern . . . whether we're talking addiction, abuse, neglect, shattered boundaries, or anything else.

The point is, you have your pattern, someone else has a different one, and most involve deep pain or scarring of our human psyche, which takes a lifetime to master. And if we really keep our eye on the ball, we might master it by the time we die; if not, we sure got through a good ton of college credits.

This perspective means that you can stop beating yourself up for doing the same dumb things over and over. Or relapsing. Or dating the same wrong type of person. Or losing your job again. Or losing your money. Or being hurtful to others. Or self-sabotaging.

Your goal next time is to simply *hurt less.* Not because you're numb—just the opposite. Instead, you'll be so aware, so clear, and so, well . . . getting bored with this whole major. A part of you will be just less interested in the pain the pattern causes. You're mastering it. The pain is less juicy, the pain is less painful, and feeling alive by experiencing the pain is less attractive.

Your goal is also to see the pattern earlier and earlier each time it pops up. It's like a door-to-door salesman who keeps coming around; eventually, you expect it, but you're getting better and better at just politely shutting the door instead of standing there getting your time sucked away as they run through their spiel.

Life majors aren't easy to conceptualize. It's admittedly a real dumbing down of a ton of psychology. But so is the concept of a *pattern.* And so are our ideas on how easy it is to break or cure a pattern.

And please, don't get me wrong—there are some forms of abuse that have to be prevented and stopped immediately. I'm not talking about *those* forms of abuse (emotional abuse, physical abuse, sexual abuse, etc.); I'm talking about the big picture *inner patterns* that ripple through each of our lives, and why they might be there, and what we are supposed to do with them instead of just getting down on ourselves for not having conquered them and be living happily ever after by the time we're thirty.

You're learning to be gentle with yourself, learning to embrace your pattern at this kind of life major that, even if it's one you would *never* have chosen, is somehow still here in your life, and so you are going to be taking these damn classes in the subject for a long time.

But, eventually, the classes will end. The life major will wrap up, and maybe someday you'll look back and muse on how mind-boggling many classes you took in your field of expertise were, and how insightful you are in it now.

And how *fucking brilliant* that diploma looks on your cosmic wall.

M.E. *School* Prompt

Your prompt is to jot down some lifelong patterns you've experienced and see if you can determine what your life major might be.

The objective isn't to solve your life major. It's simply to *see* it. Seeing a pattern is half the battle. You have your whole life to work on it. For now, just work on being gentle with yourself about it.

My patterns (things I repeatedly do, encounter, or that happen to me) and/or life major are:

_____

_____

_____

_____

_____

Ways I can be more gentle with myself around my major:

_____

_____

_____

_____

Chapter 26:
The Trifecta of Trust

You can do anything. You do it better, faster, and more competently than anyone else. Your siblings know you'll take care of shit. Your co-workers know you'll get it done by the deadline. You're so freaking competent.

I bet you do the bills at home, too, and plan the vacations. Maybe your partner does a few things, but only because you let them.

Sure, your garage may be packed to the rafters with tons of crap you should have gone through, or your yard has big brown weeds choking the cracked driveway, but it's because *it's only you doing everything,* and *something's gotta give, man.*

Being the one who gets shit done all the time when nobody else will is exhausting, but you're so good at it! Because you know that you can't count on anyone else, not really. I mean, they'll try, but usually you have to go finish or redo whatever they tried to help with. You can only count on yourself. Heck, maybe you've been doing this since you were a kid and had to buy the groceries yourself. Your parents never showed up at school meetings. Whatever. You took care of yourself. It's kept you alive.

Except now you're kinda breaking down a little from it. You're so fricking tired. You feel so guilty for that messy, spidery garage you never have time to get to. You just wish someone else would take on some of these responsibilities. But even if they did, it wouldn't be done right anyway.

Sound like you, boss?

This is the whole point of the *One Minute Manager* books and the *Who Moved My Cheese* classic leadership parables. Empower others and get out of the way. That's the only way to freedom.

People like us, though, aren't just controlling at work—we do it through our whole lives because somewhere along the line, we lost our trust in others and the world, or it got broken, or both.

Because being the One Who Gets Things Done is a very safe feeling. We don't rely on anyone else because who knows if they'll even show up to get done what needs to get done?

I bet you even have a hard time trusting the universe to help you. And by the universe, I mean life. You don't trust it's on your side. You have to fight and push and choke life to get anywhere. You do *all the work*.

Superhero, you really must be tired.

But I have a question. What do you think all those other people are out there in the world for? Are they there just to annoy, reject, and disappoint you?

Let's rephrase that: What emotional endpoints are you getting from protecting yourself by controlling and running the shit out of everything?

I bet I know: safety. Or proving to yourself and others that you're good enough (because you're caught in the *I'm Not Good Enough Show*), which is, at heart, just another way of being safe.

Safe from what? How about pain, loss, fear, anxiety, homelessness, death?

All this *being on top of shit* and *being the only one you can count on for shit* has kept you safe for so darn long. I mean S-A-F-E! like that deep, deep feeling that no one is going to disappoint you and all those bad things that could happen maybe just won't come around on your eagle-eyed watch.

You think that by controlling more, you can minimize all that bad, broken, unhappy, and ultimately threatening stuff from entering your life.

So how's that working out for you?

I know this demon well. I'm a Controller too. Knowing that I'm the only one who ever helped me get ahead, doing everything myself, figuring it out, and doing it better and faster than anyone else makes me feel safe. It also makes me feel smarter, better, and overall continues to prove to both myself and you that I Am The Best. Call it being caught in a hamster wheel of safety and self-proving; it's what we Controllers do. Maybe this is you, maybe it isn't. Maybe it's someone you know, whom you can finally start to understand.

Because the question is, *Why are we this way?*

Three Kinds of Trust

Yep, you thought we were done with healing. We aren't. There's one more area to look at, and it has to do with trust. We're going to rebuild it. You're going to realize that after the forgiveness, after the grief, after the realization of your patterns, the next thing to do is start building yourself up. And building yourself up requires boatloads of trust.

It's going to feel glorious. This is what you came to M.E. School for, after all.

As a Controller, I fundamentally lack trust in others. It got broken a bunch of times in my life through being betrayed, unprotected, you name it. I don't trust others, and I don't trust life to help me or give me what I want or need. I only trust myself. And I'm hell-bent on proving to you and me every single day just how great I am, that I am better than Good Enough because I can carry the weight of a hundred. And so I do. It's like I can't stop myself.

The upshot of this is that I'm constantly tired, overworked, stressed, blaming others for not helping (when in fact, I make it pretty hard for them to help), and blaming life for not being on my side or making things easy.

Controllers lack trust in one or more of two broad categories: They lack trust in others or they lack trust in the universe, God, life, or whatever you want to call your higher power. The third and last area where we can lack trust is in ourselves. That's why I call it the

"trifecta of trust:"
trust of self, trust of others, and trust in the universe.

Unfortunately, most of us have broken trust in one or more of these areas.

Not only is this one of the single most important segments of M.E. School, but it's often the most life changing.

See, we never really stop and think about where, when, or how our fundamental trust got broken. Instead, we single out the individual shitty events, rejections, criticisms, or betrayals we've experienced that we load onto our backs to carry. Every now and then we finger-point to one and say, "This is why I'm this way today."

Maybe you've even discovered that some kind of perpetual betrayal or disappointment makes up your life major—the breaking of trust over and over in this area has become a pattern.

But we don't think about these patterns or life majors in terms of being fundamentally a trust issue, unless it's super obvious, like having been cheated on one or more times.

I'm asking you to find the connecting thread between these three areas of trust. Which ones are broken in you? Which one is the most broken? How did these events or people break them?

I already told you that, as a Controller, my trust of others is very low. (Okay, I'm a reformed Controller today, but for the sake of example, I'm a Controller.) However, my trust of myself is very high. And while my trust of the universe has taken a serious beating, it's also fundamentally strong.

But there are subtleties. You can be a Controller and still have low trust in yourself. (I know, crazy, right! How does that work?) This happens when all the other trusts are broken, and because you've done stupid stuff over and over that you kick yourself about because your trust in your own decisions and desires is also pretty darn low. But still, you try. *You're the only one you have to rely on.* You're still a Controller, even though you may be one who doesn't trust herself very much.

Good stuff, eh? It's a game-changer.

I know you might be a bit confused, so I'm going to break each form of broken trust down to make them sparklingly clear.

We'll first look at trust of others. In the next chapter we'll examine trust of the universe. We'll get to trust of self a bit later.

Trust of Others

As I mentioned, I walk around with everything on my shoulders. I don't accept help. I rarely even ask for it. And if you do something for me, I feel sorta guilty accepting it, like I don't really deserve that unwarranted kindness, or I have to pay you back immediately somehow.

Every so often, all this stuff on my shoulders gets too heavy to carry and I break down. I get cancer. I gain weight. I drink too much wine. I melt down with my husband. I get angry at my friends. I get pissed at my employees. I fall apart.

And then, I remember: I'm acting like I'm the only one in these relationships. I'm acting like I'm the only one who knows what's going on, I'm better than you, I can't rely on you, you don't like me anyway, I don't need you, and frankly, I can't expect more than a half-ass job from you even if you did come around.

Well, guess what? When someone acts like that with *you*, you say to them, "Awesome, I don't need you either. Good luck with life."

Yet, I cast these presumptions toward all sorts of people in my life that I'm in actual relationships with. How fucked up is that. I wouldn't want to be in a relationship with someone like me.

It's really hard to extend trust to these relationships. I *plan* and *prepare* for them to disappoint me, in all their variations:

They didn't invite me to the dinner party.

They're talking behind my back.

They don't really want me on the team.

They gave me that expensive gift just to make me look cheap.

They won't pitch in and help take care of mom.

They'll ask me for money again and expect me to pay up or feel guilty for saying no.

They won't understand if I tell them I need a different kind of behavior from them in order to feel loved, or that I feel like I give way more in this relationship than they do.

They don't see my value even though I'm the one always staying after-hours to get things finished.

On and on.

Why even go there? Why do I need to trust at all, especially with all these stinky, needy, unappreciative people?

Because staying in a one-sided relationship is untenable. And I want to have relationships. I want good, healthy, strong relationships. Which means I have to redevelop *trust in others*. I have to. This is not a choice. Only if I decided to go live alone on a mountaintop would I not need to start trusting others. And I'm not doing that. My feelings about them need to be reformed, and I need to give them a shot of participating in that reform.

Somewhere along the way, many of us have been so disappointed by others that we've just stopped trusting people to like us, love us, promote us, recognize us, see us, or show up strong or reliably for us. And so we compensate by being independent and not needing them.

Maybe we got this way from always being the last one picked for dodgeball. Maybe it was having your best girlfriends suddenly and meanly dump you in high school. Maybe it was feeling like the constant outsider, never being invited to parties or fun things. Maybe you had to become this way because your mom was always out on dates or at her second job, and, if you were lucky, leaving you a peanut butter sandwich for dinner. Maybe your divorced parent didn't want to pay child support and constantly made you feel like they thought you only stayed in touch for their monthly check.

Somehow, you got it in your head that you were not wanted. Or you got it in your head that even the people who do love you are still going to disappoint you—like your partner who pretends they're not cheating, or your best friend who talks smack about you behind your back.

The point is, in a part of your life, you're a loner instead of being with the pack. And lone wolves have a harder time. There's no one to snuggle with for warmth at night. There's no one to guard the perimeter with you in the snowy forest. There's no one to share bringing home the meat with. You want all these things, but you won't allow it.

Maybe this is you, maybe it isn't. But if you're lonely, overworked, overlooked, and exhausted, chances are you have some broken trust about other people in your life being able to help you, be with you, or ease your burdens. You think they can't, they won't, or they'll do it for a while before disappearing.

How do we fix this?

First, you're going to start giving them a chance to show up strong for you. Chances are that in your retracted, controlling state, you've been systematically removing or withdrawing their ability to show up differently for you. Every tiny, daily decision you've made to minimize their importance to you, their involvement with you, or their ability to *make you care* has set the current tone for your relationship. Now, they're just doing what they feel you're expecting them to do—they presume their behavior is A-okay because you've been letting them get away with it forever.

But wait, you say. *I did give them a chance. Over and over even. And they fucked it up. C'mon, Summer, I'm right! These are called boundaries!*

Are they boundaries or are they something else, something stemming from your fear of being hurt or disappointed again? From your fear of needing to take care of yourself since no one else will? From your feeling that they'll reject you, fuck up, betray, or otherwise make you feel unwanted or uncared for?

Let's draw a distinction between *a plain ol' untrustworthy person* and *your inability to trust others* to show up for you in your life. See that subtle difference?

Chances are you long ago ditched most untrustworthy people from your life. Or in the case of family or people you can't easily get away from, you've adopted a certain protective distance. You have boundaries.

What you're left with is a bunch of people who'd actually like to make you feel good and become valued by you if you gave them the opportunity. People who'd love to help out, people who'd like to feel needed, who would love to take the lead on the project, who'd enjoy a lunch date with you, and frankly, who want to feel included and appreciated just as much as you do.

If you want these people in your life, you have to keep giving them chances. If you don't want them in your life, then walk away. But this half-assed trust thing is just wearing. It's unfulfilling for everyone. If they truly are untrustworthy, let them go. Switch teams at work. Look for a new job pronto. End the friendship. End the relationship. Be cordial at holidays and no more.

But truthfully, the number of people who are truly self-centered, untrustworthy bastards is quite low. Usually what's going on is something else: Because you got hurt at some point, you began withdrawing opportunities for those people to be close with you, see your soul, care about you, rise to their commitments, share the burden, or any of a hundred other things that'll make you release your held breath and feel trust. They never figured out that you stopped giving them these chances, and now they're just moseying along thinking everything is hunky-dory, but that you're kind of distant, never ask for help, and are maybe a little self-important.

Nobody is really getting what they want.

Okay, I'm generalizing here. But you know what I'm getting at: Do you trust that others see you, adore you, want you, enjoy you, will help you, or will delicately hold your heart in their hands like a fragile bird if asked?

If you're even a little unsure, you know what's next for you: You've gotta launch into a full-on campaign for remaking and healing your relationships. You'll make a thick and thriving community of people who're there for you and you for them.

If your instinctual reaction to this idea is "Uh, *no*. What a nice idea. But it doesn't work like that for me," then use that reaction to see just how much your trust is actually broken. Which brings us right back to our key point in this chapter, which is to ask the question:

How would my life change if I rebuilt trust in others?

Think back to earlier chapters. You know when we did that work on forgiveness? You remember when you started allowing your heart to break? You know when you started looking at your life major and realized there *must* be some villains for the "college classes" to work?

You were already working on healing your trust of others. What you were saying to yourself was "I'm going to get my heart hurt: People will still do crummy things, but not only can I handle it, I'll flourish because of it. My heart is strong and supple. My past and future are continuously in states of breaking and healing. *And dammit, to experience the love, support, and healthy teams I want to have and feel in life, I have to start trusting others again and feel that, not only do I belong, but I'm essential to them and they to me.*

Oh my God, the yumminess of this is killing me.

And maybe, just maybe, you're realizing that this is part of the reinvention you're seeking. Maybe your Dead Zone is already washing away under the realization that other people do want to see you at Painting and Poetry Night or showing up to T-ball. Or that your ex really didn't want to hurt you like that, and so on.

Regrowing trust in others is a process, but it begins with the awareness of the break. You've got that now.

So, who are you going to give the opportunity to show up differently for you? Who are you going to lean on for something close to your heart? Who are you going to risk disappointment with because in order to regrow trust with them, you *have* to take that risk?

Tell me in the prompt.

M.E. *School* Prompt

Your prompt is to do a quick check-in: How much trust are you giving each important person in your life, and do you have strong healthy teams you can rely on?

Journal on the following questions:

- Am I a lone wolf? If so, what are the limitations I experience as the result of keeping others at arm's length?

- Are there things I've taken on in my life that are draining or exhausting, but I do them since I think no one else will or can?

- Who in my life has broken my trust? Am I content to allow them to continue to inform my beliefs about trust and my own lovability? Do I continue to give them that power?

- Who am I going to give the opportunity to show up differently for me? How? What will I ask of them?

- Is there someone close to me whom I've given up on? Is giving up on them being kind to them?

- How would my life change if I rebuilt trust in others to a high degree?

Chapter 27:
Trusting the Universe

All right, not having trust with other people is pretty obvious, but this next area is trickier.

Think about your life, generally. Your hopes, your dreams—all of them depend on your relationship with, as the late, great Prince says, this thing called *life*. Call life the universe, God, Source, flow, the future, your higher power, whatever you want. It's this basic sense that life is *for* you and not *against* you, or even just totally indifferent.

This is a relationship too—it's a relationship with your future and your feelings about whether said future will give you what you want, those hopes and dreams, or coldly look away.

Most of you trust that it takes a constellation of things bigger than us to make everything you want sync up just right, like being introduced to someone who'll become your lifelong best friend, finding the right partner for having a baby, or discovering your greatest epic talent and making it grow with all the outside cash, resources, and support it requires. Sure, you worked for it, but there was something else on your side, moving things along, and popping those magical, pivotal moments into position.

That said, that trust may presently be bedraggled and broken. Your life may have scissored it into tiny shreds, and you have no idea how to get that trust back. All you know is that lately, you've had to fight for every little thing, and when things do somehow come together, well, it's felt like dumb luck. And no, you don't trust Lady Luck very much either.

After all, life may have caused you to lose someone you love. Life may have caused you to get hammered with that debilitating health condition. Life may be withholding a baby from you or even just a solid life partner. *Life sucks, man.*

The Stingy Universe

In reality, you may have lost your trust in the universe long ago. I mean, you may *say* you have trust in God, in divine timing, in life, and in your future, but in practice your universe is pretty stingy. It doesn't give you everything you want. It's fickle. It's picky. It's not fair. It periodically abandons you and makes you wait, stuck in a hole of crappiness, for months and years for things. In short, it's that bad boyfriend who stands you up, stops texting, and ghosts you for long periods. *Fucking universe. Can't trust it.*

And then it hits you: You basically don't trust that life has your back. It's disappointed you too many times for that. Which of course means you've got to do everything yourself, which is hard. I mean, you don't even know what's around the corner one minute from now. How can you possibly foresee and sync up all the potential wonderful turns and pivots of good things down the road, all by yourself?

Imagine a life in which you don't trust the universe *at all*. It's a pretty mean, small life ahead. It means luck is random. Life is random. Nothing has real meaning except the fragile things you make before they get all smashed up again under the tumbling weight of chaos that is called time.

If this is you, honey, then you are badly estranged from the universe. It doesn't matter if you *believe* in God or Source. Trusting it implicitly to act constantly and benevolently on your behalf, even when tough stuff is on your plate, is a whole other story. Because, if you did, if you *really* did, you'd have a way more optimistic outlook. You'd take a whole lot more healthy risks, and you'd know that you don't have nearly as much to fear. You'd know there was a purpose for both the good stuff and the bad. And you'd know that everything will work out. Because it always does.

Think about how many of your decisions weigh on "if only things could work out," or "if only I knew if this would go well," or "if only the universe supported me." These are all variations of you not having faith that the universe has your back. And because you lack that trust, you're back to frantically trying to control all the loose ends of your future that come hurtling at you. And you are exhausted.

You'll be surprised at how many things you either curb yourself from trying and/or grind on in frustration that are rooted in your lack of trust in life. For example, right now, as part of my reinvention, I want my life to start supporting me more as an author. Moreover, I want the emotional endpoints of feeling like what I share matters, that my ideas are worthy, that my words are catalysts for good things, and that I receive the support to write even more. Even at this moment as I sit here writing while I sip my coffee, and my foot heater pumps warm air on my toes, and my cat keeps nosing her way onto my lap, I'm actually engaging in an act of trust building with the universe. I'm writing because I'm *trusting* that someday you'll be reading this. I'm *trusting* that all the magical things that have to happen for that to come about will indeed occur. Life will help me. It *wants* to help me.

I'm working on creating trust around this because that's the kind of relationship I want to have with my future. Not only am I working on building trust that life will support my desire to write, but I'm also trying to trust that my health will stay good and that some random mutation won't spring up again and pop another tumor. Because again, I want to have *trust* in my body and life to support me and my health instead of constantly fearing for it.

Creating and maintaining trust around both of these things requires me to trust something outside me—which is the unknowable potential and power of my future and all the things, both material and spiritual, that conspire together to make it, which I call *the universe*.

My intention is to feel loved, adored, and supported by the universe.

You as well? I thought so. Then choose: Do you trust the universe or is that trust broken? If it's broken, do you want to mend it? Are you ready?

M.E. *School* Prompt

Your prompt is to journal on the following questions about your current relationship with the universe or your higher power:

Do I feel that the universe is completely on my side (supportive, abundant, and nurturing) and is trying every day to put good things in front of me?

Do my actions and the way I live reflect this belief? Or am I saying I believe it but am behaving as if I don't?

Do I feel that if I try something bold, I'll be supported?

Do I feel that life has decided I'm not worthy of something, or that it's "not gonna happen in this lifetime"?

Chapter 28:
The Universe Is My Suitor

Developing trust in other people or in the universe requires little tiny steps. Your trust in other people will gradually grow as you practice healing and forgiveness and create active moments for trust building through proactively building your relationships.

But the universe? How do you do "healing and forgiveness" with *that*? How do you proactively build trust with *that*?

You start by realizing where the trust is broken. You've already written down many of the ways the universe has disappointed you—you just wrote them out in the last chapter's prompts, and they're also buried in the "Tell Me All the Ways Your Heart Has Been Broken" exercise in chapter 23. It's where you feel life or God didn't give you what you needed. It's where some circumstance of birth or happenstance fucked up your body, family, life, or mind. It's in the way you feel that you'll never meet your twin flame. It's when life didn't give you the chance or the money you needed at a critical time. Stare at those words you wrote.

This is all your blame on the universe pouring out for all the rotten things it did to you. This is why you don't trust it.

Unfortunately, you're going to be in a relationship with your future, vis-a-vis the universe, for the rest of your life, and even beyond that. (Sorry, death does not necessarily get you out of this relationship.)

Do you want to fix this relationship? Imagine instead a partnership with the universe where you said, "You love me so much. I don't always understand your timing or your actions, but check out my emotional endpoints. They're what I'm building my life around. And I can't do it all by myself. I need you. I mean, you're going to be there anyway, so let's repair this rift. I want to trust you. I want to know you have my back. I want to feel like life has goodies planned for me. I want to know you're not against me."

Now we're talking. This is you building trust again, and you can do this with not just the universe but with your expectations of others as well. When you have this feeling of warmth, protection, and hope with both other people and your future, your fear of things and your need to control the shit out of things winds way down.

You're going to say "prove it to me" over and over, of course, as you rebuild these relationships and you know sometimes you'll be disappointed. But that's okay. Hearts are made to break. People are not perfect, and the universe can be inscrutable. But again, you don't have a choice about this, unless you intend to live in these broken relationships for the rest of your years, sweating it out by yourself. But that is not why you're here. You're here precisely *for* these relationships, in which a big merry band of us can share trust back and forth and see what we can make together.

Spiritual people always ask why we're on earth: "What's the point of life?" they ask.

The answer, relationships. Your relationship with yourself, other people, and our larger community, including earth, the universe, or God. Because you're in all of them, whether you like it or not.

Healing your trust like this is a *big, big, big* area for many of us. It's where we scream, "No! I'd rather be miserable!" than risk healing these relationships. But if you know your trust is broken, this is *exactly* where your next step is. And you know it because your A-level Controller self is actually a severe symptom of the broken parts of yourself exacting their need to make you feel safe.

And sure, maybe you're not a Controller. Maybe you're just a Doubter. As in, your lack thinking is so enormous that you simply *can't, can't, can't* believe that the universe really will take care of you. It hasn't happened before, so why should it start now?

Why? Because you were in a shitty relationship with it before. Now you're in marriage counseling with it. Now you're rebuilding that relationship to be better and stronger than ever. It takes two to tango, and I'm asking you to be the first one at the table.

Things Usually Work Out Right

Let me start by asking you to do one thing: Look at your life. On par, about how many things go right for you in a day? You know, basic stuff. You wake up and there's oxygen in the air for you. Your body works, and you can stagger out of bed in it. In fact, you have a bed, a comfy bed with nice sheets and blankets. You have a place to live, and there's food for you, clean water, and a shower. You might or might not have work, or enough money at this given moment, but you've had both in the past and surely will again. On balance, life is taking care of you. It's helped you get all these things, and 95 percent of them are good.

Sure, there are some wonky, difficult situations, like the annoying guy who lives above you who always sounds like he's dragging loud, heavy weights across the floor at 2:00 a.m. Or the fact that you need $3,000 worth of dental work and can't afford it. Or your boss, who's a micromanaging nitwit, exasperates the heck out of you.

But on balance? Can you say that in your day, every day, more than 5 percent of the things that happen to you suck donkey balls? And if they do, are those things of your making, or did the universe *force* them onto you?

I thought so. You see, we just pull out that old lack thinking too often. We spiral into negativity bias. The teensy black spot on the white paper is what catches our eye, or the tiny chip in the glass of our otherwise awesome cell phone.

But 95 percent of your day, every day, is good, and 95 percent of the time, your life is on your side, with you, helping you. Most of our worries never, ever manifest. We forget this. The universe does in fact support you, day in, day out.

One of my favorite ways to rebuild trust in life is with what I call the Universe Is My Suitor exercise.

You start by pretending that life, God, or the universe is your suitor. Yes, your loving, wanna-be romantic partner, wooing you every day to the best of their ability. And oh boy, does this partner adore you. The thing is, you've been pushing them away for a while. You've been telling them how rotten they are, how they act inconsistently. You're doubting their every move, and you're constantly challenging them to prove that they love you. And they're kind of sick of it. In short, you've taken over the relationship with your crappy thoughts and forced them into a wary corner.

What do we normally do with romantic relationships in which we don't really trust our partner anymore? We clamp down. We complain and moan. We sift through their cell phone. We brace for the disappointment. We micromanage. We tell everyone what a shithead they are, or we do the opposite out of sheer embarrassment and pretend we're the happiest couple in the world.

You don't trust this suitor, not one bit. The universe is supposed to be your partner, but, in reality, you've had to jump in and take over the whole relationship just to make it function at all.

Let's back it down a notch. Let's say you kinda, sorta trust life, but you keep ending up not letting life actually contribute much to the relationship. You trust it, but you trust yourself more. Imagine if this were a date. In an ideal world, your partner would ask you out. You'd say yes. He'd plan a sweet and romantic evening at your favorite spot. He'd remember the flowers. He'd remember his toothbrush. He'd show up to impress. And you're impressed. You relax. Someone wants to care for you, and you let them.

Now, let's pretend instead that this jerkwad universe has fucked up more than one time in the past. It has broken your heart and betrayed your trust. It won't marry you, it won't give up its other partners, and you sit and dangle in the void, feeling your inner worthiness slip away.

In fact, on the last date it arrived super late and you'd drunk way too much wine by then waiting for it. On the last date, you saw its phone flash on the table with DM's about a hookup later. Jesus, what a lousy date. But, hey, you're *stuck with it.* You and the universe, together, for freaking ever. Now what?

You think, *If it can't pull its shit together, I'll pull it together myself.* You take its 50 percent contribution to the relationship and say, *nope.*

So here you are now, doing everything in your power to tell the universe exactly what to do, when to do it, and how to do it so it doesn't disappoint you again. If you go on a date, you tell them when to pick you up, what car to drive, what color paint the car should have, how the seat should be adjusted, what restaurant you should pull up to, what you'll order and what they'll order, and exactly when the dinner will wrap up. You do this since you don't trust them *one little bit.* You've snatched their job right from their hands, leaving them powerless and you . . . infinitely unsatisfied.

Do you think your partner will be having any fun with you? Or do you think your partner will want to get away as soon as possible? Yeah, that's what happens when you don't trust and share equally with your suitor. You start to get overcontrolling and tell them you know everything. And unfortunately, a lot of what you tell them sucks, since you start lobbing boatloads of lack thinking at them.

And, if your faith in them is truly, epically ruined, you don't even ask anything of them at all. You give up. The universe is just a warm body in the ratty armchair of your life. A stale, empty marriage. Nothing more.

Ahem. Let's change this.

The date, of course, isn't really a date. It's a way of seeing how little you trust or give your partner a chance to show up strong for you. It's a bellwether for your feelings of hope that when you reinvent yourself, you have a strong and powerful partner at your side, who's likewise working tirelessly to shove good things your way. And it's a recognition that your future success or failure is intimately tied to your feelings about whether life, or God, or Source, is truly on your side or not.

So, again, pretend for a moment that the universe (your suitor) is madly in love with you. They may have drifted or grown silent, they may have disappointed you in the past, but you're going to be with them for, like, 500 more years or something and right now they are sitting at your doorstep with a huge bouquet of roses looking painfully at your door knocker and just hoping against all hope that you'll *let them in.*

They've remembered that they've seriously, madly, crazily, fallen for you. They've remembered that you are the best thing that's ever happened to them, and they want nothing more than to make it right. They realize they've *never stopped loving you.* And *never will.* And *let's forgive whatever happened in our past because we obviously weren't communicating very well. But now, we are.*

Mmmmm . . . yum. This is the kind of willing partner you want. Think, how does someone who's crazy in love with you act? How do you act when you're falling (or refalling) in love with them?

The idea is that you can't believe that the universe will give you your heart's desires if you can't even believe it would give you basic, unending, pure, steadfast, "I love you on your good days and your bad days" love. It loves you when you're cranky, it loves you when you're happy, it loves you on bad hair days, and it loves you when you're feeling like doing nothing but crawling in a hole.

And so you remember: The universe loves you. It gives you stuff all the time. It wants to show you off to its friends and family. It wants to make sure you get home safely and that your boss treats you nicely. It talks up your skills and blusters as heatedly as you do when you're complaining about your friend. It's on your side no matter what. Get it? Everything that someone madly in love with you would want for you is now what the universe wants for you, and frankly, what it has *always* wanted for you.

Now, a little caveat: Some of us were raised to think of the universe as God or a parental-style figure—do good and you'll be rewarded, do bad and you'll be punished. And life has indeed punished and rewarded us based on a prescriptive set of ways to act. And like most parents, sometimes their actions make no sense at all, and we're seemingly punished for doing good, rewarded for doing bad, or just not listened to at all.

I need you to remove yourself from this authoritarian model for a moment. God, in the prompts ahead, is your partner. I know! That can feel freaky! Almost sacrilegious! But it's such a freaky feeling that it can become a blasting torch for your remodeling. And you need a pattern interrupt.

You know that crazy, sexy, all-in, hungry feeling you have when you fall in love? That is exactly the feeling I want you to have about your future, the universe, and the gifts it's just dying to bring to you. Throw yourself in, and do this.

M.E. School Prompt

Write a letter from the universe to yourself as if your universe were your romantic partner or a suitor intent on wooing you with their love.

The universe sees you as the amazing god or goddess you are: sweet, loving, sexy, fun, creative, smart.

In this letter, the universe is talking directly to you. The letter contains everything a partner would say to someone they've fallen in love with. Pretend the universe is a real person as you write. How would you express your love for a real person?

This letter is reminding you of your worth and attractiveness on all levels: mentally, spiritually, emotionally, and physically. Your suitor is telling you how many plans it has for you both in the years ahead. It's apologizing, if need be, for those things that happened in the past that you didn't understand at the time (or still don't understand today). This is a love letter from the universe to you. Let yourself go into it.

Here's what my universe had to say to me:

> Darling,
>
> Look, lovebug, I wrote this for you. You forgot I wrote this to you a long time ago, before you were born even, but now you've found this note in a little drawer of your life, and when you read it, I know you might cry. And I'll cry

for you, and for us. I want to know how we can make things better, together, again.

All the things you've been through have pushed us apart, but I want us back together, and I'm willing to fight for it.

I am never leaving you. I may disappoint you, hurt you, even betray your expectations of me, but you and I are just the same; you're my best friend. We're together, made of one another. I don't know why you stopped believing in me, why you yanked your faith away.

More than anyone you'll ever meet, love, raise, marry, or know, it's still you and me first, my love. So let's be in love again. Trust me again. It's my promise, and I've never broken it.

Every day I wake up with you. And every night we fall asleep together. I never leave your side. I always give you everything I have. I give you the world and everything in it. I give you the solar system and every drop of oxygen you breathe.

I long for you to take it all from me, to take the gifts I have for you. It's what I'm here for. It makes me happy when you do.

I believe in you, my love. I know what you can do. I see your extraordinary power and greatness. You're made from the same stardust that I made suns and planets with. I don't ever want you to feel small. Believe me, I couldn't have chosen anyone better than you to spend my eternity with. Trust me on that.

I want to keep you safe, and I always look out for your best interests. I'll never put you in harm's way. We do everything by mutual agreement.

When you cry, feel depressed, are confused, or frustrated, it actually brings us closer because that's when you know I have your back.

I'm here for you no matter how you feel or act. You never have to keep up appearances or act a certain way with me.

My love, I support you in everything you try or do. Please let me support you. Please ask me for things. Please allow me to shower you with abundance. I want to see you shine! I want to see you happy, loved, and safe. I love you. I love you so much.

XO,
The Universe

Now write your own.

_____

_____

_____

_____

_____

_____

_____

_____

_____

_____

_____

_____

_____

_____

_____

_____

_____

_____

_____

_____

_____

PART VI:
Weightlifting for Your Soul

Chapter 29:
Things That Make You Feel Fucking Good

We're almost in the clear now. The thickest, heaviest parts are over. You did it—the demolition is done. From here on, our focus is on rebuilding: rebuilding *you*, rebuilding everything. You can't build a tall skyscraper on shaky ground, so here we are going forward, putting down a foundation so strong you could build the Empire State Building on it.

No more universe stuff. We pretty well ground that to a fine point. However, more than one student has told me that rehabbing their relationship with the universe is their favorite, favorite part of all the work we've done so far. But it gets even better.

You see, when everything gets emptied out, as it now has in you, there's a bright, clean open space. Buncha people have been forgiven—including yourself, including the universe. Buncha confining ideas about yourself have been released. You get why you've been feeling the way you've been feeling, and you also get that this is all infinitely changeable, and *that you are changing it.*

Smell that change? That's a fresh cut lawn. That's dawn sprinklers on a warm spring morning. That's the soft purr of hummingbird wings at your feeder and the bright pink of roses climbing your gate. This is you, ready to fill up on the good stuff now, the really good stuff. And to do this, you're going to remember what the good stuff is in your life, because so many things make you feel so fucking good! Why don't you do more of them? Often when we transition or grow, we become so focused on the pain of our rebirth that we forget entirely about the things that make us glow with warmth and happiness. It's like they stop existing. They haven't. You just haven't been looking in their direction lately.

This is the moment to remember—to capture—all those things that have always and likely *will* always make you feel freaking good. Get your butterfly net. We're going hunting!

Here are a ton of ideas to get your own list going.

Things That Make Me Feel Great

Watching the sunset over the hills or trees

Laughing at a movie

Laughing with a friend

Being ridiculous with my children until they erupt in giggles

Letting go of every single "have to" for a weekend

Petting and snuggling my animal friend

Letting my fingers slip into those of someone I love

Smelling the wet sidewalk in the city and feeling the vibe of life around me

Slurping ramen noodles

A long hot bath

Lighting a candle at my desk while I work

Snuggling in fresh sheets

Gazing at something beautiful

Gazing at someone beautiful—my partner, my mother, my children

Digging in the rich dark earth of my garden

Sitting for an hour on the salty wet wax of my surfboard, not even caring if I catch a wave

Swimming in the pool in the backyard, listening to the laundry blow on the line

Doing a perfect downward dog

Executing a perfect set at the gym

Catching a ride on the subway to a stop I've never exited at before, just because

Painting, coloring, sketching, beading, sawing, sewing, shaping

Writing my heart onto paper, typing my dreams into books

Playing an old song I forgot I love so much

Giving money to someone who needs it

Giving love to someone who needs it

Popping together a new scrapbook or photo album

Telling someone how awesome they are, how lucky I am to know them, how they are important

Lying on the chaise lounge on a warm day feeling like I might nap, or maybe not. It doesn't matter. The day is bliss either way.

Known Pleasures

My list could go on for pages and pages. What's on yours? And when was the last time you allowed yourself to do or experience things like this? Today? Yesterday? These aren't treats for good behavior. They're fundamental pieces of life.

These aren't **things** you do if only you felt better.
These are things you do in order to feel better.

It's easy to feel so good. Stop *waiting* for the good feelings. Go *make* them. They are hiding in practically everything. They are waiting for you to find them.

You want the emotional energy to make some excellent emotional endpoints? Well, you remember what your inner battery is? It's time again to charge it. Start by dreaming up a slew of little things that will fill your well with good feelings, then start doing them. Baby steps. Simplicity is key.

After all the deep soul-searching work we've done, this may sound like *chapterus interruptus,* peppy cheerleader rah-rah during half-time, but it's not. It's a critical piece of your reinvention. Your reinvention isn't all about hard "ah-ha" moments. It has to be balanced by delicious, gorgeous experiences and ideas that you *act on.*

I live three miles from the beach. On a day with all green lights, I can be there in seven minutes. The supple sand is soft and sinks under my toes and sometimes, after a winter storm, the whole beach fills with gorgeous black sand with flecks of gold. I can sit on this sand and let the ocean roar through me. I can feel the ebb and flow of the waves, smell the negative ions escaping the flurry of ocean spray, cast my mind into the bright sun, and dream about all the things I'm doing or want to be doing. I could do this all in under thirty minutes, the length of one sitcom, round trip.

But do I do it?

"Lavender Pajama Me" hasn't been to the beach in about eight months. And yet I ask her to rise up and relight the smoky little embers in her heart. Know what she says back?

Yeah, and with what?

My bare pantry, that's what.

Naw, honey, you gotta fill that panty with some ingredients if you want me to make soup.

Umm hmm. I remember that whole section about the Dead Zone. Go make some interesting things, I heard myself say to you.

I went and made some. Did you? Are you?

I painted a whole wall of my house bright peacock blue and hung plants on the walls.

I snuck off on a very dicey trip to a tiny volcanic island off the coast of Africa (yes, for reals), and wow did it reset all my buttons.

So yeah, I started stocking my pantry.

But what I'm saying right now is a little different.

Think of this as chapter 9's Dead Zone revisited, with a little twist, because now you're realizing that making good feelings is more than just stocking your pantry: It's *changing* you. What's more, the things on this new list are less about adding the spice of new and unique things to your life and more about returning to your *known pleasures* and allowing them to fill you up.

Every good feeling you purposely create is rebalancing the scales of your inner being. You aren't waiting for yourself to feel better or for good things to come to you. *You're making them first,* by choice. And these good feelings aren't dependent on anyone else doing, saying, giving, or being any certain way for you. No power leaks.

This is, literally, Round Two.

I don't know if sneaking off to the beach in the middle of a workday is going to light up my soul. I might feel *meh* at best as I sit and let the wind brush my cheeks. But one thing I do know: I haven't given myself this little experience in many, many months, and it's easy and cheap, and even if I have to pull my pants off my pleather chair with a large sucking sound, I will make myself go. Because back when I used to give myself this experience a lot, I was also a lot happier. So I'll go with trust and a spirit of adventure.

M.E. *School* Prompt

Your prompt is to write a list of things that make you feel amazing.

Review your prompt exercise from chapter 9, then create a new list just like mine—one filled with silly, lovely, sweet, easy experiences. These don't have to be unique or special things because this time, the emphasis is less on novelty and more on pleasure, especially experiencing known pleasures. When you finish, circle a few things to get into your agenda *this week*. You are balancing your scales.

Remember, these aren't things you do *if only you felt better*. These are things you do in *order to* feel better.

Things that make me feel fucking good:

_____

_____

_____

_____

_____

_____

_____

_____

_____

_____

Chapter 30:
Self-Love Extravaganza

All right, finally, *finally,* we return to the third and final part of our Trifecta of Trust: trust of self. I told you we'd get there. You worked on your feelings about others, you reimagined your relationship with the universe, and now here you are, staring straight into the mirror of yourself again, thinking, *I'm reinventing myself. I'm stretching and becoming someone new who's happier, flowing,* on point *in my life. I love this person. I love me.*

Self-trust and self-love are inseparable. And if you lack one, you'll always lack the other.

Yet over the years, you've probably learned how to not only mistrust your choices and desires but also how to criticize yourself and continuously raise your expectations about yourself to almost unimaginable levels.

But I do love myself, mostly! . . . you grumble.

And you do. Mostly. Except for little bits here and there. And those little bits where you don't show yourself gentle, loving affection and compassion end up being the bits that really screw you.

For a minute, let me put my tough-love "mom hat" on and tell you: I see you when you're frustrated with yourself. You think it's your responsibility to figure out everything, to fix everything, to be near perfect all the time, and to be *better than.*

I see you haranguing yourself about things you did four years ago that you just can't let go of.

Or when something goes wrong in your life? Well, it's because you're just not loveable enough, smart enough . . . something enough. (Self-blame has hints of the *I'm Not Good Enough Show*.)

Or what about those ten pounds you gained this holiday season? What a shame. *I suck*, you think.

You're a bigger critic than anyone else will ever be to you.

I'm still wearing my mom hat when I say that I hate to see you always saying such hurtful things to yourself, thinking such hurtful thoughts about yourself. I don't know why you keep doing it. Why do you always have to be perfect? You can mess up, you know. You can drink too much beer, smoke, not exercise, show up late to the family party, say dumb things that get you fired, cheat on your girlfriend when you're drunk and freak out afterward. Everyone expects it. Every one of us does dumb things. We waste periods of our lives, and we shoot off in wrong directions. We hurt people, and we hurt ourselves.

I mean, we all know we're going to mess up over and over. I don't know why you think you're so special that you *never will*, or that when you do, it's somehow *extra worse*. It isn't.

You're not special. You're not expected to be perfect all the time. You're meant to fall down a lot, in fact. Babies don't glide out of their mother's wombs winning 500-meter races. They fall and cry and, honestly, are pretty wretched and difficult sometimes for years and years.

You were a baby too, and someone was gentle with you. Why did you stop being gentle with yourself?

If I can be gentle with you, why can't *you* be this gentle with yourself? You're the only one who can talk to yourself and say, "Honey, I love you. I know you messed that up. But let's be gentle on yourself, okay? I love you. Now, how can you fix it or do better next time?"

That's all it takes. It's so simple, so easy. And yet you torture yourself with these weird crazy feelings of "you screwed up for good, you'll never make it, people don't want you, you're lazy, you can't follow through, your family can't handle you" . . . on and on.

If I talked to my child like you talk to yourself, I'd be thrown in jail. I can't imagine ever talking to a child the way you talk to yourself sometimes, it's hideous.

You look at your body, and the first thing you point out is how it's failed you, or looks ugly. Or it's old or it's fat, you can't do the sports you used to love, and no one looks at you with lust or sexy curiosity anymore.

You look at your finances and the first thing you say is "I'm so stupid. Why did I jack up my credit? Why am I always underpaid? What's wrong with me? Why didn't I do better?"

You look at your relationship and say, "I guess I have to settle for this. It's not like I can expect anything better than this."

I treat my dog better than you treat you.

What's up, honey bear? Where did you learn that? And can we drop that? Why not?

Self-Love and Self-Trust Quiz

The best way to explore your current degree of inner worth, self-trust, and self-love is to take this little quiz. Each scenario illustrates a way in which you love yourself and experience self-worth and self-trust. Just put a checkmark next to any that apply wholly and fully to your feelings about yourself. Don't check the box that you simply *agree* with. Check the box if you're actively *living* the scenario each and every day.

☐ I fundamentally respect myself, and I know that I am good and, most of all, that I'm hugely deserving of anything wonderful that life serves up.

☐ I deserve a great partner, a fulfilling career, my own creative or spiritual expression, and anything else I want to experience. I deserve it all.

☐ I deserve to choose my life for myself despite anything my family has told me, or what my current or past partners, or bosses or co-workers, or family or friends have said about me.

☐ I'm fundamentally amazing. I am beautiful in ways that only I can see, and I'm beautiful in ways that other people see too. I am not ashamed or embarrassed to say this.

☐ I often feel strong. I make strong decisions, I take strong action, and I rarely second-guess or doubt myself. I know my capacity, and I can course correct easily if I need to.

☐ I love my family and friends, but I don't empty myself or neglect my own life for them.

☐ I don't need people to prove that they love me all the time. I never get irritable, needy, or do crummy things to others just so they prove they'll tolerate it or forgive me.

☐ I rarely think or feel negative things about my body. I like how I look, how I feel, and what I weigh. When it gets ill or otherwise "breaks," I never feel a sense of betrayal or anger.

☐ I don't try to be perfect or hold back on decisions, ideas, or projects because I'm "not ready" or my project "isn't good enough yet."

☐ I can say no easily to things I don't have time for or interest in. I don't find myself getting mad at myself often for involving myself in things I don't really want to be doing.

☐ If someone talks negatively or rudely to me, or hurts me, I tell them how I feel. I don't stuff it.

☐ I recognize that I don't always make the right decisions, but fear of not making a good choice doesn't hold me back.

☐ I treat myself to the same level of forgiveness and understanding that I'd speak to my child with (if I have one). And I never talk harshly to myself or call myself names.

☐ I know my worth, and I don't hesitate to put a high monetary value on it.

☐ I'm incredibly accepting of my color, sex, gender, class, ethnicity, nationality, age, and orientation. I love everything about how I'm made and other people are lucky when I share myself with them.

☐ I let go of things easily and don't go around with them in my mind for hours or days. If I regret something, I can put it down and assure myself that next time it'll be different.

☐ I don't put myself "last on the list." If it's a weekend and I need to get stuff done for myself, I'm not doing it tiredly on a Sunday night because I gave to my whole family first, all weekend.

☐ I never gauge my "lovability" by how much others love me back. I never feel like I "give and give" or that something's wrong with me if others don't reciprocate.

☐ I easily receive all the good things people and life have for me. I graciously and easily receive money, help, compliments, and anything else people want to give me. I never question it or say no.

All right, some of those were easy to check, and some felt downright cringy, right? And many, many were ones that you wanted to check, but there was a little wobble because while you think or feel that thing most of the time, you know that there are many times when you don't.

Each statement is engaging in what we call *contrast*. Each one is the positive opposite of an unloving feeling. By seeing if you can't hold or identify with these positive feelings, you're lighting up the fact that you hold the opposite.

What we're looking for are any holes in your sense of self-confidence, self-worth, or self-trust. These are the holes we want to fill with a new set of feelings because, as they get filled, the little garden of yourself begins to grow wild with blossoms and heavy-hanging fruits.

Look at the items you couldn't check. Right there, those are where your lack of self-love or self-trust are peeking like polka-dot panties out your pant waist.

Which brings us to the central question: *How do I fix it?*

Going forward, you're going to pay rapt attention whenever horrible words or thoughts arise in you, and then you'll tell them you're done letting them be inside you. And then you replace them with the feelings you want—the feelings embodied in one or more of those statements: compassion, patience, trust, affirmations of worth.

This is where you roll your eyes and think, *If it were only so simple, Summer, you'd put every therapist out of business.*

You're right, I would. Except that even though it's a pretty simple idea, it's much harder to execute. It means you have to catch yourself in the midst of your negative, critical, or unworthy lack thoughts or feelings the moment they arise, at times when you say things like "God, I'm always late, what's wrong with me? Ugh, I hate my turkey neck jowls! I can't believe I let myself lose custody of my kids. I should never have sold that house. I should never have started dating that guy. Why can't I ever stop drinking diet cola?"

These very specific thoughts about your imperfection, unworthiness, or stupidity are baked in so deep that they just hum along in the dark depths of you waiting for a choice moment, then they rise up like whales to the surface as you criticize or hate on yourself.

This goes way beyond the *I'm Not Good Enough Show.*

This is the *I Downright Hate and Mistrust Parts of Me, My Body, or My Life Show.*

And like all the other forms of trust we've looked at, this form (your self-trust and self-love) also got broken in you at some point (or many points) through the dumb decision, failure, or icky fuck-up . . . on and on.

Your **trust** of others got messed up when someone hurt you.
Your trust of self got messed up when you hurt someone,
that someone even being yourself.

Now, shift. You forgave others, why not forgive yourself? Why not forgive yourself every single time one of these wretched bastard feelings pops up?

This means you're going to immediately begin practicing feeling very different feelings around these specific self-harming barbs: You're going to generate heaps of deep, compassionate understanding. You'll practice feeling trust. You'll carry a constant, loving desire to be kinder to yourself. You're going to tell yourself, "I'm gonna be my own mama, my own papa. I'm going to be the lovingest, most supportive, biggest cheerleader to myself because I can't wait for anyone else to do it for me. I mean, why do I keep asking people I love to give that to me when I can't even give it to myself?!"

Good question. How can you expect others to give you the love, respect, trust, and admiration that you don't even adequately give yourself?

Be Gentle with Yourself

You start by being gentle with yourself.

Then you begin rebuilding trust in yourself. This is no different than all the other emotional endpoints we've practiced, except these particular emotional endpoints are grounded in self-love, self-trust, and self-acceptance.

Right now, I want you to get really *specific* about what you want to love and trust about yourself. You're going to love all your nooks and crannies, all your bits and pieces. Love your wide hips. Love your wide smile. Love your past decisions, even the piss-poor ones. Love your intelligence. Love your crankiness. Love you, all of you. The imperfectly perfect you.

And once this bird of self-love really gets flying, you're going to rediscover all the things you really want to be, have, or do that your unloving feelings previously crimped, and there'll be no one and nothing telling you "you can't."

We've been cultivating your self-love and self-trust through many of the prompts you've already done in M.E. School: grieving, forgiving yourself, forgiving others, being gentle on yourself about your patterns and life major, recognizing the inherent and good pain of ceilings, accepting that you're between the reefs, reconciling yourself with the universe, ridding yourself of fear and lack thinking, increasing things that give you joy.

Self-love and self-trust sprout quietly and surely when the rain of *other* kinds of inner growth have worked their way through the soil of you. You've already felt how feeling forgiveness of yourself and others somehow resulted in deeper self-acceptance. When you create a strong, healthy boundary, the side effect is a slight rise in your self-love. When you grieve, the side effect is a little more self-compassion. When you stop controlling, the side effect is a heaping tablespoon of trust.

We're just putting the final touches on this by generating some self-loving, compassionate, emotional endpoints around very specific parts of you by catching those ugly bits as they breach your surface. Your prompt will help you with this.

M.E. *School* Prompt

Review your checklist, then spend some time feeling into those statements that you hesitated to check, or which you wanted to check but knew you'd be simply agreeing with instead of actually living them.

Remember when I said every statement you couldn't check can reveal the contrast or the gap between your actual feelings and how you want to feel? Choose some of those statements and make them be about something very personal and specific. Then write down the positive contrast to your chosen selections.

For example, if you can't agree with the statement that begins with "I let go of things easily and don't go around with them in my mind for hours or days," then you'll choose a specific, current situation to apply that statement to, such as: *"I can't believe I screwed up that presentation so bad at work yesterday and forgot the project deadline. Ugh, why did I do that? I keep thinking about it."*

Then you'll find the opposite of dwelling and circling on self-blame about your poor preparation and missed deadline. Your contrast is: *"I let go of that mistake at my presentation easily and didn't go around with it in my mind for hours or days. I trust myself to do better next time. I feel compassion for myself."*

Chapter 31:
Pretzels Are Only
for Eating

Now that you're starting to rebuild your self-love and self-trust, we're finally heading back into the rich harbor called "having boundaries." Because without boundaries, you're sunk. Your self-love may have filled your boat with goodies, but your lack of boundaries allows them to be eaten by rats. Let's stop that cycle. Let's examine boundaries with a concept I call "pretzels are only for eating."

Life Stealers

One of those obvious things that ends up not being obvious is this: everybody gets exactly one lifetime, all to themselves.

Yes, one. Dad got his, Mom got hers, your brother and sister got theirs, your spouse, friends . . . everyone. One life, all to themselves, to do absolutely anything they want with it.

Just close your eyes and think about that for a second. Let the idea go deep.

Yet we all have someone who thinks they can have not only their own life but ours too. They want you to do what they tell you to do and think how they want you to think. They criticize you or call you dumb or ignorant or selfish if you choose to do, think, or be any different than what they expect or approve of. They carry their own choices over into your life and try to mandate that you choose them too. What's more, they expect you to do gobs of things for them or constantly give them money or time, and then they berate or coldly condemn you if you refuse.

How utterly selfish, don't you think?

Lives are so precious. And here they want to have control over *two*—theirs and yours. They're thieves who already have their own life, but they want to steal yours as well. Who gives them the right?

No one. Not a single other person can tell you how to live, what career to go into, or whom to marry. They can't tell you what political party to follow or how you should spend your weeknights. They can't tell you that the only way you'll be a good person is by giving them money, not seeing that friend of yours, wearing certain clothes they prefer, or any of a hundred other requirements.

But, oh God, how they try.

When a case of life stealing gets really bad, you find yourself in some kind of relationship with this life stealer, and you end up spending gobs of time just figuring out what they want from you, how to make yourself more desirable to them. You obsess about how to make them happy, and fret about accidentally doing something to upset them.

Hear this: You don't need to become a pretzel for anyone. You can be seen for who you are, as you already are (no changes required), and loved. If the person you're with or born to doesn't approve, then they need to go do the things *in their own life* that they want you to do. It's not your job to follow their orders and carry out their expectations. There is not a single person on earth who can enforce the idea of them being in charge of you.

Hey, if it's your mom or dad who's the life stealer, I get it. A lot of us have families that really stick together. It's like a code has developed that no one dares to break—a code that shaped generations before you about whom to marry or what job to get.

But remember, codes change. People expand and grow and all changes aren't bad, like your family expects them to be. They're just different. Like, maybe you don't want to become an engineer. You're totally unsuited for it. Maybe you want to decorate houses instead, and interior design is your *thang*. Sometimes we have to be the sand in the oyster, the one element that causes the family's old, struggling, worn-out tune to expand and take on new harmonies and nuances. You're it! You got picked for that job by your very nature, and no, it isn't an easy task. But that's your role—the expander, the introducer, the one who increases the family's adaptability instead of narrowing it.

Sometimes the life stealer isn't family. It's that person you fell in love with or best-friended. This person is so amazing . . . *argh how can you be as amazing as they are?!* Well, easy. They tell you exactly how: Don't see that friend anymore, change your hair, keep your body looking a certain way, don't have those silly hobbies. "Do it for me, honey."

You begin to form a list of all the things you should no longer do, think, or be interested in. You have another list for people they don't like whom you need to minimize or cut out.

Your partner, who once treasured you for *you,* now treasures you for how well you adhere to their new ideas for you. And you, well you may have just accidentally gone along with that. Because after you got together, the criticism began. The subtle hints of not being good enough for them or anyone else. The guilt inducing began too: "Why won't you do this for me? Is that other thing more important to you?"

Your response? How about this: "I *am* doing this for us. I'm bringing in variety. I'm challenging your insecurity, which you want me to coddle. I'm helping you grow, babe. This other thing isn't more important than you, but it's part of me, and I brought it with me, and if I have to keep shutting down these parts of me, then you won't really have *me* anymore. You'll have a watered-down facsimile of me."

You can keep going too: "There's a lot of things I brought with me and that are part of me, and I want to keep them as long as they don't truly hurt you. If I've got some bad habits or personality traits, I'll work on those. But my friendship with so-and-so? That doesn't hurt you. It does challenge your insecurity though. What about my interest in XYZ things? When did that go from being a cute part of my personality to something stupid about me?"

This, my darlings, is what creating healthy boundaries looks and sounds like when you have a life stealer around. It means that when anyone tries to get you to say, think, or feel something, remember that we each have our own life and get to do anything we want with it. Nobody can co-opt your life with their ideas.

And further, if someone tries to badger you, punish you, scold you, or make you feel like shit for doing "terrible" things to them (say, by not following their orders or coddling their prickly, shaming, judgy, or perfectionistic personality), remind yourself that these are just the tactics or traits they've discovered that have given them great payoffs with other people, so they do these a lot now.

But they no longer do them with *you*.

Boundary Baiters

There's a lesser, lighter variation of life stealers whom I call "boundary baiters." These are the people we more normally associate with trying to infringe on our lives by demanding more than they give in constant, small ways. They're the ones to whom we overgive, the ones we can't say no to, or who cajole, guilt, or berate us into doing things we really don't want to do. Your boundary baiter could easily be your romantic partner, parent, friend, kid, boss, or brother. Heck, even your tenant or child's teacher can pull a variation of this shit on you.

One of my clients, Tera, had a gardener boundary baiter. This gardener would yell at her, demand extra money she didn't earn, get pay advances for work not yet done, and choose what yardwork she was and wasn't willing to do. Tera was afraid of seeing the woman's explosive temper or sullen resentful looks if she asserted her needs. The thought of firing this gardener was unthinkably scary. It sounds silly, I know, but it always looks silly to an outsider. To the person in the relationship with the boundary baiter, it's been a slow, invisible slide of gradually being more and more taken advantage of. It's hard to see it.

It can also look like any of these situations:

"I don't have money for rent. I don't have a job. I don't have money for food. You have to help me. I know you will."

But this is what you say every month.

"Yeah, I know, but every month you're okay with it, so . . ."

"I expect you to check your e-mail on the weekends and after-hours. You need to be on call at all times for anything I need."

But then I'm working 24/7, I'm never really off.

Or how about, "He really needs to move out, but he just won't! I don't know what else to do!"

How about you take all his stuff and box it up and leave it on the porch?

"I could never."

Oh, but you could.

Or perhaps, "She always says she's so sorry afterward, and it'll never happen again. But then it does. Over and over."

So next time it happens, tell her you're done. Through. Over it. Outta here. It ain't acceptable. No more chances.

"But that's cruel. She won't have anywhere to live without me."

And when did this become your problem? Because if it really were your problem, you'd fix it like that, I say, snapping my fingers for emphasis. *But it's her problem, and you're enabling it to continue. Some friend you are.*

Your boundary baiters will be dumbfounded and pissed when you don't respond like everyone else does to their guilt-inducing, fear-inducing, self-trust–crippling behaviors.

And you know how you can tell if you've got one of these? Just tell me now if you feel any of these feelings with someone: guilt, shame, anger at feeling used, secrecy, lack of self-trust, compromise to the point of giving up something you love. Each of these emotions is a blinking red light that warns you that you've just succumbed to letting them have a piece of your life.

But what if you love them. *Loooooooove.* Don't you do things you don't like, and sacrifice, for people you love?

Mmmm, sometimes you do. No one likes caring for their partner or parent through cancer, but they do it because they love them.

But always tip-toeing around, not sharing your true feelings, not sharing your wants and needs clearly, and holding cauldrons of bubbling anger inside you? That's totally different territory. You've discovered that this person's love, friendship, or service is incredibly conditional. You've become accustomed to this highly conditional relationship.

And trust me, you can live without it.

The sweet breath of cool oxygen you'll take when you get out of this straightjacket will be dizzyingly freeing.

But I know you're afraid of the fallout. Remember chapter 7, "Fear of Feelings"? As soon as you create a healthy boundary and your boundary baiter (or life stealer) encounters it, you're going to feel fear—primal, soul-screeching fear. You might fear their angry disapproval, or you might fear that they'll leave you. You might fear that you'll feel guilty if something bad happens to them without your ever-protective stance. You might feel afraid of the confrontation itself when they discover that you changed the rules. In other words, you're fundamentally afraid that your boundary will make you feel awful. Why enforce it when all these bad feelings might arise?

Well look, you already have a ton of bad feelings. It's just that you're the only one spinning in circles with them while your boundary baiter gets to feel happily oblivious. And you're worn out—totally pooped, feeling like you're always not good enough or always feeling guilty, or both of those at once.

Your efforts haven't resulted in anyone truly being happy, self-sufficient, compassionate, or loved. Why keep giving your life away?

Go get your life back.

Be the sand in the oyster,
be the challenger who helps your friend, family,
or partner expand. Because that is real love.

In the prompts, I'll ask you to identify your boundary baiters and pretzel-making life stealers. Then you'll write down your new boundaries you'll create to keep all of you safe and growth filled.

As you encounter and address people and places that need boundaries, then enact those boundaries; you'll discover a rare and delicious feeling: inner strength. And this strength? Well, it leads to self-love. You are finally protecting *yourself*, and your whole being feels it.

M.E. *School* Prompt

Your two-part prompt is to identify people or things who "make" you feel guilt, shame, anger at feeling used, or like you have to keep secrets, like you have to change something vital about yourself, etc. Then create healthy boundaries to address them.

Part One: Journal on the questions below to identify these people and situations in your life.

- Who makes me feel guilty or that I'm a bad child, partner, spouse, or friend if I don't do something they think I should do?

- Who makes me doubt myself or tells me my feelings are wrong and theirs are right?

- Who does things to me that I know I shouldn't tolerate, but I do?

- Who's made me compromise to the point of giving up something I love?

- Who takes my money, takes advantage of my good nature, or otherwise uses me or my assets without giving back much (if anything) in return?

- What things are sucking my time with little or no reward (other than making me feel guilty if I don't do them)?

- For whom do I do things because "it's family" or "it's expected of me" even though it's painful?

Part Two: Choose several of your most emotion-packed answers from above, then write down next to them how you can effectively address and enforce boundaries. You can also use the Be Wrong exercise from chapter 21 if it helps you think differently about what is and isn't possible.

Ask any of these questions as you come up with your solution: *How can I change this? What boundaries will I create? What or who will I say no to? Where will I stand my ground?*

Here's an example of how to answer each part. Let's say you chose to answer this question: "For whom do I do things because 'it's family' or it's expected of me, even though it's painful?"

Part One Answer:

> Every year I'm expected to fly to my brother James's house in Idaho for Christmas. I hate it. He smokes, he's an alcoholic, he abuses his dog. His wife and kid are not nice people. My mom wants our family together, so I go. But I feel miserable the whole time. In fact last year, James got super drunk and started a big fight on Christmas and called me a bunch of names.

Part Two Answer:

> My healthy boundary: I tell my mom that next year, everyone is invited to my house. She'll be upset since it means she might not see James, and she doesn't like her routine changed. She

says she's still going to James's house even if my family doesn't show up. So, there's that: blowback from Mom, and feeling like she'll pick James over me and my family, again, which hurts. To enforce this, I'll tell Mom I'll pay for James's airfare to my house. I'll also tell Mom that I love her and want to see her, but if she chooses to see James instead, then I'll come over to her place on New Year's and we can start a new tradition together, but that it will still hurt my heart, and I'll have to explain her decision to her grandkids.

Chapter 32:

I Love Myself, but You Loving Me? That's More Difficult

M.E. School is almost over. You're in the final stretch. It went fast. Well, maybe it went fast, or maybe you put the book down for a month or eight because *damn, Summer, that really was a slog through the middle.*

I know. That's what self-growth sometimes is: a long slog through the middle. You're slogging through it to get through the equally sloggy, middle part of your life. My hat's off to you. You're doing really well.

But now, here we are.

Do you know that almost a year has passed for me? It's October, and I'm thinking about hanging Halloween decorations and getting all my spooky on. I never get trick-or-treaters—our street is empty and dark. But my heart is a warm fireplace with witch hats and cinnamon-scented candles. My heart is also open to being gorgeously and deliciously loved.

I had to work on allowing myself to receive this kind of love and nurturing from others. Being a great receiver is something I'm continually expanding into.

I know this book might seem like a constant cataloging of my own weak points, but there it is: I'm human. I'm not out of the woods yet either as I take myself through this process yet one more time. So if you're fretting that you aren't even close to your reinvention, don't worry. Be gentle with yourself. Learn to receive with me.

The Cancer Story

It's 2015, and my twelve-year-old daughter, Lexi, is sitting on the bed with me eating chocolate-covered strawberries. I'm lying down with a pocket of cadaver skin sewed under my chest muscle just under what used to be a breast nipple but which is now an empty pocket of wilted, sunken flesh, cleaned out like someone scooped all the ice cream from a carton. I have blood-filled half-inch tubing running beneath my skin and down my ribs, sticking out of my skin, which I'm supposed to empty into the toilet every few hours. The draining goop looks like raspberry sauce with cottage cheese. But it's just the leftover juices from where my breast used to be. Oh yeah, I had a mastectomy. Oh, yeah, I have cancer. And it has spread.

Every day this week, my friends have been bringing us meals. It's only the fifth day after surgery and already my refrigerator is stuffed full. My bestie Jen sent the chocolate strawberries. I have bouquets of flowers surrounding my bed and heaps of cards on my table.

And part of me wants to text everyone and tell them to stop sending things, stop coming for pity visits, and stop bringing food because I'm fine, goddammit. And then another part of me reminds me that I still need help just putting my clothes on or brushing my hair.

I need to explore something that's popped up that I'm struggling to understand, which is how to receive.

What a joke, I think, that I've practiced personal growth for twenty years and made so many breakthroughs, but even so, here I am rubbing up again against that same ceiling: I can't let someone freely give me something without feeling a sharp sense of discomfort, embarrassment, or mistrust. *I suck at receiving.*

You want to know how I discovered that? I found it in my urge to mumble to my friends to stop bringing my family food.

I found it in the feeling of guilt that comes up when I think to myself that my friends sure treat me better than I treat them.

I found it when I think, *We don't need you to clean the kitchen and do laundry. C'mon this isn't a big deal. My family can figure things out for a few months.*

I feel it when I think to myself that I have so many people who care about me, and how little I hardly ever go out of my way for them in return.

It makes me think about everyone I know who's had surgery too, and I didn't sign up to bring them family dinners, take the kids for a few hours, or send them flowers. All I can focus on is how selfish I've been in my friendships.

And then, too, I think about all the lovely e-mails, tithes, and thank-you gifts I receive from strangers who tell me I helped them think differently, see their lives differently, take their power back, wake up, and totally change their lives.

I think about how in the past I've taken pleasure in their gratitude for about five minutes, then let it drop from my thinking. After all, it's hard to really receive that. What if I become an egomaniac? I tell myself, "Better to not receive than risk becoming a complete ass."

I know this sounds like crazy talk. But all our ceilings sound like crazy talk to someone who doesn't share them. And not being able to receive is a grand, big ceiling—one I'm going to have to break through if I ever want to feel the pleasure of true, balanced friendships, as well as the pleasure of allowing life and the universe to support me. And the joy of actually, full-heartedly accepting the rain of blessings, prosperity, and treasures that I keep telling the universe I want to experience.

But I can't even savor these chocolate-covered strawberries because I feel guilty and bad that my friend brought them, and I know she barely makes more than minimum wage, and these probably equal four hours of work for her.

This emotional ceiling of mine makes me focus on how little I do and how not good enough I am even when I do as much as I humanly can, and how I shouldn't be feeling happy about getting all this attention and love even when it's, *ahem*, deserved.

A giant, "I'm not good enough" and "I can't receive" subroutine that's been playing in my system for God knows how long has reared up . . . again.

I've manifested a beautiful circle of people around me, but I can't let them give to me. I can't even trust that my friend is taking extreme pleasure in me eating these strawberries, that this is exactly what she works for . . . to be able to show her love to others.

I wonder where else this same subroutine is playing out in my life and in what I'm trying to create?

I wonder, *where do I succeed but feel unworthy to receive the full extent of what I've made? Where else do I long for more money, more freedom, more of anything, but when it comes to me, I gently push it away like tapping a floating balloon with my fingertips?*

This is right at the heart of the dilemma so many of us are in.

We work so hard to create, flow, receive, manifest abundance . . . and then when it arrives, the other hidden script pops up and says, "Nope. You don't deserve this. Don't be selfish. Don't you feel like you're inconveniencing these people?"

"Don't you feel like you're taking more than you give?"

"Don't you feel like you'd be charging too much?"

"Don't you feel like they could do better elsewhere than with you?"

"Don't you feel like you shouldn't need to ask for help with this?"

"Don't you feel like you don't need that much?"

"Don't you think you're taking advantage of your situation?"

"Don't you feel like someone else probably needs it more or deserves it more?"

Or a million other ideas pop up.

I'm having to do some massive revisioning of my thinking. I'm having to consciously accept that I must be a good friend. I must have been worthy and helpful. Or I wouldn't have this circle of amazing people around me.

They are proving it to me by simply being here.

I need to move past this ceiling, and my body created the opportunity to do so. I have to be able to receive the bounty and nurturing they want to give to me.

Because if I don't eat these strawberries and warm up these dinners for my family, how else can my friends feel the pleasure of giving, helping, and nurturing? Isn't it selfish of me to only and always be the giver, never the receiver?

I truly have been selfish, just not in the way I thought. I've been *giving, giving, giving* to make myself feel good about myself, while robbing my friends and family of the same pleasure.

I decide to become a wonderful receiver.

But sneaky me, I have a trick to use: Every time I feel guilty for receiving, I'm going to remind myself that receiving is also giving. By receiving, I'm giving someone pleasure and a feeling of meaning. I acknowledge their empathy and generosity.

I'm no longer selfishly denying the people I love the ability to show their affection to me. I'm no longer making it all about me and my insecurities. I'm making it about them and honoring and receiving and accepting their offers of love.

I'll be basking in every nice piece of mail that comes my way, in every surprise gift. I'll recognize the sender and honor the deep sentiment that caused them to send it.

I'll accept compliments and actually let myself believe them, since I honor that the giver is a smart person whose words are truthful and count.

I'll accept bounty in any and all forms, trusting that the source of it is taking joy and pleasure in my receipt of it.

My receiving will be a form of giving that, while it seems like cheating, is the best I can currently do.

The Unselfish Act of Receiving

Ah, so that's my story. That's the day I woke up to that particular ceiling in myself and decided to barrel through it. And you know what? Since then, I have become a much better receiver.

For instance, nowadays one of my friends always brings all the food when she and her family come over. At first I thought, *Well my food must really suck. Maybe this is her way of not eating it.* And then I thought, *Maybe she knows I don't really care for cooking, but she does.* And finally, I thought, *Maybe bringing meals is her way of showing love, kind of her love language, and she knows how grateful and appreciative I am for her bringing it. It's a win-win.*

And that is just a tiny win. The bigger wins we see come in other forms, like when you negotiate your salary at a brand-new job. What if you asked, "How much am I willing to receive?" instead of "How much do I think I deserve?" Because you'll probably low-ball your value (that ol' self-love, self-worth thing!) when you say, "What do I think I deserve?"

Whereas, "How much can I receive?" allows you to open your mind to the idea that maybe this company sees a lot in you, and expects you to counter their initial offer, and will be a little disappointed if you don't counter high enough since the kind of people they want to hire should all be strong self-advocates.

"How much can I receive?" allows you to think less about the value of yourself in all kinds of situations and instead lets you think about the pleasure and joy that life or others will have in giving to you. It's a pretty gorgeous way of turning things around, isn't it?

But to do it, you have to practice being a great receiver. Most of us have a lot of crummy ideas built up around people who receive well. We call them greedy, rich, or full of themselves. Or we say they were born into it, like some tycoon's daughter or the son of a famous actor. There's rankle and envy. We don't like great receivers. But we'd sure like to be one.

You'll want to change your perception about what being a great receiver truly means. Being a great receiver can be steeped in humility and gratitude. Being a great receiver can be your gift back to the people you love, since you know you'll never take advantage of them. They can trust you to receive from them. Isn't that a great feeling?

Me enjoying those strawberries is how I want to think of myself as a great receiver. Me loving my friend's meals is me being a great receiver. Me allowing the universe to plop down a big win at a raffle is me being a great receiver. Now scale that up. There's not much difference between strawberries and raffle tickets and the much bigger stuff that comes in the form of "I got the job! I got the fat promotion! I got the handsomest man! I charged $20,000 for that service and got the contract!"

You get the idea. Just like we reshaped our relationship with the universe, I want us to be rethinking our relationship to receiving. Get good at it. Get real, real good. And to get good, *practice.*

And if you discover while practicing that you have a follow-up pattern that tells you, "Sure I can receive, but it'll just be taken away, I can't count on it, or I'll lose it," then go back and look at our chapters about patterns. Maybe you have a big one around good things being taken away, or disappearing, or not lasting. Be wrong about that.

Chances are that at least part of your reinvention will involve you being able to become a great receiver. Many of us are born as great receivers (remember the birthdays when you wanted every gosh darn thing in the *whole* toy store?), but we lose the skill as life batters us along.

Now, reclaim it.

M.E. *School* Prompt

Your two-part prompt is to notice where you long for abundance, wealth, riches, and bounty, but distrust or reject it when it arrives in any of its millions of forms.

Part One: Journal on the following questions:

Where do I deny others the pleasure of giving to me? Why do I reject it?

Where do I have ideas about what's "too much" or not appropriate to receive?

When do I feel guilty about accepting something good or wonderful?

Do I feel like receiving means taking from someone else? Do I believe there really isn't enough to go around, or that I'll be selfish or greedy if I receive from others?

Part Two: Feel the emotional endpoints of deserving everything good by choosing something that you want to allow and receive. Close your eyes and feel a wealth of that good thing pouring in, even for a few fleeting seconds. It feels right and good to receive it. Instead of rebuffing or rejecting their offers of help or gifts, you open your arms wide. You have been asked to take something, hold something, and that is a precious request. You accept with joy.

Chapter 33:
Caution! Other People's Beliefs Ahead!

A few years back, I received an e-mail that accidentally sent me down someone else's path for a while before I found myself again. You ever do that? Lose yourself inside someone else's beliefs about you?

What'd happened is that in one of my blog posts, I'd used the word *pissy* to describe something . . . well . . . *pissy.* As in: whiny, immature, and self-centered.

A critic sent me hate mail saying she was promptly unsubscribing from my blog due to my "white trash language." (Apparently, she didn't know that *white trash*, unlike *pissy*, is an actual racist term, definitely worse than *pissy* from a social angle.)

She really needs to get a life instead of writing e-mails like these, I thought (with lots of eye-roll emojis).

However, fast-forward a few years to when I found myself sitting with my fingers dangling over the keyboard one day in a hot writing frenzy of another article, having the sudden realization that I hadn't used the word *pissy* in a blog or e-mail ever since. Nor had I used the words *monkeyballs, asshole,* or any other word my friends who know me would say I use with unusual regularity and gusto. My blogs had been pristinely clean ever since that one piece of hate mail.

Yet there I was, writing, with my fingers frozen. The word *pissy* just wanted to come out so badly. Oh God, the sentence was perfect for it.

And that's when I realized I had just found a limitation in my thinking that I had put there myself, that the Pissy Lady had so graciously gifted to me. A limitation that was freaking ridiculous.

Remember how we talked about "limiting thoughts?" Well, I had one. And boy was I mad because, not only did I have one, but I'd allowed some nasty stranger to give it to me, someone I didn't even care about and probably would not like if I met her: Pissy Lady had caused me to unconsciously doubt and censor myself for *three fucking years*.

Boy-o-boy was I pissed. Pissed at myself that she'd snuck through and impacted me after all. She'd helped me form a hidden limitation that was something like "Smart girls don't use foul language in their writing," or "Don't alienate your readers or you'll never grow a following," or "Keep everyone happy by watering it down a bit, Sum."

If I were reading a blog post I didn't relate to, I'd have just moved on. But this person got deeply triggered, and this is where things get dangerous. She wanted me to get triggered with her, hence the e-mail. She wanted me to feel how she feels. And it worked. I began to subconsciously adopt this other person's opinion about how I should behave.

I'd let this stranger have power over me, from inside me. Then I'd begun to fail to be me and became a little more like her.

Holy mother's marmalade.

When someone else is telling you how to think and feel, and who they think you are or should be, if you believe them even the teeniest bit, you start living a little less like yourself and a little more like them. These beliefs, which are not your own, become your own and end up forming the inner limitations inside you.

Imagine that we all have these sort of limiting beliefs inside us that either allow us to do, feel, or have something . . . or not do, feel, or have something. These limiting beliefs are like walls that channel us down certain paths of possibility and eliminate other paths. We're rats in a maze choosing one corridor over another, restricted by high walls of belief.

Our inner walls are framed, often invisibly, by the input and reactions of everyone around us, and those channel the way we express ourselves in the world. Pissy Lady had accidentally helped construct one of mine when in response to her, I had begun flowing down a channel of "smart girls do/don't do this" and "make everyone like me, even people I don't like or respect." It had seriously been impacting the quality of my writing, my authenticity and message, and even my own self-respect. Pissy Lady had won the moment I took in her judgment and altered course. To please the few, I was sacrificing the many, including my own self.

This also meant I'd been unconsciously favoring the sensitive, censorious, and judgmental types over the creative, fierce, and open types every time I wrote *monkeyb***s* instead of *monkeyballs*. This made no sense. And it's sure as monkeyballs not me.

There's no point in trying to manifest growth if you're constantly limiting and restricting yourself into only diminished channels or paths that you often unintentionally and unconsciously accept from other people.

And critically, you have to *see* these paths before you can evaluate whether they're working for you (meaning leading you to the prize, my pretty rat!) or restricting you from ever even desiring the prize in the first place, because someone, somewhere has helped wall it off from you, based on their feedback about who you are, what you should want, and how you should behave.

This is one of the reasons why you've seen so many juicy, weighty, eyebrow-raising f-bombs in this book. I have reclaimed my power and now sing freely again.

It's time to find your own limitations. Find those walls. See how they got created. See if you can trace them back to where they began. If you can't trace them, no biggie, you can still ditch them. Just pull up the floorboards. Start looking. It's crazy rewarding when you do.

What you're actively hunting for are beliefs about yourself or your behavior or goals that you didn't thoughtfully create—instead you accidentally or unknowingly took on *someone else's beliefs about you* and made them your own.

The result is you get to be more you, less them, and you become that beautiful, open, radiant essence of uniqueness that you are meant to be—uncluttered by other people's limited beliefs that you've self-internalized about who you are.

Yes, what we're really talking about is inner authenticity and shedding self-internalized beliefs that fundamentally don't belong to you.

For instance, maybe your mom always told you to "marry a rich guy." And so you tried. And it didn't work out. But now that you look back, you realize what your mom was really saying was "Marry a rich guy because you'll never be able to support yourself or a family on your own." Which is why you didn't end up trying to become a scientist or a senator or whatever you once wanted to be. You instead took on her beliefs about you and made them your own. But they're *not* your beliefs. They're hers. Give them back.

Examine this idea that a lot of things you believe about yourself were accidentally and inadvertently patched together from other people's ideas of how you should look, think, or act. And more importantly, do you love and value those people enough to trust the guidelines they gave you? Or are those guidelines stunted, restrictive, foreign, mildewy, dated, or inappropriate for the challenges you face today?

You are a bright, authentic being singing with starlight. Remember the letter from the universe in chapter 28 reminding you that you're made of stardust? Well, you truly are. Iron, water, calcium, selenium . . . it's all in you. And it's the same exact stuff that makes the stars. The universe is infinitely patient, waiting to see how you'll express yourself through it.

If there is one gift the universe has truly given you, it's the ability to do or be anything you choose. Yes, our outer circumstances and physical biology limit us and give us all different game boards to play on, but *how you play the game* is strictly 100 percent your choice.

Remember, too, that your internalized restrictions aren't created only from other people's criticism. You pick up ideas from your culture, the Internet, TV, media, and more. Ideas about what weight you should be, how you should style your hair, how much money you should be earning, and what to think about the president or your local cannabis rules. We do a lot of things just to *fit in* when in fact the things we're doing don't fit us at all.

No wonder we feel tired; that's a lot of fitting round pegs into square holes, as they say. It never really works, even though we pretend it does.

I invite you to break free, reclaim some bits of yourself, shed other people's sneaky restrictive beliefs, and feel what being *you* is like.

M.E. *School* Prompt

Your two-part prompt is to think about the things you don't allow yourself to do, be, or express, then envision yourself as a fully independent self-realized being.

Part One: Journal on the following:

☐ What are some of the limiting beliefs I hold about what's right or wrong for me, how I should act, what I should want or desire, etc., that feel small or restrictive?

☐ Is this really what I believe, or is this someone else's belief that accidentally got stuck to my shoe? Did I inadvertently internalize their judgment and make it my own?

☐ Do I trust and admire these people enough to want to keep their beliefs? Did their beliefs work out well for them and lead them into happiness, success, and love?

☐ Are there any other ideas I have that I suspect may not be my own that I picked up from any other place (society, culture, social media, stereotyping, etc.)

Part Two: Write a short journal entry about yourself as if you were fully expressed. Nothing and no one limits you. How would you be living? Where would you be living? What would you be doing with your time? You can say what you want, love who want, work where you want._____

_____

_____

_____

PART VII:
Dive! Dive!

Chapter 34:
Unstructured Space

Now that we're in full swing of the rebuild—yes, you, we're rebuilding you—here are some suggestions for how to create the most optimal environment to do it in.

It starts with the sky. Right up there in the blue—see that? That's right. A whole lot of nothing. Maybe some wispy clouds or even big booming thunderheads. But it's just water vapor. It's a bunch of big empty space up there.

In art, when composing a drawing or painting, you're taught to look at the negative space, also called white space, as much as at the actual thing you're painting or drawing. Be aware of the emptiness surrounding your brush. It counts too. It's part of the composition, even though there's nothing there.

Think of your life. So busy with all this rushing around: to-do lists, goals, places to be, money to earn, work to get done, people to see. You scribble your black pen onto every tiny bit of white on the paper. And then you ask, "Where do I go next?"

I don't know. There's no white space. It's all full. There's no room for anything new. No room for dreams or new directions.

Some days when I feel totally overwhelmed, like I'm getting nothing done and going nowhere, and like knocking off one more thing on my list won't make a darn bit of difference, I remember unstructured space. White space. I look around in my life and see that I have none. How will I ever feel revitalized or inspired if I don't even have the space for those feelings to arrive?

Walk out to your patio. Sit in a chair. Gaze at the blue sky. Let random thoughts flutter through. Obsess, if you will, on a problem or two. Then let them go. Wait until the stillness enfolds you. It may take a while. You're pretty keyed up. You get up and put your phone inside the house. You put your feet up on the outdoor table. There, that's better. Now what?

Nothing. Just be nothing. Do nothing. Need a nap? Take one.

Wake up. Now what?

Nothing. Be nothing. What you discover is space. Emptiness. A place for new ideas to form. You're giving life moments to reach you. You're giving the whisper of new ideas a thin silver streak of nothingness to ride in on.

You—always so busy. Nothing can reach you. You're so full, so preoccupied. Stuffing your head with texting and Netflix and arranging to pick up the kids and getting the chores done and finishing your deadline at work. Every single second is full. You can't even stand in a line without pulling out your phone.

But not now. You're bored. You hate feeling bored. You reach for your phone out of habit, but it's not there. You sit in the white space. You become aware of the undrawn-on parts. The parts you've been looking for.

How do they come to you?

An idea floats in. Or a random, silly thought. Or a keen sudden observation.

Some ideas come so quickly you lose them. Others stay awhile and nest in the eaves of your mind.

Little birds of inspiration fly through the uncluttered space. But you have to be still, open, and empty to see them. They bring intuition, inspiration. They pop open decisions that have been long on hold. They flash insights into problems longstanding.

You hate being idle, doing nothing. But inside the nothing is a flock of ideas.

Stay long enough to find them.

M.E. *School* Prompt

Your prompt is to go sit somewhere for a minimum of thirty minutes and do absolutely nothing. Alternately, take a long drive and don't play any music or even think about touching your phone. Your goal is to find the white space.

Chapter 35:
My Future Self

Close your eyes for a moment. Imagine it's one year from now. Where are you? Who are you with? What are you doing? Where are you living?

Chances are it's a bit hazy. It's filled with *"How the heck do I know?"*

Go back to the emotional endpoints you identified in chapters 7 and 8. Some of those were pretty juicy. Some felt really good. You were finally getting a sense of the feelings you've truly been shooting for all this time, even if you don't have the path toward them yet.

Speaking of paths, remember the easy road versus the hard road of chapter 13? *Mm-hmm, yeah.* You pick the easy road. Your little easy-road backpack is strapped on tight; you just spent thirty minutes in unstructured space, and maybe an idea or two popped in your little head.

Now what?

Now, you discover the Future You.

The Future You, or your Future Self, is the person you want to feel like a year from now, or five years from now. Anytime in the future, really. She's peaceful, content, prosperous, safe, joyful . . . you can add any emotional endpoints you want to that person. You know, too, that feeling these things means that whatever situations had to enter your life to give you these feelings have indeed arrived. And any situations that had to resolve themselves in your life to give you these feelings have indeed resolved.

This Future You isn't about accomplishments, exactly. You haven't necessarily checked off a list of to-dos that got you through your Life Goals list. Instead, you've allowed life to unfold and guide you into the perfect people, situations, and circumstances that support, allow, and build all those wonderful emotional endpoints. You've been practicing feeling (pre-acting or Flowdreaming) these emotional endpoints, swatting resistance out of the way, and discovering all kinds of interesting new ways to reach your feeling goals. You've been in the captain's chair, steadily pointing the way, even as the sea of life billowed you here and there. The billows are okay since you have a sail and wheel. In other words, you've been working with the universe, not against it. You direct, the universe swells, and the boat that's you moves ever closer into all the feelings and experiences you want.

Describing the Future You and how to build it is one of my favorite parts of M.E. School. When my king mind gives me a list of options or things to do, or tells me what my "shoulds" are, I tell it to just chill because while yes, I'll pick something on that list to pursue, I also know that life itself is going to keep giving me even better things to choose from. And why? Because life knows what I'm looking for. It knows my goals. I'm infusing my life every day with good energies like a tea bag steeping in tea. New and even *more* aligned things will crop up.

Because that's the key: My Future Self isn't really in the future at all. It's right here, right now. To get those emotional endpoints hopping and cracking, I need to begin feeling them right now, this moment, starting . . . *now*!

There is no "waiting for things to change." There's no "it'll show up soon." There's no "eventually I hope I get this."

No, no, no. I feel all the things happening now, already, right now, around me in my life. Think about those easy chill-happy things on your list from chapter 29: "Things That Make You Feel Fucking Good." Except now, I'm not just thinking about injecting a few known pleasures into my life to balance the scales . . . no, I'm thinking about the feelings I intend to feel from *here on out,* and the things that might happen that lead to them.

Each time I give myself this treat of feeling my Future Self, I'm squeezing more of its feelings into my life and energies—think about the tea bag again. It can't help but turn the water around it into flavorful green jasmine or sultry Darjeeling. Your life is becoming more *orange-blossom oolong* by the day.

Right now, my Future Self is feeling something like this:

I'm feeling curious and excited about the interesting opportunities that have flooded in. In fact, I can't remember when I last felt so much curiosity and expectation surrounding my work. Something has happened that has revitalized or redefined my job. I feel something new peeling open for me, revealing a whole new world where I feel more than welcome—in fact, I'm the star guest! My creative juices are sizzling and alive! But none of this is overwhelming, in fact, it's the opposite. It feels right, somehow just totally right. My life feels calm and focused. I have plenty of time to stretch out into slower days that still feel fulfilling. I have time, freedom, and fewer and fewer "have to's."

And that's just my work life! I also feel healthy and fit. My heart thumps with healthy gusto, and my body feels svelte and graceful. I love the feeling of seeing myself in a pretty dress in the mirror and feeling delighted at how slim, healthy, strong, and great I look and feel.

Not only that, but I feel at peace over how my daughter has settled happily into college, and my heart swells with delight at how quickly she's acclimated. I feel content and have released her . . . all pangs of loss are settled. My son and husband are delightfully fulfilled, and I feel myself spending lots of time with them, having even more time for enjoying our lives together. We travel, we're healthy, and I feel like these are some of the best days of my life.

And finally, I realize that I'm financially in the best place ever. All worry, fear, and doubt about the safety or abundance of my future finances are settled. Something wonderful has happened that has allowed me to pay everything off and have tons of cash left over. My finances are strong and steady, with no chance of ever dipping. I have released all fears about my future financial well-being. I am safe. I have more than enough and always will, and as I mentioned, there's no overworking or stress at all in my life. It's all good.

I could keep going for pages and pages, but you get the picture. Notice how everything is feelings based, even the things that are specific, like my daughter starting college, or paying off my bills. I *feel* great about releasing my daughter into her future. I *feel* safe and secure with my bills all paid off.

And some statements are purposely vague, like when I say, "Something wonderful has happened . . ." that's when I'm giving acknowledgment that it's not my job to know the specific thing required . . . that's the universe's job, not mine. I'm not going to steal my dance partner's steps and dance for both of us.

And see, that's the trick of it: You want to choose specific areas to feel good in without being too specific about how you'll reach those feelings in them. Notice I didn't say, "I get a $500,000 contract and pay off my house." Nope. I'll let the universe handle the *how;* I just tell it the *what.*

Creating Emotional-Energetic Blueprints (aka Manifesting)

I bet you were wondering when I'd get back to this. Probably 90 percent of M.E. School students believe in the concept of manifesting, which I touched on by giving you a very non-woo-woo way of understanding it back in chapter 7.

But now that we're talking about your Future Self, you need a larger and more nuanced interpretation of manifesting, which is the idea that by using inspired action, pre-action, and your emotional endpoints, you end up having enormous sway over your future.

You are the captain of your boat, setting the course and navigating your direction (the feelings and successes you want to experience). The universe is the ocean (the vast swell of opportunities, other people, and life itself that you get to work with as you move toward those feelings). Everything you're learning in M.E. School is making you a badass captain, which is why you're now ready to put some components together to create an energetic-emotional blueprint for your life.

Think about describing the outline of your future like an architect drawing up house plans that the universe will dutifully follow. You sketch the blue ink on the white paper in rich, long strokes. You tell your life the shape of your "future house."

The construction crew on the ground? They're the universe, willing to haul in all the lumber and cement you need (the components necessary for you to build the life you want), only they don't know what to build until you show them (via your emotional endpoints and pre-action).

Your emotional endpoints form the lines in those blueprints. You sketch your intended future feelings, and life lines up all the right details to match. Life likes to be in alignment with how you feel. Your future is responsive to you, a reflective mirror. What you *are* is what your outside life *reflects back*. As you change, the things that are reflected back to you change in tandem.

What's currently present

outside you in your life is a

direct **reflection** *of what's inside you.*

Happy rich girl on the inside mirrors plenty of money and opportunities outside. Serene, satisfied guy on the inside mirrors peaceful, supportive, relaxing life circumstances outside. That's why you're pre-acting and pre-sponding all those emotional endpoints. It ain't just to feel good; *it's to force life to encounter you that way and respond in kind.*

What you feel is what you create, and "manifesting" is just the idea that you can be an active participant in this as opposed to just passively receiving whatever is thrown your way. Life contains order and chaos, and you get to be the deciding factor about which you receive more of.

You're ready to start creating your Future Self. We'd have done it earlier, but see, I didn't want you dragging Backward-Looking Girl into it. Or your Plan B. Or lack thinking. Or popping the *I'm Not Good Enough Show* on the downstairs TV.

But now you've brushed those away, like cobwebs cleaned from a window sill, with your newfound awareness.

Tell me about your Future Self. Be mindful that if you include specific *things*, you should still focus mainly on the feelings those things will give you. Stay aware that the specific things you mention might not even happen, or might become a moot point when something even better happens!

For instance, what if you say: "I get a better job that pays more and is way less stressful."

Okay, that's a *thing*: a better, higher paying job.

The feeling goal of that thing? "I feel less stressed. I feel full with money. I feel happy and engaged."

Now what if your life has decided that getting you those feelings would be *waaay* easier if it could just give you that well-paid fellowship for four years of studying, complete with a housing and childcare stipend for you and your whole family? You'd get an advanced degree and all your expenses paid for four years. Not a job, but also not too shabby? Yeah, you'd take that? Okay then, let your suitor, the universe, do its job and give you whatever is the best and easiest road, even if it's different than the road you have in mind.

Magic Phrases

One of my favorite things I add to any Future Self work is called a *magic phrase*. I have many magic phrases that I've stumbled on over the years, but my favorite is probably "this or better." Each time I feel "this or better," I'm acknowledging that I really have no idea what my easiest road may look like, and sure I picked some specific goals (write a book, teach a course, etc.) that I think will get me to my emotional endpoints, but ultimately, I want those things or *whatever is better.*

"This or better" is something I can't yet see, don't even know to ask for, something that only gets lined up after I complete the stuff currently in front of me, and so on. But *that*. I want *that*: whatever is better.

M.E. *School* Prompt

Okay, are you ready to sketch your Future Self? Your two-part prompt is to write about your Future Self, then feel it. Make the blueprint.

BONUS POINTS: Spend twenty minutes in unstructured space to let new ideas leak in before you even pick up your pen. Then, let 'er rip.

Part One: This technique is called "By This Time Next Year." Answer some of these as you sketch your Future Self. Focus on how you look and feel *by this time next year.*

- What's going on? Who's in my life, and who's not?
- Where do I work, or do I work much at all?
- How are my family, my partnership, and other good, close, or intimate relationships?
- How are my health and appearance?
- What are my finances like?
- What are some of the biggest feelings about myself that have shifted?
- What's been permanently and beautifully solved?
- What new, beautiful things have begun?
- Have I managed to create good balance in my life and with my time and stress level, or my mental and emotional health?

Part Two: Spend a few minutes feeling your emotional endpoints sparking out of you like the bright glowing tips of a sparkler in your fingers, lighting your future ahead of you. Recall "emotional reconditioning" or Flowdreaming from chapter 8, and let the emotions ripple through your body. Steep the tea bag. Be this person, now.

EXTRA BONUS POINTS: Feel these feelings every day. Make it your new practice.

Chapter 36:
What If . . .

There now, Future You. I know a few things on your list felt fantastical, but many felt pretty logical and sound. In fact, you were decidedly cautious, even a bit conservative in your sketching. After all, you had a one year timeline. What could be solved, changed, or grown, realistically, in just a year? Oh sure, you tossed in a few big-ticket items, but generally, you feel like you've got a working plan.

Now let's mess with that. No kidding. Let's mess it all up.

Maybe Evelyn's story will show you what I mean.

Evelyn's Egg

Evelyn and I are on a call together. She's a lovely, dark-haired, forty-three year old, single, with a good but boring job working as a dealership manager for the auto industry. And the only thing she really, really wants is a baby. Her life never quite lined her up with a partner who was willing to have one. Her eggs are aging. Eventually, in vitro became her only option. And so she tried. She took the drugs, did the procedures, and watched as egg after egg didn't stick. No sticky eggs.

After seven years, there's just one last egg on the ice—the runt, the one that has the least chance of sticking.

Her dream of becoming a wife and biological mother has dwindled into guilty, heart-aching moments of pouring through baby magazines like a dieter scarfing chocolate, and sitting home each evening eschewing dating or any more attempts at "finding the right guy" because it is just too painful. In short, she's really, really depressed, and it comes through in the tone of her voice. It's quiet, hesitant, pockmarked by large silences, and occasionally bitter.

Evelyn's Future Self feels things like "I live with peace in my heart and feel content. I focus on my work, feeling how it fills me up with purpose."

What's unspoken is that *a baby would fill her up with purpose. A baby would make her content.*

So we open up her What If list.

Your What If List

This What If list is a very different exercise than By This Time Next Year.

Here's the critical difference: Instead of holding your desires into a "reasonable" time frame of what could really happen for you and by when, in this exercise, you go balls-out and write down any and every amazing thing that you'd love to have in your life. No censoring. No ceilings. You write down things you aren't even sure you really want, except that they just sound cool and fun.

"What If" means that anything is possible. And you don't have to choose between them, plot your way to get them, or ask yourself if you're picking the right one. "What If" means you instead tumble feet first into a swirling eddy of magic, and the What If that jump out are all seeming impossibilities that nonetheless arrive. And yes, What If can include miracles like the last sticky egg.

I wrote my first What If list about my career back in March 2009. These weren't goals, just possibilities that I opened my mind to. (My actual goals were much smaller!) This was about seven months prior to when I got fired, almost divorced, and found myself crying into those wadded-up tissues at my therapist's office.

I remember going outside one late afternoon with a big, yellow legal pad of paper and propping myself up on the chaise lounge by the long side of my pool. I just began to write. I may have had a glass of wine beside me.

I still have the list, and while much on it would seem boring to you if I were to list it all, just know it encompassed crazy stuff like:

What if I grow my very own million-dollar publishing company?

What if I have a huge podcast with tens of thousands, no, hundreds of thousands, of fans?

What if I find an even better company to work at, that pays me 100 percent more than I'm making now? No, 200 percent more!

What if I'm paid and flown to speak all over the world about Flowdreaming?

What if I'm able to buy a bigger house for me and the kids?

What if my husband stops acting like such a dick and we get our shit together and feel in love again?

What if I stop acting like such a pity-party mouse turd and naturally, without even trying to, instead feel super inspired, super happy, and thankful for everything I have?

What if I pick up the guitar and start playing music again? What if I even record a few songs?

What if I get a call from a producer who wants to do some cool-ass, self-help reality show with me?

Astonishingly, by year's end, a series of huge changes ensued that brought me close to, or past, many What Ifs on the list. Remember, when I wrote this, *not one of these things was happening.* Not a one.

Within another year, 90 percent of the wild, outlandish What Ifs on my list actually came true. I would never doubt the power of a What If list again. It's the wild hammer that cracks the rock that reveals the waiting gem inside. Until you strike the blow, you have *no idea* what your life is longing to offer you.

Looking back, a few of my What Ifs don't seem crazy at all now because they *actually happened* instead of being outlandish. But remember, in early 2009, I was miserable, in pain with a bleeding inflammatory disease I didn't yet know I had. I was exhausted and being emotionally pelted and raked over daily at work. I'd even just been kicked off my own online network, one that I'd built from the ground up as a webinar and podcast host . . . and guess who my replacement was! It was my right-hand man, my own employee. They took my spot right from under me! And I discovered they were also going to high-level management meetings that I just happened to learn about afterward. Everyone heard the exit door flapping but me.

Plus, I was getting zero support at home. My partner, as you recall, was leaving the house at 7 a.m. and coming home past midnight most days.

Did I mention I had dropped to about 105 pounds without even noticing? Friends, when you lose weight without even noticing, you *know* things aren't right.

My book, *Flowdreaming*, was out, and yes, I had a popular radio show around it and lots of sweet fans and new clients who wanted to learn more about what I was doing. But that, my dears, is where I was at.

Hence, me sobbing outside on the chaise, drinking wine, writing up a crazy list of things so unreal I laughed as I wrote, laughed *and* cried. This is what you do when everything implodes.

And then everything changed.

My business, Flowdreaming, had just been idling, waiting for my full-time attention. And by the winter, it had grown substantially as I threw myself into my own newly self-employed work. As a result, my "salary" paying my-self was, incredibly, doubling what I'd made at the publishing house. Then, it tripled. And finally, quadrupled.

My kids now saw me every day from morning 'til I tucked them in with songs at bedtime. I was able to take breaks on my own schedule to teach art at their preschool.

A couple of TV producers even called me about a reality show. They canvassed my friends to get all the dirty gossip on me and I guess it wasn't enough, since I ended up being "too boring" to build a show around. Which is probably a blessing.

I spoke in Ireland and London. I was flown to the Dominican Republic to headline a big festival. I was being paid to speak.

My husband and I got our acts together; I stopped sniveling, and he started coming home. In fact, he *lost* that lousy job that had given him his excuse to stay away. I was secretly happy about it.

My What If list was now my *This Shit Happened* list.

Now remember, none of this "just happened."

I worked my ass off.

But I also *pre-acted* my ass off, meaning I did all my inner growth work as ferociously as I tapped out marketing e-mails and got on calls (well, after my morning cry).

But the tiebreaker? The big unknown asteroid that brought in things I could have never seen because I felt too small to even think about receiving them? The asteroid was my What If list. It was like the universe was looking at that instead of my daily to-do list and saying, *"Now that shit is where it's happening!"*

Each year, I've made both a This Time Next Year and a What If list as a result. Not all the things on the What If list happen, nor do they usually hap-pen as quickly as the first time when I was hitting the biggest wall of my life, but some of them *do happen.*

Your What If list is not magical thinking. It doesn't mean sitting on your ass waiting for things to just drop into your lap. Rather, it's allowing some bigger ideas to be acknowledged in yourself and by the universe. It's taking the lid off so a few drops of the *wondrous* can sink in and become *actual possibilities*. It gives permission for things to happen that you hardly even believe could happen.

Because damn, you just wrote them and thought them. And now life is craning its neck around to see how *you just changed the game with those thoughts.*

And Evelyn?

Evelyn, make your What If list. We all know what's gonna be on it.

Evelyn's What If List

I use the last egg and it sticks.

I have a healthy pregnancy and a very healthy, full-term baby!

My job totally supports me and makes it easy for me to transition into motherhood. I feel so blessed to have my team around me.

Not three months ago, Evelyn reached out to me. We'd done some mega sessions together, done some Flowdreaming, and had a long conversation with her body.

And the runty egg stuck because the runty egg wasn't so runty after all. It was a healthy, full-term baby boy. Her only boy, her only child, and one who'll no doubt be attending the finest schools and all Evelyn can lavish on him.

But you knew this story would have a happy ending.

Your What If list is where you unleash all your wildest, long-forgotten fantasies. It's where you dream of what you'd feel like if everything went *100 percent right* in your life for no less than a year . . . maybe even five years, or ten! Nothing is impossible. Lift your sights above "win the million-dollar lottery." Lift them to things like "I feel set for life. I have all the money I need from benevolent, abundant sources."

Reach into the highest crevices of your mind and feel into those things that would be wild, spectacular, life changing . . . and fun. Most of all, fun.

When you have finished your What If list, put it away somewhere special. Tuck it in your bra drawer. Put it with your kids' report cards. Stick it in the box with last year's taxes. Then take your phone and set a one-year reminder. On this day, a year from now, fish out your lists and look at them. What's changed? What hasn't? You'll be blown away—that is, *if* you do the work, this work that we're doing here together, right now.

M.E. *School* Prompt

Your prompt is to write a wild, fantastical, soul-delighting What If list.

Unleash all your wild, crazy ideas for your life. These are things that you normally think are "too good to be true," or that you have no idea how they'd come into your life.

Begin each new idea with "What if . . ."

_____

_____

_____

_____

_____

_____

_____

_____

_____

_____

_____

_____

_____

Chapter 37:
Brave Action

Tammy is the sweetest Southern girl. Her husband is in the military and they move every year. She also has six kids. Six! And she is not to be underestimated.

As a full-time mom moving every single year, you'd think she'd just be packing and unpacking boxes, constantly vacuuming Cheerios, cleaning up cat throw-up, maybe getting a mani-pedi every now and then, and generally just be yelling at one kid or another. I mean, it has to be exhausting! But no, she's out each dawn practicing for her 5k runs. She's volunteering at her kids' schools. She's all over everything, and into it all. And in a recent conversation, she told me this. "I do a brave action every day." Except she says it with a thick Southern accent, like "Ah do uh brave action ever day."

I am intrigued. What is this "brave action?"

"It's when you do something you don't wanna do but that makes you feel so stra-*rhong* inside."

I'm used to thinking in terms of "inspired action." I rant at my clients every day to *go take some inspired action right now!*

Inspired action is when you do something that just feels good, feels right. It may or may not move you toward your goals. That's not the point. The point is that in order for life to serve you up with new choices, you have to move through the ones you've already got in front of you. More on that later. For now, we stick with Tammy.

"So what kind of brave actions do you do, Tammy?"

"Last night I wore my prom dress to an officer's ball."

You didn't. An officer's ball. Her prom dress. Those events are formal and dignified. I cannot even imagine.

"My prom was in 1999."

It's still early, and I'm quietly laughing into my coffee.

"Why would you do that?" I ask.

"Because it was hard. It was *verah* uncomfortable. And I still fit it even though I looked like a *who-re*."

I wonder how short her old prom dress was. And I'm envious it still fits.

"My husband was so proud. All the other girls are gonna do it next time."

Tammy is a badass. Legit, she can claim that. If you wear your twenty-two-year-old prom dress to an officers' ball just because you like feeling brave, then you get the gold star, honey.

I've been addicted to brave actions ever since this conversation. I don't know if Tammy made the idea up or if it came from some super popular author whom I somehow missed hearing about, but brave actions are da bomb.

Do them.

Do them because now that you're feeling fired up, a little freer in yourself, and ready to make some moves, you might be asking, "Just what moves do I make, Summer? You know, besides feeling the emotional endpoints? Besides grieving and crashing through ceilings and all that?"

Exactly! When do you make your life start *moving*? What does it take to get the ball rolling?

Brave actions are the baby steps to other kinds of action, including inspired action. Brave actions help you wiggle into the cold pool water on a hot day. Brave actions build your trust muscles and unplug you from the inertia of just drifting.

If you're single and haven't even thought about sexiness in years, a brave action is to notice the hot guy gassing up next to you at the gas station and make eye contact and bravely comment sweetly about his nice . . . truck.

If you're constantly overworked at work, a brave action is to tap on your boss's door and ask if you can set up a little time together to talk about some ideas you have for where you can go next with the company.

If you've been pushing back the fear that your lower back really is fucked-up, and if it is, you won't be able to work anymore in Loading and Deliveries and then what (eek!), then your brave action is to book an appointment with your doctor and get the damn X-rays.

If your ex never brings the kids back on time or is always late coming to fetch them, your brave action is for you all to simply not be home after the allotted time.

If you're embarrassed that your knees look so saggy and veiny and your dark leg hair catches the sunlight so you haven't worn shorts in five years, your brave action is to put on a pair of those shorts and go stand in line at Starbucks for twenty-minutes, allowing strangers' eyes to run down your legs.

See where I'm going? Brave actions can be big or small. They all share the same common trait, though: They push you into a Grow Zone. They let you feel that moment of being uncomfortable, of stretching.

Inner power is a muscle. It can atrophy.

It can also **grow** and **strengthen.**

A brave action strengthens your muscles.

Doing lots of small brave actions eventually makes that medium-size action seem less big. You've built up to it. It feels handleable. And doing your medium-size brave actions makes that big brave action likewise less big feeling. You're ready. Your muscles can lift it with ease.

The same, by the way, is true about making big scary decisions. Have you made a bunch of smaller brave decisions on your way to the big one? Are you feeling the pleasant boost of confidence and delight at how these smaller choices worked out? Are your recent months littered with tons of medium-size decisions that were also hard, but you made them? If so, then you're ready to make the big one!

Let's start with some strength-building, confidence-building, brave actions right now.

M.E. School Prompt

Your prompt is to keep a log of any brave actions you take over the course of a week.

A brave action reverses a power-stealing situation or causes you to feel a good kind of uncomfortable growth. You must feel a tingle of bravery. And before you do each brave action, remind yourself that it'll be filled with ease, divine timing, and flow.

Here's an example of a great list:

Date What I Did

9/2 I wore a blouse I love even though I know the color looks horrendous on me, and it shows too much boob.

9/3 I said no to organizing the school picnic. (I'd normally feel guilty saying no to this.)

9/4 I had a date with myself: dinner, movie. I've never taken myself out alone before.

9/4 I had an overdue conversation with my mom.

9/5 I cleaned the garage and got rid of a lot of stuff from my past. It was hard.

9/6 I committed to starting a side business (no more thinking about it!) and bought the domain.

9/7 I asked my boss if I could work from home permanently. The convo wasn't as scary as I thought.

9/8 I made a phone call I dreaded. It was to the IRS.

Now it's your turn to brainstorm ideas.

☐ "My brave actions this week or month will include . . ."

_____

_____

_____

_____

_____

_____

_____

_____

_____

_____

Chapter 38:
Inspired Action

As mentioned, brave actions and inspired actions share the same family history. You do the brave ones even when, *especially* when, you can't find the *inspired* ones.

Being stuck is such a sucky feeling. I know because I felt it on Day One of beginning M.E. School and this book with you. And yes, the year has changed, and I feel a great deal more open, fluid, and accepting of everything happening and where I may be going next, but the problem is that I still don't know where I'm going next.

I have three possible directions I could move toward in my life at the moment, and I keep landing on them like a confused fly landing on three equally delicious cookies. Or three equally terrible cookies. I'm not sure I want to go in any of the directions. But they're all I can see right now.

So I buzz between them in a state of emotional paralysis. Meanwhile, the pressure is mounting. I can't keep doing nothing. I have bills to pay.

I think you know the feeling.

Thing is, I want to make the *best* choice. The right choice. The one that'll create a solid win.

And I don't know if any of the current options will create that win. I'm stuck.

When we reach these points of reflection, we often stall out and just wait for the magic, right answer to appear. Or we look at our options and decide they all suck, choosing, "None of the above" and sitting out the game until, we hope, a new set of options rolls around.

Back to my example: Do I write more books? Do I keep plugging away with my business? Or do I go back to school for a degree in psychology? Torment. Which path will most likely be the easy road and the one that leads most effortlessly to my clearly defined emotional endpoints? My Future Self is like a phantom excitedly giving me jazz hands, bouncing around somewhere in front of me, after I've made the right choices leading to her. *But how do I know what choices to make? I can't tell what she's saying!*

In reality, while I think I have at least three choices (or maybe more if I throw even more ideas in), in fact I have only *two* choices right now: Either I pick one of the three-plus directions and just go for it, or I decide to stay in my standstill, waiting for life to change around me.

If I decide to wait, I risk not paying my bills. So, there's that.

I choose to pick a route. I feel ambivalent about it. I don't feel it's going to do all that great, actually. My oracle cards tell me the direction will be a flop. All signs point to "no" or are at the very least ambivalent. Fuck it. Here's the deal:

Only by proceeding forward *into action can my life reveal a new set of choices.*

Yes, I snuck that same phrase into the last chapter. Now, we're opening it up.

Remember those old "Choose Your Own Adventure" books? (Yes, I'm that old.)

Well, each book starts with a chapter that ends with a choice. If you pick A, you flip to page 15 to continue the adventure. If you pick B, you flip to page 25. The idea is that there are multiple story lines and they all lead to different endings. You pick the story line based on your choices at each pivot point.

Right now, I'm facing an A-B-C pivot point. All the options suck. But I pick one anyway since the story can't advance until I do.

Only by choosing can I get to my next set of options. Once I make a choice, I allow a whole new set of ideas, options, and directions to flood in.

Life *requires you to* act *so it can give you new feedback. Period.*

Lag Time

Waiting for a perfect choice or direction usually means getting frozen in the snow. You can tell if you're already frozen in inaction by how long you've been sitting in the exact place of paralysis or discomfort, mulling your choices (or lack thereof).

Hate your work? How long have you been hating it? You've been hanging at the almost-to-the-last page of your choose-your-own-adventure chapter, unwilling to make a choice. You're waiting for life to change around you, make the decision for you. That is a power leak position. That is what's called *lag time.* Lag time is the precise amount of time between when you identify a problem and the moment you begin to fix the problem. We often identify a problem over and over, failing to notice that we got stuck in identifying it and never moved to the next step: addressing it. Addressing it almost always means taking an inspired action.

How long have you been longing to get back to the gym and maybe finally get a fit bod? Oh, so two years of lag time around that? Two years of constantly being mad at yourself for not making time for your body and prioritizing your fitness? Then make a choice, take action, end the power leak of being mad at yourself. Only by grasping a direction and going for it will life open new doors. Maybe you'll get to the gym and decide you hate it, but while there you run into an old friend who is bonkers about ballroom dancing. Or kickboxing. And you go with them to a class and fall in love with it. And you fall in love with that new dancing partner too. And now your life is back in motion, offering you new directions and solutions.

Not taking action is like sitting inside your home behind closed doors, closed windows, no phone, and no Internet and expecting life to offer you new choices. To get some new possibilities swinging your way, you've got to get up, get outside, grab the mail, and go walk to the park, metaphorically speaking, even though none of those are things you actually want to do.

Here's the takeaway: you can't get on the most luscious, lucrative path until you start to take some action—and here's the clincher—*any action*.

Yes, any action. Even the one that seems not great.

Regular Action vs. Inspired Action

Our biggest mistake is to sit in fear, waiting for the perfect opportunity or best direction to reveal itself. Guess what: All the current choices have already revealed themselves. You just don't like any. I hear you.

And yes, I guess you can wait for the creaking wheel of life to spin and force you into a new position. But honestly, that's a slow grind. It means waiting for your boss to get fired so you have the potential of a happy workplace. It means waiting for your doctor to tell you to get to the gym or get on medication, now. You don't want to wait for outside forces to make the choices for you. You want to take your power and make a choice yourself.

Or you can just wait and watch life pass by.

Me? I don't have time for that. Do you?

If not, then pick a direction; make a choice. Once you begin doing this, finding the elusive unicorn of actual *inspired* action becomes easier.

Action feels *inspired* when you want to do it. Action is just action when you don't want to do it.

Ideally, you want to take
enough action that the chessboard resets and
more opportunities for inspired action start showing up.

Inspired action is when something feels good, feels right, and makes your toes tingle and your pits sweat with anticipation. Your heart flutters, you're a little bit scared, but damn if this thing you're about to do works out well, then . . . whoa, you're golden.

It's a feeling that's unmistakable. You're drawn to it. Pushed to do it, to choose it. You can't explain why. Your friends shake their heads and your parents wring their hands.

Inspired action isn't always a bird that flies in from the heavens and whispers in your ear, so don't wait for that. Sometimes inspired action can simply mean doing your list of long-standing "shoulds," as in, you *know* what the next scary step is. It's been on your Should List for a while. But your brave action quota was low, and the inspired action felt too big. But now you're ready to leap.

Choosing Toward

Another way of looking at it is by using an idea I call "choosing toward."

For example, let's say I do pick the choice of writing more books, and even novels, as my path of choice toward that Future Self of mine. That's the inspired action I'll take. It's also a brave action since I'll be putting a lot on the line with no guarantee of any payoff –double whammy!

Now, each day I look at my list of things to get done, and I notice which things on my list bring me closer toward my goal of reinventing myself as more of a writer versus things on my list that take me away from that goal.

My list right now is positively full of things that are doing anything but taking me toward writing. My daily list has me calling website developers to fix broken stuff on my website. My list has me figuring out why iTunes isn't showing all my MP3s for sale like they're supposed to. My list has me developing more and more content for my webshop.

And so I begin asking a question about each thing on my list: "Does this bring me closer to my goal of writing more, or does it move me away from it?"

This question is a litmus test. My goal is to begin choosing toward my writing career more and more often, and to notice the long stretches of hours, days, or weeks when I'm not.

Writing to you, right now, at this very moment as we head into the final chapters of M.E. School is definitely choosing toward my goal. And damn, it feels good. It feels *inspired.*

You're choosing toward things every day. And it's so tempting to say, "Yeah, but I've got to do this and that to pay the bills!" Granted, going to work behind the counter of your local retailer pays the bills, but it means every hour you're there, you're choosing away from your goal of being a fine artist.

On balance, what direction are you **choosing** toward during the bulk of your time?

It can be really, really surprising to notice the direction in which our choices are taking us. Even more surprising is how well this one simple question works to instantly crystallize your choices into ones that feel inspired versus ones that are leading you backward (or simply maintaining a holding pattern).

Doers and Dreamers

Now that you know what both pre-action and inspired action are, I want you to see them as sister and brother sitting on both sides of a big universal teeter-totter. They balance one another. One is essentially *nonphysical action,* and the other is *physical action.*

This means that all the emotional, energetic blueprint making and pre-acting that you do should be perfectly balanced by joyful physical action. I know, it's so tempting to spend time on the one you like and ignore the one you don't. All of us are naturally inclined to one over the other. We doers love to make stuff, produce, work. We often work ourselves to burnout, in fact, and can't figure out why working harder or being stricter with ourselves didn't get us where we wanted to go. What we doers really need is some juicy, soft pre-action. Our life wants a blueprint so all the construction guys know where the heck to build instead of just crazily throwing up bathrooms and bedrooms in a flurry of constant, undirected, hard work.

On the other hand, we dreamers bask in creating the fantasies and feeling-scapes of what we long for. Our desires and ideas are hot and wild, rippling through us with joy or anguish. But the idea of putting in physical effort . . . well, we get locked up in paralysis, stuck, unsure, waiting. Action feels unpredictable, hard, and often pointless. Action has led to failure and rejection.

You know which type you mostly are. And yes, you are also a bit of both.

If you're predominantly the doer, then these last few chapters about action probably seemed like solid, self-evident advice. If you're a dreamer, then you totally swam in delight through the first chunk of M.E. School, but these action chapters kind of sucked.

But inner growth and transformation need both from you in equal measure. Only playing on one side of the teeter-totter is ineffective.

I often tell my students that you can hop on foot and you'll get somewhere, but if you use both feet in equal measure you can run . . . even sprint. And this is the point in M.E. School when you begin sprinting.

M.E. School Prompt

Your three-part prompt in this chapter is to review your potential paths and then come up with either action or inspired action to begin choosing toward them.

Part One: Ask yourself, Am I more of a doer or a dreamer?

Part Two: What do you want to see change, grow, or get unstuck? See if there's any obvious inspired action around it. If not, then start taking any action. Get the ball rolling. Journal on these two questions:

☐ Which paths (if any) am I currently considering to start creating movement, change, or growth in a new direction or as part of my reinvention?

☐ Is there any inspired action I feel called to do?

Part Three: Begin choosing toward your goal. Ask this question before you make any and every choice in front of you: "Does this thing bring me closer to my goal of (fill in the blank) or does it move me away from it?"

_____

_____

_____

_____

_____

_____

_____

Chapter 39:
Falling off the Fear Cliff

Deep breath. Here it is, the cliff.

You're panicking. You're actually thinking of doing something this book suggested, and now here you are. You want to grow, transform, and reinvent yourself into your next, happier self, but now that your nose is pushed right up into doing it, you think: *Ugggghhh . . . but everything will get so messed up, Summer!*

Shhhh. No it won't.

Nonetheless, you're suddenly backpedaling, asking yourself why you want to make these risky, probably stupid moves. What have I talked you into?

It doesn't matter what you're thinking of doing, we all know the powerful after-party effect where we suck our innards into a tight little ball and second-guess the shit out of our decisions because we are scared.

You're about to take a brave or inspired action to the next level. You're about to commit to some emotional endpoints that you have no idea how you'll achieve. You've decided to lay out your heart on the universal altar of trust and just hope that you're making the right choices and that life will, in fact, gently care for you.

To that end, maybe you're about to dump your old friends. Maybe you're about to sign the legal papers that will change your life. Maybe you're deciding to move across the country. Perhaps you're about to spend a gob of retirement savings on something you've always wanted but never dared to give yourself. Or you're about to finally tell someone the truth. Or maybe you're about to make a pivot that was two decades in the making.

But now, come to think of it, whatever pain or longing pushed you to want to do or choose these things has slacked off.

You think, *Whoa now, maybe I'm reinvented enough already. I'm feeling better. Why do more? I really can coast a while longer. What's the rush? I mean, it feels like I'm doing okay—not great—but better. I'm back in the* Good Enough To Get By Zone.

You feel like you don't even need to do this "growth thing" anymore.

Not only that, but now you think about how much this new choice or thing or direction will drain your savings and inflate your debt. You think about how your family won't speak to you again, or how disappointed your parents will be in you. You think about how selfish you'll be, how irresponsible. How you can wait it out. On and on.

You've utterly forgotten what led you to your decision to act, or, if you still remember, you're working furiously in your mind to downplay its importance and up-play the "I can't justify this" lack thinking that's now engulfed you.

I mean, Dead Zone? *What Dead Zone?* Come to think of it, you've managed just fine in this stuck, stifling, unhappy, unfulfilling, empty place for a long while now. You can manage a little more.

The sheer truth is that you're just afraid—blindly freaked-out—and very, very willing to backpedal to some seemingly safer point . . . which you've done about a bajillion times before.

I call this, "reaching the fear cliff," and when your toes are clasping the edge of it, then your growth has truly begun.

Fear cliffs like this can be found everywhere in your life, constantly. We all have cliffs like this inside us, but usually, they're more like a series of small drop-offs as opposed to a full-on cliff. It's where our known world meets the unknown, and all we can do is freeze up. We aren't in the Grow Zone yet, nor are we between reefs. The ceiling, too, is still above us. The power leaks haven't yet been plugged. We approach the cliff of change, then hang back.

We're on the *lip* of the Grow Zone ready to take off between the reefs. It's the *precipice* of deciding to shatter the ceiling. And now you want nothing more than to backtrack. The fear cliff is too high, too scary, and taking the jump is likely to kill you.

Here's why the fear cliff is so freaking scary and why we bring ourselves to the brink of change again and again and then fall back: It's because we are approaching the true unknown.

You remember me telling you that our pasts have conditioned us to project that our future will be mostly like our past, because our past is all we have to frame our future by. For instance, if all you ever saw, felt, or experienced was the color red, then how could you really know if blue was going to be good for you? How do you know that blue exists at all? Why would you even attempt blue? Why not just try to make red better?

We're biologically made to be unable to sense a future that feels much different than where we are right now. Or if we can sense it, it's dreamlike, unreal. We have nothing to reference it by other than magazines, movies, and however we imagine our friends and family's lives might be.

Close your eyes right now. How does your dream future feel? You saw your Future Self already, and you want to be them. But what's ahead is truly unknown—you have no past reference point for it having never experienced it before.

It's easy to project familiar things forward. But the unknown? Not so much.

For instance, I can easily imagine finishing work tonight, making dinner, and going to bed. I've done that thousands of times. But when I imagine dropping work, buying a last-minute airline ticket, and being on a Costa Rican beach by this evening to start my new career as a travel writer, I balk. I've never traveled on the fly like that. I've never sold a travel article either. The whole idea goes from a shimmery longing in my heart to suddenly feeling weird, scary, and highly untrustworthy.

This is why we down-talk ourselves right off the fear cliff over and over.

Our old self is popping up and saying, "C'mon, get back to where you were. You like to be in what's known, not what you "might" turn into or what "might" happen. There are no guarantees. Go back to where you were, dummy. At least we know what's there."

Stop and think what this means. If we're creating our future based on what we experienced in the past, can you see how this leads us to a Groundhog Day effect?

What's worse is if you made a bold choice in the past and it failed, then when you look at all your future potential bold choices, the fear cliff will say to you: "Bold choices lead to failure. You've been here before. Step back, walk away."

But if you listen and walk away, then your future can't ever change, because you keep anticipating and attempting to avoid what you know happened in the past, and therefore *you never let a new shape take flight and emerge*. Your future is thus condemned to be almost completely repeating your past fears and experiences.

You can guess what the end result is: You feel perpetually stuck. Whenever you try to change your stuckness, your fear cliff screams at you to stop. And so you do, which leads to more stuckness. And then it leads to yet another approach to the cliff . . . until someday . . . someday when it finally gets to be just too much . . . you throw yourself off.

And that's exactly what it feels like: falling.

Falling into uncertainty. Falling into the unknown. Falling into new forms and possibilities that you haven't yet experienced. Letting go into trust, you're propelled off the fear cliff by hope, faith, and oftentimes by pain, all mixed up together, but only after the emotional value of *change* finally eclipses the familiar fear of the cliff.

And that's where you land: At the bottom of the fear cliff is *change*. It's possibility. It's where you haven't been before, where there are no guarantees. It's an end to stuckness. It's the start of newness. It's where you stop programming your future based on your fears from the past. It's the end of Groundhog Day. It's where all the riches lie.

Getting through a fear cliff is the hardest thing you face in life. You do it while your heart whispers and begs for change, yet your head shouts and bullies you for submission. Eventually, you pick who wins, and if it's the leap that wins, then you win too.

You'll discover your last bit of transformative inner knowledge through *seeking and finding* your fear cliff. And once found, *embrace* it. Dive.

Embracing it means taking the leap. You can teach someone how to dive by standing on the board and modeling the right form, but no one really learns to dive until they just . . . dive.

And baby, we have strengthened your dive muscles for perhaps weeks or months now. You're ready.

But I can't guarantee that it won't still feel messy.

We all know that transformation can be erratic, even though we're desperate for it to be neat and tidy. We want our transformation cool and linear so we can see the result clearly, right there in the distance—structured, precise, and guaranteed.

But transformation isn't neat or linear. It's often shaky and wild. Things crumble. Things slip from your grasp. Last year, I found a perfect way of describing it: "I'm trying to hold up the avalanche."

But you just can't.

You flail, beat your fists, and try oh-so-hard to control and force and mash things into that way you want them.

But transformation is messy. Sometimes the mountain has to come down.

Sometimes on the other side of the mountain you find a meadow, a stream with golden fish, butterflies, and safety.

And sometimes there's only a scruffy trail that you still have to walk on a ways until you find those butterflies and that stream. But they're there.

Transformation cleaves you in half, into pieces, and orders you to reorganize into your new shape. It whispers to you, "The old shape isn't going to work anymore. How often do I have to explain that to you?"

Stop trying to hold back the avalanche with your little fists.

Step away and allow it to come down.

And use this book as a rope, as a handrail, as you work your way through the mountain.

And yes, you can also take what I call "tiny bites" if the avalanche scares you. Yours might be a slow-moving avalanche—just one little rock blipping down at a time. One little thing changing here, then another there. You'll still emerge transformed, no matter the pace.

M.E. *School* Prompt

Your prompt is to identify one or more fear cliffs inside you.

Use the prompts to explore where and when you've felt them before, and if you have lack thinking pulling you back from the one up ahead. Or maybe your past leaps have worked out spectacularly well. In that case, hurrah, let's do it again!

☐ What are my current fear cliffs, and what are they stopping me from doing or becoming?

☐ What fear cliffs have I approached before?

☐ What would "diving into" or embracing my fear cliff mean for me?

☐ If I do want a lot to change, do I think everything has to break for that to happen, or can I take tiny bites instead? (Remember chapter 20: "You Will Fix It When You're Ready to Fix It.")

☐ Am I supporting myself through this process by continuing to "go to the emotional gym" often, like I learned to do in chapter 8 with the concepts of pre-action and pre-sponding? (If not, go back and reread chapter 8.)

Chapter 40:
You Are a Gift

Is this it? Have we really come to the finish line?

Indeed we have.

About a year has passed for me. Right now, it's the day after Christmas, and I'm happy to tell you that all my clothes are on. *Er,* I mean I'm not in pajamas, or sweats, or otherwise dragging my ass around the house, bowed by the weight of future uncertainty while pining for a reinvention.

If, like me, you moved slowly through all the ideas in M.E. School, then a lot has probably happened to you as well. You got to play with the concepts and apply a few ideas here and there into real-life events as they unfolded. You might even be ready to fire off an e-mail to me, letting me know which concepts and techniques worked and which ones fizzled like a dud firecracker.

But we know you probably read all this in a few days or weeks (or if you got busy, months), which means you're staring at this chunky manual for change and wondering what the hell to do first.

First, go back to chapter 1. If you've skipped the prompts so far, then start over. Journal on them or download the worksheets. Skip the ones you just can't figure out or are unwilling to do. But remember, each chapter in this book is stacked to build onto the next. The gold you're looking for is often hidden precisely in the places where you've been unwilling to look for it before. You can literally follow the chapters and feel how your thinking shifts and the next steps become more obvious.

The inner work is what creates the change. You go to the gym to build your muscles, and by golly if you go, your muscles *will get stronger.* The same is true for you, right now: You're going to the gym of your heart and mind, and cleaning, forgiving, repairing, healing, strengthening, and rebuilding them. Your transformation will emerge just as your biceps will pop from all those curl-ups.

When I first began teaching M.E. School, I was so excited about sharing the various ideas and techniques for things like creating your emotional endpoints, pre-acting, and finding power leaks that I failed to see the forest for the trees for a long, long time.

"The forest for the trees" is a phrase I explained just a few days ago to my teenage son. It means you're so focused on the little stuff that you fail to see the context—the big stuff—that all the little parts fit into. Because when you're up close, the little stuff looks as big as a tree, and so you think the tree is everything. It's not. The forest is everything.

Here in M.E. School, the phrase means any handful of ideas, prompts, vocabulary, or ways of seeing things may be a tree for you: huge, exciting! But ultimately, all these ideas fit into the the Bigger You—the Forest You. The Forest You changes slowly, tree by tree, over the seasons. Yet each day, what you pour into the forest of you is *incredibly important.*

M.E. School has just uprooted and replanted a big patch. Your spindly maples have been replaced with strong oaks with a thousand acorns ready to spread through your life.

After three or four years of teaching, I realized that the bulk of my students were often women in their mid thirties to mid sixties. Huh. I figured it was because women normally seek help; dudes do not. They probably related to me, also in my forties. However, I saw a scattering of men too—ones brave enough to open their hearts and touch the broken parts inside. Because that's what had happened to us all, I realized. That's our forest: Something had withered or broken in our forests, and we were intent on putting things back together in a new, different, happier form.

Sometimes it was their hearts that had been broken, or their finances were broken, or their marriages, even their sense of self. What they really, really wanted was to rebuild themselves. *Rebuild their forest.*

It always started with pointed feelings of "I'm stuck," or "My last kid just left home for college," or "I never learned how to earn my worth, make the money I need for retirement, and now I'm freaking out."

There was always a particular pain point that goaded them forward. And so, we'd take the pain point and begin unraveling it to see what treasure it would yield.

Oddly, it was other things, not the pain point, that would often change first. I liken it to trying to get the hands of an old grandfather clock to start moving again. Just pushing the hands around on the clock is like tackling the pain point. It moves the hands—temporarily. But to get the whole thing moving, you have to open the back of the clock and look at all the other, seemingly unrelated moving parts: the gears and wheels.

So we'd look at something seemingly totally unrelated to the pain point and free the stuck gear. Things like looking at your self-trust. Or finding and plugging a power leak. Or learning how to find your emotional endpoint. Or learning how to anticipate and create ease and flow. Each bit we freed, fixed, and oiled began getting the gears moving. And then one day, *voila!* The hands on the face begin moving on their own.

What it comes down to is knowing, ultimately, that you are worth every drop of time and every penny of investment you pour into yourself because you are a gift. Yes, a gift.

The "you" that you're **building** is the you that you're giving to everyone and everything else in the world.

You are the greatest gift you could give to us all. You deserve to make your gift, *you*, spectacular. Clear. Happy. Free. Loved. Loving. Secure. Giving.

And in return, isn't it crazy remarkable that you woke up today to reciprocate a gift from the world of oxygen, sunlight, and a body to live in?

What a remarkable thought.

We tend to think of the world as something we have to blunder through, step carefully in, and figure out.

We forget how the world spreads its arms for us and offers itself up to us with every breath of air we take into our lungs, with every morsel of food we nibble, with the sunlight warming us and flooding our bodies with metabolic activities that keep us running smoothly. God, how beautiful that is.

But what we forget even more is that every day we get to *gift ourselves* to the world. We get to say, do, feel, and think things that by the very act of doing, we *put out into the world.*

Wow, the world must really trust us, even love us, to willingly receive so much from us each day, then give us back a whole new next day to do it all again.

And even crazier, 100 percent of everything we do in a day is self-directed. I mean it comes 100 percent from *you*. It's whatever *you* choose. Talk about being in a power position. That, baby, is you.

Isn't it funny how we squander that? Or forget it? How we feel like all the things we do are because other people made us, or said we had to, etc., etc.? Well, not anymore. Or at least, not as much.

The world is waiting for your every thought and every action. Each moment is like finger-painting in wet sand—whenever you do something, you sculpt a little bit of life.

What are you giving the world each day? Like, the majority of the time?

What you're giving is *you*. And what's in *you* to give? That's entirely up to you.

Reread that if you need to really understand that thought.

It means that if you make yourself into something that's bright, secure, loving, and beautiful, then that is what you deliver every single day to everyone and everything around you. I can't think of something more honorable, compassionate, and loving to do for the world and everyone you care about. If everyone in your neighborhood or your town showed up this way, can you imagine how things would change? And isn't it crazy that "personal growth" and "self-development" are two of the greatest, most loving acts you can do for others? It blows my mind.

The one thing you have to remember here, at the end of M.E. School, is that you *truly are a gift.*

There's a Japanese concept called *ichigo ichie* that author Frances Miralles explains well:

Pronounced ichigo ichie, its meaning is something like this: What we are experiencing right now will never happen again. We must value each moment like a beautiful treasure. We must become moment hunters.

Each moment, you give the gift of yourself to the world, and in turn the world gives you once-in-a-lifetime moments that are never, ever repeatable. A simple act of finishing the last sip of your coffee is different from any other sip any other day. Similar, yes. But always unique, treasurable. How gorgeous a thought.

You are a unique moment happening to the world, and the world is a unique moment happening to you. And these moments move forward, irreplaceable, second by second. Meaning your forest shifts and blows with the winds of life, and you get to decide in every second how you'll be or feel in it. How astonishing. How powerful. *You* are that powerful.

Right now, there's something in your life you want to heal, do, be, or have. It may be as huge as building your own business, or it may be as simple as coming to peace in your heart. Your number one goal, your only and ultimate goal, is to make this happen. It's the gift you want to make next for the world, it's the moment you want to savor once in all its uniqueness.

To hold anything back is to squander yourself and your gift to the world.

But you do not squander.

You are fierce and fearless.

You are gentle and kind.

You're courageous when you need to be.

You're giving and compassionate.

You're thoughtful and loving.

You're smart and attractive.

Your interests and hobbies are fascinating.

Your mind is fascinating.

And your gorgeous body is a temple.

If anyone, *anyone* has ever told you otherwise, *they are dead wrong.* One hundred percent, completely wrong. It means that person also failed to know that about themselves, so how could they possibly recognize it in you?

Please use every idea you've learned here, every technique, everything, for the rest of your life. Use it in your current transformation and in the next and the next because you will change again. You will get stuck again. And you'll grow again too. You just have some better tools for it now.

Remember the "easy road." Remember Plan A. Remember emotional endpoints and Flowdreaming. Remember your boundaries. Remember your What If List.

And mostly, remember the gorgeous inner power that flows through you at all times like a ceaseless thundering waterfall.

Because, congratulations! You have now officially finished M.E. School.

Until we meet again, with blessings and love,

Summer

M.E. *School* Prompt

Your final prompt is to ask the question, "How am I happening to the world?"

What are you gifting it with? What is your next step today? Because out of everything you've written through M.E. School, this is your ultimate discovery: *knowing who you want to be as you gift yourself to the world.*

Journal on this.

_____

_____

_____

_____

_____

_____

_____

_____

_____

_____

_____

_____

_____

To the Awesome People

This book baby was a hard pregnancy. Unlike my other books, in which I felt pretty self-satisfied going in and being able to teach at a safe, intellectual distance . . . well, in this book, I had to get personal. Really, really personal. My past, my story. I had to own my fuck-ups in black-and-white because you need to see exactly how I've surmounted them and continue to overcome and transform even in the face of the craziest few years any of us have ever experienced.

This book demanded that I get raw and open. I can't tell you how many times I almost erased entire paragraphs, entire sections as I worried what people and places from my past might think. I even said pretty unflattering things about my husband. *(Sorry, honey, it's for the greater good!)*

But that's exactly what caught my attention: I noticed that I was still willing to pull back and hide pieces and bits—the ones most objectionable and likely to get people mad at me.

I always tell my students that if you want to do Really Big Things, you have to *get over yourself.* Getting over yourself means you can't let your freaked-out, fearful self shut you down. You have to say, "Whelp, what I'm doing is bigger than me. I serve it. And letting my scared little ego get in the way is only going to keep me small."

It's less about fearlessness and more about knowing that when you have a true gift to share, then your own needs for approval, being liked, and being safe *must* take a backseat. So I tried to do this.

The way I tackle this is with a team—great people who both tell me when I hide and who cheer me when I get something right.

Here are a few of the people who helped me get through the fear, who felt a call to read my early drafts and generally tell me what worked and what sucked. I love you all.

Jessica Ballenger, your early feedback was instrumental in shaping this book, and your friendship all these years has comforted me more than you know.

Diane Goodchild, Mama Tiger and powerful goddess, thank you for your feedback and continuous encouragement.

Amanda Keene, your ability to find typos and perseverance to carefully note the, what. . . hundreds (?) of them was a true test of grit. Thank you.

To Michele Martin for seeing the prize inside this manuscript. I could not have found a better ally and steady hand.

To Darcie Abbene for heroically picking up this orphaned book and spit-shining it into shape. Your insights and suggestions have been invaluable.

To Larissa Henoch for gifting this book with a beautiful and thoughtful design.

And last, to *you*, dear reader. Your bravery in taking this journey with me lights my heart and nourishes my soul. *Thank you.*

About the Author

Summer McStravick is a personal growth coach, author, podcaster, and creator of Flowdreaming®, a mind-body technique for manifesting and growing inner emotional strength.

Her books and podcasts have been used by over 180,000 people to transform their inner emotional landscapes as well as their external lives. Her intimate, boutique program, M.E. School®, has brought almost a thousand students through its virtual doors, creating extraordinary and positive change in their lives. Find Summer's work at Flowdreaming.com, in her podcast, and in the Flowdreaming app.

Summer's also a cat mama who loves to garden, collect crystals, and get lost in a good fantasy novel.